Ellen H. (Ellen Hardin) Walworth

An old world as seen through young eyes

Travels around the world

Ellen H. (Ellen Hardin) Walworth

An old world as seen through young eyes
Travels around the world

ISBN/EAN: 9783741196294

Manufactured in Europe, USA, Canada, Australia, Japa

Cover: Foto ©Andreas Hilbeck / pixelio.de

Manufactured and distributed by brebook publishing software (www.brebook.com)

Ellen H. (Ellen Hardin) Walworth

An old world as seen through young eyes

MILAN CATHEDRAL.

AN OLD WORLD,

AS

SEEN THROUGH YOUNG EYES;

OR,

TRAVELS AROUND THE WORLD.

BY

ELLEN H. WALWORTH.

"How beautiful the world is! and how wide!"—LONGFELLOW.

NEW YORK:
D. & J. SADLIER & COMPANY,
31 BARCLAY STREET.
MONTREAL: 275 NOTRE DAME STREET.
1877.

To my Mother,

Mrs. ELLEN HARDIN WALWORTH,

WITH

UNMEASURED LOVE AND RESPECT,

I 𝔇𝔢𝔡𝔦𝔠𝔞𝔱𝔢

THIS ACCOUNT OF MY TRAVELS.

PREFACE.

When I was about to start for Europe with my uncle, mother and I decided that I should write long letters home on the rainy days and between-times of our trip, which she would keep together until my return. They would answer every purpose of a journal, and at the same time keep her informed of our whereabouts and adventures.

From the time I landed at Glasgow I wrote nearly every week; but we travelled about so constantly that news from our friends was often long in overtaking us. I had no idea that my letters were being printed, and was very much surprised, at Florence, to hear a friend say he had read one of them in an American newspaper. It was not until we reached Rome that I heard from home that they were being published regularly in the *Albany Sunday Press*. This was news indeed! But Albany seemed very far away, and I was soon absorbed in the idea of going on around the world, which had not suggested itself to us before; so my impression of being before the public was very vague, and I continued to write as usual. In fact, these long letters, written at odd times and in odd places, had become to me a part of the pleasure of the journey.

PREFACE.

After reaching home I spent a portion of the summer vacation, before returning to school, in arranging my printed letters with appropriate pictures in a scrap-book. It seemed but a step from the scrap-book to the published volume, and the next vacation was spent in linking together the disconnected history of my journey in its present form.

E. H. W.

SARATOGA SPRINGS, *April*, 1877.

CONTENTS.

I.
AWAY.

School-girl fancies—Their fulfilment—Summoned home—The decision—Only a valise—Passports—Uncle and "ditto"—The steamer—Bound for Scotland—The leaving and the left—Adrift 1

II.
AT SEA.

"We met by chance"—Overboard—The Captain's cabin—Petrels and porpoises—A cozy tea-party—Old Neptune's shower-bath—"Fifth Mate"—Pilgrims—Sounding—A roundabout dance—A marine poem—Ship-croquet—Tag—An impromptu masquerade—Land 7

III.
SOUTH-EASTERN SCOTLAND.

The Clyde—Dumbarton Castle—A gray city—Bonnington Linn—Cave of Sir William Wallace—"Land of Burns"—Faster than Tam O' Shanter—Loch Lomond—A pony-ride in the clouds—Exploring Ellen's Isle—Following in the footsteps of Roderick Dhu and Fitz-James—A village of know-nothings—Scotch children—Stirling Castle—Familiar faces 18

IV.
RAIN AND RUINS.

The "Iona"—Three hundred and fifty-two days of rain—Kyles of Bute—Genuine Highlanders—The hunting season—Fingal's Cave in a storm—Birthplace of Christianity in Scotland—The Caledonian Canal—Drip for drip—A banished clan—Lads and lassies—A tiresome rest—We differ—Once more in the Lowlands . 30

V.
EDINBURGH AND THE HOME OF SCOTT.

Heart of Mid-Lothian—Memories of Mary, Queen of Scots—Edinburgh Castle—Abbotsford—Sir Walter Scott's study—His collection of antiquities—His tomb—Melrose Abbey . . 40

VI.
THREE CITIES OF IRELAND.

The Irish Coast—Jaunting-cars—A wild Irishman—Dublin—Across the country—Lost in Limerick 48

VII.
KILLARNEY AND BLARNEY.

Among the Lakes of Killarney—Cottage of Kate Kearney—Gap of Dunloe—"Old Weir Bridge"—Muckross Abbey—A sudden squall—"Boots"—The Blarney Stone 52

VIII.
ENGLAND.

North Wales—Chester from the walls—A labyrinth of railroads—The great Cathedrals—Witchery of York, solemnity of Peterborough, and grandeur of Ely Minsters—The "Dark Ages"—Cambridge and Oxford—"Great Tom"—Kenilworth and Queen Bess—Desolation—"Where are they?"—Stratford-on-Avon—Shakespeare from his cradle to his grave—Inn of the Red Horse—Souvenirs of Washington Irving 59

IX.
LONDON.

Visionary companions—"The Golden Cross"—Panoramic pictures—Westminster Abbey—Houses of Parliament—Bewildering collections—An artist's generosity 74

X.
THE TOWER.

The Thames—The Tower of London—Traitor's Gate—Spectres—Bloody Tower—The little Princes—"The block"—The Horse Armory—Trophies—St. Paul's—Dover and the Channel—Leaving the British Isles 80

XI.
BELGIUM.
Misunderstandings and mistakes—Desperation of a Bostonian—Bruges and its Belfry—A voice in the dark—Romantic Flanders—Ghent—"Market Day"—The Grand Béguinage—Antwerp art—Eau de Cologne, and O the Cathedral! . . . 86

XII.
UP THE RHINE.
The first glimpse—Pleasure-seekers—Sunday at Königswinter—The way we walk—Legends of the Drachenfels—An island nunnery—Romance of Rolandseck—Thirty-three ruins—Sunset on the Rhine—Out of Dreamland—Mayence Cathedral—Charms of Heidelberg—Fooled!—Lager in Ruins 94

XIII.
NUREMBERG AND MUNICH.
In Bavaria—Antique charms of Nuremberg—Modern art of Munich—A dance on a scrubbing-brush—Palace of the King—The Royal Chapel—Porcelain pictures—Beauty on the walls—The Glyptothek—Colored statues and stained glass—A giantess—A warrior—From Munich to Ulm 104

XIV.
SUMMIT-GAZING.
Switzerland and the Tyrolean Alps—A legend of Lake Constance—German roofs and Swiss cottages—A peculiar introduction—Zurich at night—Mountains in the air 114

XV.
SWISS VALLEYS.
Enthusiastic tourists—Ragatz and Chur—A French landlady, Swiss maid, and German doctor—Lucerne—My window—The Rigi—The lake—William Tell—Washerwomen of Geneva—Mount Blanc 119

XVI.
UPS AND DOWNS.
"Letters from abroad"—An adventure—Martigny; its strange music—Valley of the Rhone—Across the Simplon by moonlight, daylight, and lightning—"Where the river runs"—The gorge—In safety—The storm rages 126

XVII.
MILAN AND VERONA.

Sojourners at Lago Maggiore—Fun over turtles—Milan, a spider's web—Cathedral contrasts—Tomb of Saint Charles Borromeo—Galleria Vittorio Emmanuele—A Christian church of the early times — St. Ambrose and Theodosius — Reversed—Da Vinci's masterpiece—Other pictures—Verona—More churches—" Scaligers "—The Amphitheatre 135

XVIII.
A WEEK IN VENICE.

The Grande Canale at sunset—The "Stars and Stripes"—The Piazzetta—Scenes on the great Piazza di San Marco—Venice at night—The Bravo—The Lido 146

XIX.
ART.

A dreary scene—Bologna—A pilgrimage church—Opinions about pictures—Guido Reni's Mater Dolorosa—A ride through the tunnels 153

XX.
CITIES OF ART.

Florence—American studios—The Uffizi—San Marco—Pisa—Perugia—An amusing book—Italian fountains—Perugino—Assisi 159

XXI.
CHRISTIAN ROME.

Fumigation—The Pantheon—St. Peter's—The curtain lifted—Afterthoughts—Ascending—Bird's-eye view of the Vatican—Three pictures; many statues—A visit to Pope Pius IX.—The Catacombs 169

XXII.
BEGGARS, BEAUTIES, AND BONES.

'King of the Roman Beggars"—Morro—Barberini Palace—Beatrice Cenci—Church of the Capuchins—A ghostly retreat 184

XXIII.
A LETTER TO THE CONVENT.
Saint Francis and Saint Clara in connection with Assisi—Shrines at Rome—The catacombs illuminated—Under churches . 190

XXIV.
PAGAN ROME.
A blind guide—A moonlight ride through ruined Rome—Sightseers 197

XXV.
NEAPOLITAN SURROUNDINGS.
Overlooking the Bay of Naples—Stillness of Pompeii—Beautiful dwellings and grim inhabitants—Capri—The Blue Grotto—Baja—Volcanic regions — "Round the world," perhaps ! . 201

XXVI.
FROM BRINDISI TO ALEXANDRIA.
Brindisi ; the Harbor, the House of Virgil, and the Appian Way—Adriatic Sea ; the "heel" of Italy, and the outlines of Greece—New Year's Eve on the blue Mediterranean—Bay of Alexandria—Scenes from an Egyptian window 209

XXVII.
EGYPT.
A world of wonders—Palm trees—Spring in the valley of the Nile—Oranges everywhere—Arabs at work—Their houses—Donkey-boys, costumes, sais—A great mosque—Cairo in general—The Pyramids and Sphinx at Ghizeh—Tombs of the Caliphs . 214

XXVIII.
UNCLE'S CHAPTER.
His account of the Coptic Catholics as we saw them in Cairo—An ancient rite—Cathedral of the schismatic Copts—Their queer customs—Traditions of the Holy Family in Egypt—The house they occupied—The Sycamore Tree 225

XXIX.
THE DESERT AND THE RED SEA.

A bashful young man—Mounting a camel—Land of the Children of Israel—Desert scenery—Suez Canal—The steamer—Moses' Well and Mount Sinai—Down the Red Sea—Entering the Tropics—Strange Lights 235

XXX.
INDIAN OCEAN.

Tropical dreaminess—Sham dangers—A dinner that won a fortress—Mermen and their chant—The heat—Peculiarities of Aden—Incidents of Ocean life—The "Southern Cross"—A ditty 243

XXXI.
A CINGALESE HEROINE.

Odd sights and scenes—Mahometan sailors—Christina the Cingalese girl, and little Evy—Saved from death—Broken English—A passing cloud 250

XXXII.
SCENES IN THE TROPICS.

A sunset on the Arabian Sea—Point de Galle—An old Spanish priest—A Buddhist temple—A country-ride in Ceylon—The "Australia" and the "Delhi"—Bay of Bengal—Penang lawyers—Hot, hotter, hottest! 255

XXXIII.
CHINESE TOWNS AND THE MONSOON.

Singapore—The mermen again—Chinese Pagoda—Almost an accident—The China Sea—Hong-Kong—Chinese New Year—Sampans—A few people—Between China and Japan . . 264

XXXIV.
UNCLE'S OTHER CHAPTER.

The martyr-field of Japan—The modern missionaries and their work—Results of St. Francis Xavier's labors—Twelve thousand native Christians discover themselves to the Bishop—Others inaccessible—Japanese sights—Vestiges of a Jesuit martyr at Yedo 275

XXXV.
THE JAPANESE.

Queer !—Fusiyama—Japanese art—Curiosity—Japanese houses and customs—Gin-rik-shars—Daibootz 283

XXXVI.
YEDO.

Mud—Temples of Shiba—Hair top-knots—Atogayama—The "burnt district"—A chowchow house—A Japanese theatre—A day gained 291

XXXVII.
TWENTY-FIVE DAYS ON THE PACIFIC.

The waves rise and the rain falls—How we passed the time—"You savez"—Sea-birds and their flight—April Fool's Day 298

XXXVIII.
CHINESE EMIGRANTS.

The "Alaska" and her Captain—The Chinese kitchen, cabins, and opium-smoking room—Joyful messengers—The Golden Gate—Counting the Chinamen—Ashore at last 303

XXXIX.
FROM SAN FRANCISCO TO SARATOGA.

The Golden City—A kind old Dutchman—The sea-lions—Across the country—Sierra Nevadas—Salt Lake City—Prairies—Home ! 309

LIST OF ILLUSTRATIONS.

MILAN CATHEDRAL,	*Frontispiece.*
THE EMBARKATION,	4
THE QUARTER-DECK, AT SEA,	8
LOCH KATRINE,	20
MAP OF THE VICINITY OF ARDNACHEANACHROCHAN HOTEL AT THE TROSSACHS,	26
FINGAL'S CAVE,	34
EDINBURGH CASTLE AND SCOTT MONUMENT,	36
HIGHLANDER,	39
HOLYROOD PALACE,	40
EDINBURGH CASTLE, AND GRASS MARKET,	41
THE OLD TOLBOOTH,	42
ABBOTTSFORD,	44
DRYBURGH ABBEY,	46
THE GIANT'S CAUSEWAY,	48
DUBLIN, FROM PHŒNIX PARK,	50
ROSS CASTLE,	54
IRISH JAUNTING-CAR,	58
YORK MINSTER,	62
ELY CATHEDRAL,	65
KENILWORTH CASTLE,	68
WARWICK CASTLE,	71
SHAKESPEARE'S TOMB,	73
LONDON BRIDGE,	74
WATER-LILY, ZOOLOGICAL GARDENS,	76
HOUSE OF PARLIAMENT,	77
THE TOWER OF LONDON,	81
RHEINFELS,	94
STOLZENFELS,	96
RHEINSTEIN,	98
OBERWESEL,	100
RUINS OF THE DRACHENFELS,	103
THE WALLS AND MOAT, NUREMBERG,	105
THE SPLUGEN PASS,	120
LUCERNE,	124

LIST OF ILLUSTRATIONS.

CASCADE—ALPS,	130
MILAN CATHEDRAL,	138
VENICE,	147
THE RIALTO,	150
FLORENCE,	159
STAGE-COACH,	163
BAPTISTRY AT PISA,	164
CATHEDRAL AT PISA,	166
CASTLE OF SAN ANGELO,	170
THE LAST COMMUNION OF ST. JEROME,	173
THE NILE,	175
THE TORSO OF HERCULES,	177
ST. PETER'S, VATICAN,	179
LAOCOON,	181
BEATRICE CENCI,	186
THE COLISEUM,	198
RUINS OF POMPEII,	202
BATHS OF POMPEII,	204
EGYPTIAN WOMAN,	215
SHEPHERD'S HOTEL, CAIRO,	217
MOSQUE, EGYPT,	220
A STREET IN CAIRO,	222
DAHABEIH—THE NILE,	223
A CARAVAN,	237
SUEZ CANAL AT ISMAILIA,	239
NIGHT AT SEA, INDIAN OCEAN,	245
SINGAPORE,	265
CHINESE TOWERS,	268
CHINESE VISITING,	270
TEMPLE, WITH TOMBS OF THE MIKADOS AT KAMAKURA,	280
FUSIYAMA,	284
A JAPANESE GARDEN,	286
DAIBOOTZ, THE GREAT STATUE OF BUDDHA, JAPAN,	289
A CHINESE STREET SCENE,	292
GOLDEN GATE, CALIFORNIA,	306
MISSION CHURCH, SAN FRANCISCO,	310
" " RESTORED, SAN FRANCISCO,	311
THE MORMON TABERNACLE,	313
NIAGARA FALLS,	314
RAPIDS OF NIAGARA,	315
WALWORTH HOMESTEAD, SARATOGA SPRINGS,	316

I.

AWAY!

SCHOOL-GIRL FANCIES—THEIR FULFILMENT—SUMMONED HOME—THE DECISION—ONLY A VALISE—PASSPORTS—UNCLE AND "DITTO"—THE STEAMER—BOUND FOR SCOTLAND—THE LEAVING AND THE LEFT—ADRIFT.

KENWOOD, a beautiful convent of the Sacred Heart, is perched on a thickly-wooded hill overlooking the Hudson river. Eight or nine busy, happy months had already passed since the summer vacation. It was June—too warm and lovely a month, I thought, to pore over books. Sitting at my desk in the study-hall, how many times my eyes wandered from the pages before me to gaze listlessly out of the window—over the little village of Kenwood, over the green cabbage and potato-fields, and across the sparkling blue river down which the great white "day-boat" was steaming its way towards New York, and little tugs were puffing here and there. I heeded not the shrill whistle of the train as it rushed across the fair landscape, bound for the great West, leaving behind a trail of snow-white smoke which floated a moment in the air, then vanished. Even the giant Catskills which guarded the southern horizon—the only dreamy, elf-haunted region in this section of the New World—standing in misty contrast to the busy, enterprising scene before me, were unable to arrest the flight of my school-girl fancies, and bring my thoughts back to the task before me. But after all, my mind is not so far away from my lessons as one might suppose. Look at the books on my desk—the open atlas! I was studying it a moment ago, but now I am gazing far over, beyond those gray Catskills, where the map of the whole world is laid out before me; and see! my History of England, with all its romance, my Mythology of Greece and Rome, and all the books of travel and adventure I have ever read, are twining themselves through my Geography lesson. It is no longer a dull, flat page. The mountains rise towards the sky; the rivers flow rapidly to the great surging ocean; the yellow and red of the different countries turn into green fields, with winding roads leading to picturesque ruins—or else scorching, sandy deserts, with oases and palm trees; the little round dots grow into magnificent cities with spires and domes, streets crowded with strange-looking people, and picture-galleries lined with wonderful faces peering at me from the time-worn canvas—the works of the Old Masters. Such was the vague picture I drew for myself that day of the Old World—that far away, enchanted region. Everything was misty, veiled, indefinite, unsatisfactory—I only knew that the reality must be beautiful, wonderful. I should see it all some day—yes, some time in the dim future, so I told myself. When? how? with whom? These were questions to be answered when the time came. Little dreamed I that even then a message was speeding onward through the mail—a message for me which was to answer the when? how? with whom?

After dinner, when we were all out at recreation, Madam appeared, coming from the house with a package of letters in her hand. She was soon discovered and hailed with a shout from the children. The next moment she was surrounded by a crowd of eager faces, and amidst a profound hush one name after another was read slowly and distinctly, each being followed by an exclamation of delight from the happy recipient and a groan of disappointment from the others. The last letter having been claimed and carried off, I was about to walk sadly away, when Madam called my name.

"Nelly," she said, "I have just received a letter from your mother. You are to go home on the two o'clock train—run quick and get ready!"

To my startled look of inquiry, she answered, "No bad news; your uncle is going to Europe."

There was no time for explanations, and away I ran, delighted at the prospect of a few days at home. Uncle was making his farewell visit, and of course I was going to bid him good-bye. In the convent parlor I found some one waiting to accompany me. A few hours on the cars brought us to Saratoga; a few minutes' walk and we were in sight of the dear old place under the pine trees. My little brother and sister who ran to meet us exclaimed:

"You're going to Europe!" "Yes, going with uncle." To my incredulous shake of the head they only protested the more, and led me forcibly into the house to see for myself. All was soon explained. It was true! Uncle had a year's "leave of absence" from his parish. He was going abroad for health and recreation, and had offered to take me with him. We were to start in two or three weeks. "Are you willing to go?" I was asked.

"Willing! indeed I am willing."

"But are you not afraid to go away from home for so long?"

"No, no," said I. "Is a year of travel longer than a year at boarding-school?"

And so it was decided I should go.

I looked on complacently while mother planned and

purchased my necessary outfit with great good management, and I wondered to see so many things packed away in a small valise, the only baggage Uncle wished me to take. Afterwards, as the various articles of our wardrobe wore out, we replaced them with whatever available garments we could find in the place we happened to be visiting, so that on reaching home after our travels we were clothed in the raiment of many countries.

At Albany I accompany Uncle to the bank to sign my name to the "letter of credit." In New York we wait several days for our passport, in which my resemblance to my uncle is curiously demonstrated. He is described as having brown hair, blue eyes, aquiline nose, small mouth. I am described as "ditto." The points of difference, nevertheless, are quite as striking as those of similarity: he being very tall—I very short; his hair just lightening into gray—mine just darkening into brown.

We make no plans beyond the immediate voyage, determining, like the veritable truants we are, to follow the bent of our inclinations when we reach the other shore of the Atlantic. The final preparations are made; and on a bright summer morning, Uncle and I, each with a valise, a shawl-strap, and an umbrella, stand among the passengers on the deck of an ocean steamer about to sail for Scotland. The wharf is crowded with people, and we are leaning over the railing, talking with the friends who have gathered to see us off. Suddenly the signal to move is given: "All aboard!" roars a harsh voice, and amidst the rushing of many feet, the clanking of chains, the hauling of ropes, the puffing of steam, and the muffled rumbling of machinery, we move slowly out to sea. Handkerchiefs are waving; friends are gazing anx-

THE EMBARKATION.

Face p. 4.

iously at each other, many, perhaps, for the last time; and farewell messages are sent from one to another across the rapidly increasing space between the leaving and the left. Voices can no longer be heard, and the handkerchiefs wave more frantically than ever; faces fade in the distance; individuals become indistinguishable; we see only a dense, dark mass of human beings with a waving white surface. I continued to watch one handkerchief, lower than the rest, which my little brother, standing near the edge of the wharf, has been waving ever since we started. We strain our eyes in that direction until we can no longer distinguish the place where they stand, then slowly turn away to watch the scenery.

I shall never forget my last view of New York, nor how strangely I felt as the city gradually disappeared in the distance until nothing was visible but a confused mass of buildings, with spires and domes rising here and there. We were soon past Governor's Island and the Narrows, then Sandy Hook, and now we were really on the ocean, with no land in sight, save the low banks of Long Island, which stretched along on the left as far as the eye could reach. These also grew fainter until nothing could be seen but a pale streak of blue along the horizon, which was lost sight of entirely, about six o'clock in the evening. O, the feeling of desolation that comes over one as the last point of *terra firma* disappears below the horizon! Country, kindred, all, are sinking, vanishing into the sea with the fading shore—away from one's grasp, out of one's sight. It is as if the great, blue dome of heaven were pressing down the land until its base rests on the water, and sea and sky meet, clasp, mingle, and lock one into a vast, mighty prison, to toss about helplessly until the great blue curtain shall be lifted on another shore, and the portals opened into strange countries.

But now I stand leaning over the stern of the vessel, looking back, and trying to pierce the thickening twilight, to see—ocean and air, ocean and air, to feel—that we are drifting away, away, away!

II.

AT SEA.

"WE MET BY CHANCE"—OVERBOARD—THE CAPTAIN'S CABIN—PETRELS AND PORPOISES—A COZY TEA-PARTY—OLD NEPTUNE'S SHOWER-BATH—"FIFTH MATE"—PILGRIMS—SOUNDING—A ROUNDABOUT DANCE—A MARINE POEM—SHIP-CROQUET—TAG—AN IMPROMPTU MASQUERADE—LAND.

WHILE still buried in these melancholy reflections, I was startled by a tap on the shoulder. I turned round, and what was my delight on recognizing Mary M., a former school-mate! "Why!" said I, "what a pleasant surprise! I had no idea you were going abroad."

"Yes; father has often wished to visit his old home in Ireland, which he left when he was a very little boy. We are going there now, and shall land at Londonderry."

"What an interesting trip it will be for you!"

"Indeed it will! But you—I thought you were still at the Convent."

"So I was, until the other day, when I started off in the midst of a half-learned lesson. Do you remember how, at recreation, we used to dance round in a ring, singing,—

"'The bear went over the mountain,
To see what he could see.'

Well, following his admirable example, I am going over the ocean for precisely the same purpose. But isn't it fortunate we happened to meet? It will make the voyage so much pleasanter."

"Yes—and see! father has discovered your uncle, and is talking with him."

As neither of us were in a very lively mood that evening, we remained standing at the stern and amused ourselves studying geography in the clouds. The increasing motion of the vessel caused Mary to feel "rather uncomfortable;" so, loosening a very pretty salts-bottle which some kind friend had fastened to my chatelain, just as we were starting, I was about to offer it to her, when, alas! the ship gave a sudden lurch, and it slipped from my grasp as I caught at the railing to steady myself; a faint cry arose of, "Salts-bottle overboard!" No one, however, went to the rescue, and the little beauty was consigned to a watery grave.

Mr. M. had the captain's state-room, but he arranged so that Mary and I could have it together while he took a berth somewhere else. This cabin was larger than the others, and had a little book-case with drawers, a shelf, and a cupboard, besides the usual conveniences. The berths were not one above the other, but mine lay against the side of the ship "fore and aft," with the little round window called the bull's-eye directly over it, while Mary's was across the state-room, at right angles with mine, and served as a seat in the daytime. Although our quarters were so comfortable, comparatively speaking, I made very little use of them, for the ocean air seemed to invigorate me, and as soon as I went on deck, although I might feel a little squeamish (as an old Scotch lady on board expressed the first symptoms of sea-sickness), I revived immediately. Several ladies on board determined to resist resolutely "paying tribute to Neptune" (as the final overthrow is nautically termed), and though all fought bravely against it, I was the only one from whom he did not receive his dues.

The Quarter-Deck at Sea.

Face p. 8.

The crisp, salt sea air gives one an appetite which is not appalled by five meals a day, served as follows:

Oatmeal porridge at 7 A. M. (to which I generally preferred a morning nap.)

Breakfast at 8.30 A. M.
Lunch   " 12.30 P. M.
Dinner   " 4   P. M.
Supper   " 7   P. M.

The first night that I "went to bed" in a "bunk" it suggested the idea of lying in a coffin, but before long I found that it was large enough to allow me to be tossed about. My first action on awakening in the morning was to open the bull's-eye and inhale the cool, fresh sea-breeze. Mary and I then began to examine our premises. We struck a bell by mistake, not knowing what it was. When the boy came, we did not wish to appear green, and asked for water as an excuse.

It rained all that day, and stormy petrels, or Mother Cary's chickens, were following the vessel. When they found something in the water, they would gather round and seem to dance a jig on the waves, and then walk over them with their feet spread out like fans. Porpoises were also seen in the distance. They looked like little pigs turning somersaults in the water.

Before lunch, Mary played on the piano and sang, many of the passengers joining in some national airs. In the evening the captain invited five or six of us into his cabin on deck to take tea with him. It was a very cozy scene as we sat round the little steam-heater, listening to the captain's wonderful stories about his adventures off the Algerine coast; and we were waited on by a funny, wild-looking little cabin-boy who jumped as if he were shot every time the captain gave him an order. Even the drizzling rain and the heavy fog seen through the open door failed to damp our spirits.

As the bells sounded eleven, every light on the steamer was extinguished, and all retired save the officer on watch, who continued to pace slowly up and down the bridge.

I awoke in the morning to find the state-room very close. On opening the bull's-eye I received an unexpected mouthful of salt water, for the waves were very high. The vessel was rolling and pitching dreadfully, and it was all I could do to dress and go out on deck. I took a run up and down with the captain, who was the only man who could stand steady. Then I felt very adventurous. Mary and I wished to go to the bow of the boat, where the spray was dashing over, and before any one had time to say no, we were off. Just as we reached the forecastle, she gave a plunge, and a great wave came dashing over the bow; but we stooped down and clung to the mast, which protected us from the force of the wave, so we only got a delightful shower-bath. In the meantime we were so completely covered with the spray that those we had left at the other end could not see us at all. The captain was alarmed, and thinking we might have been washed overboard, ran as fast as he could toward the spot where we were still crouching. We just tumbled into his arms as another wave sent the prow of the vessel high into the air, and the mist began to clear away so that we could see.

It became rougher and rougher, until we were obliged to take refuge on the monkey-deck. Only six or eight of the passengers, including Uncle and myself, were not sea-sick, and we sat there all day watching the waves dash over the main deck. A cold, piercing wind was blowing furiously, and I was wrapped to my ears in shawls and cloaks. I can not describe the grandeur of the ocean on that day, lashed about as it was by the furious blast, nor the feeling of exultation that tingled in every fibre, as we rode triumphantly through those angry waves. One moment we were high in the air on an immense swell, and before I could catch my breath, the whole deck was under water. Notwithstanding the stormy weather, on the following day I was the first lady on deck. The captain said I was a first-rate sailor, and promised to make me his "fifth mate."

My friend Mary and I spent a part of the evening in a little sitting-room appropriated to the stewardess. She was a Scotch girl, whose English was at first difficult to understand, but as there were many of her countrymen on board, the accent soon became familiar. She was very fond of "Robby Burns," as she called him, and often quoted his poems. This evening she sang many old Scotch ballads and songs with the real national brogue, which made them sound very sweetly.

Sunday we were near the Banks of Newfoundland, and it was so foggy we could only see a few yards around the ship. The shrill fog-whistle sounded in our ears every few minutes. After awhile it cleared off a little, the wind shifted in the right direction, all the sails were hoisted, and the vessel glided majestically over the water.

We found that among our passengers was a woman and her nephew, a little cripple, making a pilgrimage to Lourdes, in the hope of obtaining his cure. She had been hoarding her small savings a long time to make this journey. Truly her faith deserved to be rewarded!

Rough, wet, foggy weather continued for several days while we were on the banks, and, as they sounded many times, I obtained a little black pebble that came up from the bottom of the ocean. The lead our sailors used was a patented affair, with a little wheel that stops revolving when it reaches the bottom. There is an index at the other end showing the depth of the water by the number of revolutions the wheel makes. Attached to the lead is some greasy substance, and the pebbles and sand adhering to it show the kind of bottom; when nothing comes up, the lead has touched solid rock.

One evening when the fog had cleared away we went on deck after nine o'clock, and the colored lights of the sunset were still lingering in the west. As we steered further to the north, the days became even longer. When we came down from the "cold light of stars," the bright saloon presented quite a pretty picture— the passengers grouped about the room and engaged in playing whist, muggins, chess, cribbage, and other games. They were all very quiet, and the captain, who is full of fun and a real jolly Scotchman, wished to rouse them; so he asked Mary M. to play a polka, and, choosing me for a partner, we began to dance very fast indeed. The captain was short and very broad, with a merry, sunburnt face, and this evening he wore his tight little uniform coat, which made him look shorter and more comical than ever. It was no easy thing to dance in a room with three long tables and four brass posts, while the ship was rocking. He was very expert, however, and understood the motion of the vessel so well that he knew just when to turn a corner (and there were plenty of them) without being jolted against something. We fairly flew around, in one door and out at another, until every one was in a roar of laughter. It caused a great deal of fun, and after that evening they danced quite often. The captain taught us several Scotch country dances.

The officer on watch during the night would sometimes tell us of the glorious sunrise he had seen. In a moment of enthusiasm we all determined to rise early the next morning to witness one. The following poem was written by our first mate in honor of the great occasion:

AN OCEAN SUNRISE.

AT THREE O'CLOCK IN THE MORNING.

The passengers had orders given
The mate, the previous night at seven,
That one and all wished to be riven
From out their bunks, and upward driven,
To see a sunrise in the heaven
    At three o'clock in the morning.

At half-past two or thereabout,
Sure there he was, without a doubt,
Rapp'd at each door and gave a shout,
Advising all in terms devout,
To rise, and see the sun "turn out"
    At three o'clock in the morning.

Of sleepy-heads there were a lot,
Who vainly tried to leave their cot;
But sleep the upper hand had got,
And chained them firmly to the spot.
So covering up their heads, forgot
    'Twas three o'clock in the morning.

Still there were plenty who arose
According as they did propose,
And dressed themselves in—goodness knows!
I think 'twas principally bed-clothes,
Eager to see Apollo's nose
    At three o'clock in the morning.

Miss Walworth rose, and Miss McHugh,
Miss Logie, and Miss Wilson, too—
The latter daily robed in blue;
But somehow she had quite fell thro'
Her style, and dressed in something new
    At three o'clock in the morning.

Miss Mills and Mrs. Buel were
With Mrs. Strauss, assembled there,
Upon the monkey-deck, I swear,
A-shivering from the morning air.
It was a wonderful affair
To see them with disheveled hair,
Watching an ocean sunrise rare,
    At three o'clock in the morning

Miss Achurst and Miss Parsons both
Got up at last, though very loth,
And came on deck, arrayed in—troth,
A something like a table-cloth,
    At three o'clock in the morning.

Of gentlemen we'd quite a crowd,
With voices chattering very loud,
And who unanimously vowed
They felt, indeed, extremely proud
They'd seen the sun begild a cloud,
    At three o'clock in the morning.

There Father Walworth, Mr. Hughes,
Behind a "bull's-eye" small did choose
The beauteous sunrise to peruse,
Protected from the chilling dews,
    At three o'clock in the morning.

But Mr. Galbraith didn't mind
The dews, the shower, the bracing wind,
For fortunately he did find
A sure protection from behind
A lady fair, who was so kind,
    At three o'clock in the morning.

Fully an hour they had to sit,
Before the "glorious orb" thought fit
His watery lodging-house to quit,
And show himself a little bit,
Until I really think, that it
    Was long past three in the morning.

And just as he began to rise,
Tinging with gold the eastern skies,
Unfortunately—bless my eyes!
A rain-shower took them by surprise,
'And penetrated their disguise,
    At half-past three that morning.

They waited—well! it must be said,
Till they got wet from foot to head,
And then they all got up and fled,
Skedaddling every one to bed,
    At half-past three in the morning.

    Sea air is not very good for the complexion, and after a few days in the wind everybody had a red nose; the skin soon began to peel off, giving one much the appearance of a baked potato. Mine was worse than any of the others after that day on the monkey-deck.

    A pleasant pastime was a game called shuffle-board, or ship croquet. One of the sailors chalked a figure very much like hop-scotch on the floor of the deck. We played with round, smooth, flat pieces of wood, instead of balls; and long sticks widened at the lower end to push them along, took the place of mallets. It required a very steady, straight shot to knock the blocks on a high number, and, besides, one had to watch the motion of the vessel, or they rolled off to one side. One evening a sailor played on a bag-pipe while the others danced a Scotch jig on the deck.

    The rough, stormy part of the voyage was now over. Day after day we drifted on in happy listlessness, and although the wind blew, and the sky was blue, and the ocean was bluer still, the merry little band of passengers never once yielded to the blues. Thrown constantly into each other's society, and sharing alike wind and waves, fog and sunshine, fear and frolic, they became more and more like old familiar friends. Even some of the more dignified married ladies occasionally joined the captain and the young people in playing "tag" around the deck — in and out doors, up and down hatchways, until I doubt if the fishes and the sea-birds ever before witnessed such sport, or heard such shrieks of laughter breaking upon the calm and stillness of the ocean.

One evening, when amusements began to lag, some one suggested that we should get up a masquerade for the following night. The idea was greeted with great applause, and all agreed to join in the fun. A committee of ladies, with the "fifth mate" for spokesman, then marched off to gain the captain's approval. A little coaxing brought him over to our side, and entering heart and soul into the spirit of it, he did much more than we had expected. The next afternoon the saloon was cleared of everything but the four brass posts, and was draped artistically with American and British flags, while a handsome throne was erected at the farther end. A reverend and dignified gentleman spent the whole day making comical masks of brown paper and colored paint. The costumes were composed of whatever materials happened to be at hand—traveling wraps, bright-colored petticoats, sheets and pillow-cases, bed curtains, paper, night-caps, sailor-clothes, etc. We formed ourselves into "mutual aid" companies of four or five, each band to keep their own costumes secret, and as all were thoroughly masked, the fun was immense.

At eight o'clock in the evening the summons to appear resounded through the vessel. Strange, wild-looking forms issued from the state-rooms and placed themselves in order of procession along the narrow passage. "Queen Victoria" was enthroned at the end of the saloon, surrounded by a brilliant retinue, and smiling graciously and majestically upon her grotesque subjects, as they appeared two by two, and were announced in stentorian tones by the captain.

Doctor Punch, Mother Goose, Captain Jinks, Pocahontas the royal squaw, Hoky Poky, and the Heathen Chinee, appeared in quick succession. Next came a gentleman with a prominent nose, decked in red flannel tights and a waving plume, who strutted proudly on in the conceit of personating Romeo. But unlucky slip! the captain roars out, "Roman nose!" and in this character the crestfallen gallant kneels before his queen. He was followed by the Girl of the Period, by whose side hobbled Old Mother Hubbard of a very different period. But, behold! A mighty nose, consisting of a raw Irish potato of enormous proportions, appears upon the scene, followed by Solomon Levi, its happy possessor. It requires all the muscular exertion of the said gentleman to keep himself on "even keel," under such a weight of responsibility. A Merry Andrew with a Nun, a Quakeress hanging on the arm of Captain Jack of the Modocs, now enter, followed by many others.

Merry Andrew and Mother Goose begin the dancing by an original jig, followed by quadrilles, Virginia reels, country dances, and polkas, which were danced in quick succession until it neared the "witching hour of night," when witches, ghosts, and goblins joined in singing "Auld Lang Syne," and vanished from the scene.

But our ocean days were rapidly drawing to a close. The frequent sails, the land birds, and the preparations on ship-board, all told us we were nearing our destination. When land first came in sight we sat watching it all day. We passed between the northern coast of Ireland and several islands on the other side. We did not stop at Londonderry, as we expected, but went directly to Glasgow to catch the tide and get in a day sooner.

I think two weeks are long enough to be at sea.

III.

SOUTH-EASTERN SCOTLAND.

THE CLYDE—DUMBARTON CASTLE—A GRAY CITY—BONNINGTON LINN—CAVE OF SIR WILLIAM WALLACE—"LAND OF BURNS"—FASTER THAN TAM O'SHANTER—LOCH LOMOND—A PONY RIDE IN THE CLOUDS—A GLANCE FROM SEA TO SEA—EXPLORING ELLEN'S ISLE—FOLLOWING IN THE FOOTSTEPS OF RODERICK DHU AND FITZ JAMES—A VILLAGE OF KNOW-NOTHINGS—SCOTCH CHILDREN—STIRLING CASTLE—FAMILIAR FACES.

WE passed up the Clyde very early in the morning, and were all on deck to see the scenery, of which we had heard so much. I was greatly disappointed; it could not be compared with the Hudson. The river is very narrow and hard to navigate, and the water a muddy, coffee color.

We passed Dumbarton Castle, or, rather, all of it that remains. It was built on a high, rugged rock that stands out boldly in the water. I am not sure whether it is a peninsula or an island, but in either case, it looks impregnable. A part of the old wall and batteries are standing near the base, and directly over them a more modern house has been built, which looked, to me, more like a soap factory than anything else. This was at first pointed out as the Castle, and all the romance associated with it was immediately destroyed; but as we advanced, so that we could see the other side of the rock, a turret and a few stones, one above the other, became visible as the ruins of this great stronghold of Scotland.

When, at last, we disembarked, we had to stand in the rain while a Custom House officer examined our baggage, and it was yet many a day before we "set foot on *dry* land.". After a time of dreary waiting, we managed to get a cab and drive to the hotel.

Glasgow is the smokiest, foggiest, sootiest place I have ever seen. The houses are all built of gray stone, and everything is gray—the streets, the pavements, the sky, and the smoke. After seeing more of it, however, we found it to be a very handsome city; large, well-paved, and, with the exception of the streets near the river, very clean — much cleaner, indeed, than many of the people. Everybody looks "as old-fashioned as the hills," and the lower class of women and children, all go barefooted. I think the "bonnie Scotch lassies" are very few, for I never before saw a more homely set of young women. We visited the old cathedral, a magnificent Gothic structure, with a massive, mysterious, and ghostly crypt. It is difficult to form an idea of what it really is, without actually seeing it; and the pictures for sale, make it look like a handsome railroad depot.

From Glasgow we made a trip to Lanark and the Falls of the Clyde, which was very interesting. The village itself is a quaint old place, with thatched roofs and crooked, irregular streets, while the whole country round is a perfect picture. After dining at the Clydesdale Inn, we drove about two miles in a phaeton, over a beautiful road, hedged in on either side, and made of crumbled red sandstone, which contrasted very prettily with the green grass. We then reached the gates of Sir Charles Ross' estate, through which the Clyde flows. There we had to leave the horse, and walk, with an old man for a guide, who strided on before us with a stick and an umbrella. This reminds me that the people here never think of going out without water-proofs, umbrellas, and all the conveniences, or rather, inconveniences, for damp weather; it rains almost constantly, sunshine being an exception. We had gone only a few steps when it began to pour, but we continued to follow a winding path, finding ourselves one moment down near the water's edge, and the next, upon a high precipice, looking at the river a hundred and twenty feet below. At one place we had to cross a narrow ledge, with the water roaring and foaming under our feet, to reach Sir William Wallace's Cave. It is a round, smooth opening, niched deep into the rock, where the great Scottish hero hid himself away for some time, to escape the search of the English. If discovered in that retreat, he could defend himself against a whole army. Being directly over the rapids, it can not be reached by water, and only one at a time can approach by the rocky ledge, across which we now cautiously·retraced our steps, after picking an ivy leaf that grew near the mouth of the cave. At another place, we passed over a little iron bridge on to a rocky island, and just as we looked down on Bonnington Linn, the principal fall, the sun burst from behind a cloud, making the water sparkle and dazzle like a shower of diamonds, and causing a rainbow to appear through the mist. To the right are these falls, and wild, steep precipices on either side of the river, with the jagged ruins of an old castle on the shore; while to the left, just above the fall, the water runs as smooth and clear as glass, with green banks sloping gently towards the river, and cattle and sheep grazing under the trees. It was a remarkable contrast.

One day we went to Ayr, to see the "Land of Burns." The cottage where he was born is a little whitewashed, thatched house of two rooms. The one in which he

LOCH KATRINE.

Face p. 23

first saw light (he did not see much of it, for the only window was about a foot square) was the smallest, and contained some of the old furniture — the wooden dresser, the broad fireplace, and the little bed built back in the wall.

We went inside the Burns Monument, and saw the old Bible he presented to "Highland Mary," and various other relics.

Alloway Kirk is not very large; it has no roof, and one end is overgrown with ivy. The old bell is still hanging over the front of the building, and we looked in through the window where "Tam" is supposed to have watched the witches. We then followed down the road to the old bridge "where Maggie lost her tail." It was very amusing to hear an old man, our guide at the Kirk, repeat snatches of "Tam O'Shanter," as he pointed out the scenes of the poem. He jabbered it off so fast that before we had time to look in the direction he indicated, he had finished the whole scene of the witches, and Tam was safely over the bridge. Burns' poetry is hard enough to *read* and understand, but when an old Scotchman rattles it off, it is like Hebrew.

We left Glasgow in the cars, or carriages as they are called, for Balloch, which is just at the foot of Loch Lomond. We met a charming English lady and gentleman in our compartment, who continued to travel with us several weeks. Scotland is noted as a place for meeting pleasant people, and we were particularly fortunate in that respect.

We took passage on a little steamer at Balloch to go up Loch Lomond. This lake is wide at the southern end, and contains twenty-three beautiful little islands. As we wound in and out among them, a new vista opened every moment, and a continued series of exclamations were uttered as the scene varied. At length the lake became narrower, the islands almost disappeared, and the banks on either side became high and mountainous. We were soon among the Highlands, with mountain after mountain appearing in every direction, rising, as it were, out of the lake; some smooth and rounded, others steep and precipitous. The steamboat stopped at several landings, where a few pretty little houses were built in a valley, at the foot of some high peak. About an hour and a half brought us to Rowardennan pier, lying directly under Ben Lomond, which is the highest mountain but one in Scotland. We landed at the spot where Rob Roy stood and waved good-bye to Frank Osbaldistone, when he was leaving the Highlands. The small hotel, where we took lunch, stands on a level piece of ground near the lake.

It is a walk of four miles and a ride of six miles up Ben Lomond. Uncle and I went on ponies, while the gentleman who accompanied us walked. He was used to such tramps, being an Englishman and having climbed a great deal in Switzerland. I held on to my pony and was not at all frightened, though he went over places where one would think no man or beast could keep his footing; he knew the way better than I did, so I made no attempt to guide him. These ponies had a peculiar fashion of stopping to eat grass or ferns, even at the most dangerous places, and it was impossible to prevent them. It became quite ridiculous; and once I tried, just for fun, to see how many I could count between each bite. "One, two, three, four"—down goes the pony's head! I begin over. "One, two, three, four, five, six, seven"—there it goes again! I could not get above ten, so I gave it up; and turning to the Scotch boy who acted as guide, or rather walked in the rear of the ponies, which took the lead and seemed disposed to have their own way generally:

"Have they been fed this morning?" I asked.

"Yae, lassie," he replied.

"Well, what is the matter with them then?"

"I dinna' ken; it's a way they hae."

This lad seemed to think that all difficulties, whether relating to ponies, mountains, clouds, or anything else, were settled, by remarking, conclusively, "It's a way they hae." We soon found that mountains had "ways" quite as tantalizing as ponies. Just as we thought we were nearing the top, another ridge would appear, more steep and rugged than the last, and so we were deceived again and again, until we thought we should never reach the summit. We continued to climb up, up, up, until we invaded the region of the clouds; there they lay, all around us. A thick, heavy cloud had taken quiet possession of the very summit we were striving to attain. What! baffled by a cloud? No, indeed! So we rode boldly into the very midst of it, mounted the last ascent, and stood on the topmost peak. Ah! but we were baffled. That ugly, gray monster, not content with hiding the entire view, wrapped us closer and closer in his damp cloak, causing the moisture to penetrate to the very skin, and we felt his cold, clammy touch on our faces until we shivered from head to foot. The wind, too, seemed leagued against us, cutting us through and through with its sharp, bitter blasts; and it was some time before we discovered that, on the contrary, it was doing us good service. It rent asunder the gray curtain before us, now here, now there, and before the tattered fragments could come together again, we obtained glimpses of the lakes, the mountains, and the sky, which were only the more bewitching because so transient. Finally, collecting all its forces, the wind rushed up the sides of the mountain; the heavy curtain was lifted bodily from its resting-place, and as it rolled slowly up, up, up, till it floated high above our heads, the whole grand panorama of about one-third of Scotland was before us. There, just at our feet, lay Loch Lomond, smooth as a sheet of glass, with every island so distinct that it was impossible to realize that they were more than three thousand feet below us. Beyond, we counted eight successive chains of mountains, each rising higher than the last. To the south could be seen the river Clyde and the bold rock of Dumbarton Castle, and further still, the ocean and the Isle of Arran. Eastward, the dim outline of Stirling Castle was barely visible; and, straining our eyes to the horizon, we fancied we saw the Firth of Forth, mingling with the sky. Thus we could take in at a glance the entire breadth of Scotland, from sea to sea. The mountain on which we stood breaks down on the north side in a precipice of two thousand feet, at the foot of which is a beautiful green valley, where the river Forth has its source in a mere mountain rill. We saw Loch Katrine, Loch Ard, the Loch of Menteith, and several others equally beautiful, lying in shadow among the Highlands, in different directions.

We reached the hotel again at about six o'clock, with a wonderful appetite for dinner. But it was fully a week before I recovered from the aching effects of that pony ride.

Late the same evening we went rowing on Loch Lomond. When we were some distance up the lake, Uncle determined that we should sail back. With an oar for a mast, and his blanket-shawl for a sail, which was held by the little boy who rowed us out, and who took the place of cords, pulleys, and fastenings, we sailed swiftly down the lake, while our English friend sat behind and steered with the other oar.

The next day we left on a steamer for Inversnaid, where an open coach, crowded with twenty people, took us through a beautiful glen. Inversnaid burn, a stream of the most romantic sort, runs through the glen, while the road winds up and down through all kinds of perilous places and enchanting scenes, until we reach Stronachlacher, at the head of Loch Katrine. It would be worse than useless for me to attempt a description of this lovely lake or its mighty portals, Ben An and Ben Venue, which seemed now to frown, and now to smile upon us as we passed between them, close to Ellen's Isle, then hurried on through the Trossachs, and just at nightfall reached the Ardnacheanachrochan Hotel, built with turrets and towers in the Scotch baronial style, and situated on Loch Achray. In this wild retreat, we remained a few days to study out the scene of the "Lady of the Lake." We walked leisurely through the Trossachs, which is not very wonderful after all; only a beautiful, rugged glen, such as are seen frequently in the United States. Uncle was disappointed; from Scott's description, he had formed an idea far beyond the reality. This, however, was the only spot where the great "word-painter" deceived us by using a little "poetic license." In every other case we found his descriptions, even in the minutest details, perfectly true to nature.

At the end of our walk, we took a little boat and rowed over to Ellen's Isle, where, with some difficulty, we landed. It is a very wild place, and required careful stepping to keep our feet, for it has black, slimy places so overgrown with fern and heather, that one moment I found myself high on a rock, and the next down—"goodness knows" where, and I didn't know how. I enjoyed the expedition very much, however, and while returning, I took one of my first lessons in rowing.

Every mile of the ride to Callander was in some way connected with the "Lady of the Lake." We passed Lanrich Mead, where the clans gathered; then the place where Roderick Dhu whistled, and his clansmen sprang up before Fitz-James, and as suddenly disappeared in the tall heather; also Coilantogle Ford, where the duel was fought; finally we followed for some time the course of the herald who bore the Fiery Cross.

We reached Callander at noon. Here we met Mr. H——, a lawyer of Albany, and an acquaintance of Uncle's. He had been accidently separated from his nephew, in the depot at Stirling, and, having telegraphed to let him know where he had stopped, was expecting him on the next train. He said that fortunately, he had drawn some money the day before, and handed his nephew five pounds. Uncle immediately took out a five-pound note and bade me keep it in case of a like accident. It remained in an obscure corner of my purse until we reached home. Mr. H—— told us that we had happened on a very "unlucky spot." We soon witnessed the truth of the assertion.

Before we left Callander (which was as soon as possible), we concluded that it was the most remarkable spot we had yet visited. In the first place, it was almost impossible to find anybody, as neither clerk, waiter, nor landlord were visible; secondly, they did not seem to know anything when we did find them. They could not even tell us the names of the mountains immediately surrounding the village.

After being directed in a dozen different ways, and stumbling into various back-yards, we at length succeeded in finding the old Roman earth-work, which was thrown up in the time of the ancient Britons, and although great trees have grown on the top of it, the shape is still discernible.

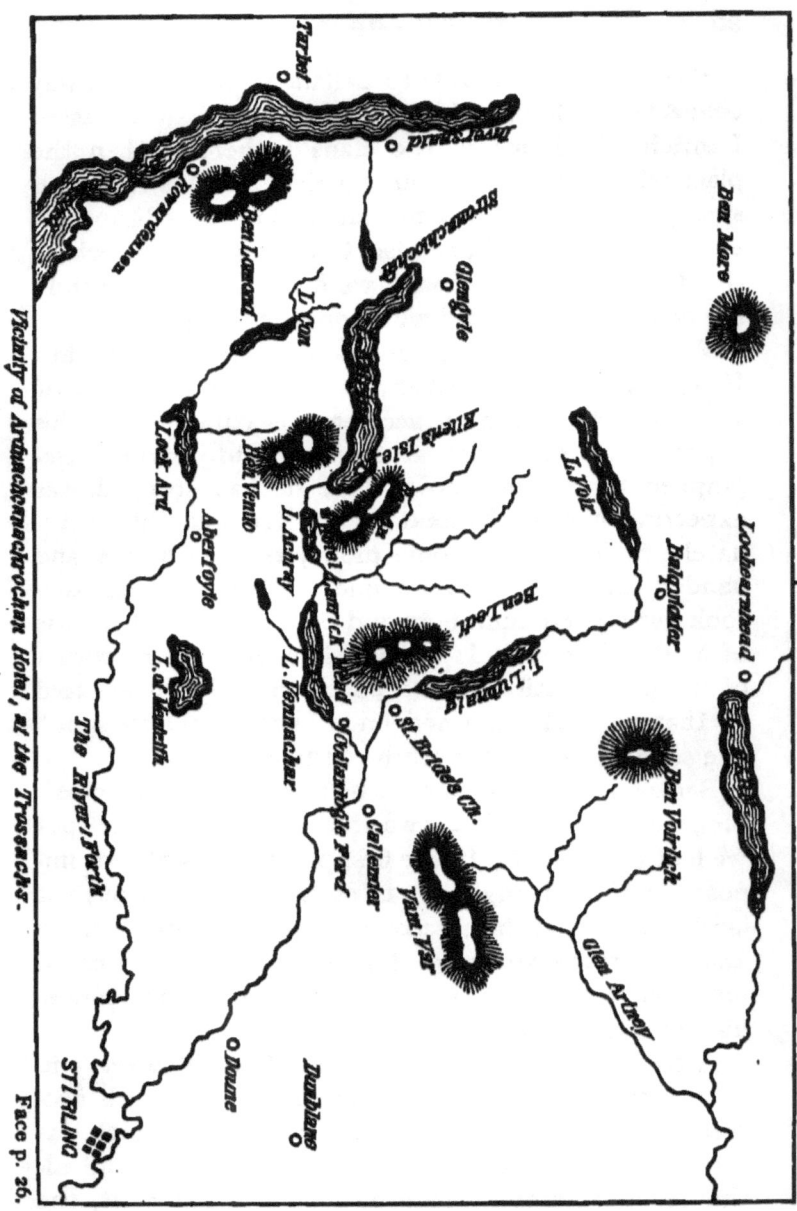

Vicinity of Ardcheanacrochan Hotel, at the Trosachs.

Face p. 26.

We had intended to ascend the mountain of Uam Var, but as nobody could tell us which one of the surrounding peaks bore that name, we were obliged to give up the project in despair. An expedition in search of some falls in the neighborhood, proved equally unsuccessful, and we came back after a long walk up hill, without having seen anything, and with wet feet and a cold in my head. By this time we were completely disgusted with Callander, and finding that a northward train left at six o'clock, we decided to take it. After much ado, the bill was at last obtained and paid, which we afterwards found to have been somebody else's; and various other difficulties being overcome, or overlooked, we finally started, caring little where we were going, just so it was away from Callander.

The country through which we were passing was filled with associations of Rob Roy. Our only fellow-passenger, a Scotch gentleman who declared himself a descendant of the Stuarts, a rival clan, had no very high opinion of our hero. He considered him as rather a disreputable character, and took great pride in pointing out the spot where a great-uncle of his had fought with Rob Roy and forced him to beg his pardon. We stopped at a little station on Loch Earn, and after waiting an hour for the coach, in a Scotch mist—which is worse than rain, hail, or snow, for it penetrates everything—we reached our night-quarters, where we had a good laugh over all the mishaps at Callander. By the way, I lost my umbrella there.

Loch Earn pleased us more than any of the Scotch lakes, and after taking long rides and walks around it in various directions, we started for Stirling in a stage-coach. As we passed through the little towns on our way, all the boys and girls, and babies, would stand by the road-side with their mouths wide open, yelling at the top of their voices. I suppose they were shouting at the enlivening sight of twenty-eight people on the outside of the coach, packed as close as sardines. As we rode through one village, a whole crowd of children ran after us, even little tots hardly old enough to walk. The gentlemen threw them pennies, then watched to see the "bairns" all run for them. When the money fell in the fields, how fast they scrambled and tumbled over the fences! One little girl got more than any of the others, for she could beat all the boys at running. We were going so fast that it was very hard for them to keep up with us, and for every conquest she made, she was greeted with a "hurrah!" from the gentlemen on the coach. Nearly all the Highland children go barefooted, and the boys wear plaid, or gray kilts, and little odd-looking jackets.

Stirling Castle is grand, gray, and enchanting; full of gloomy old stories, with cells and dungeons to match. Here, was the room where King James murdered Douglass, and the window through which the body was thrown. There, was the square opening in the ramparts through which the unfortunate Mary, Queen of Scots, as a prisoner, looked down upon the tournament ground below. Yonder is the cell described by Scott in the death scene of the brave Roderick Dhu. As we stood looking up at a heavily-barred window, the guide told us how one of the kings of Scotland, when he was a baby, was let down in a basket from a window of Edinburgh Castle and stolen away in the night; then how those who stole him brought him to Stirling, and put him in that room with the grated window.

From Stirling we went to Glasgow, having made a complete circle since we left it. When we reached the cozy little Hotel Blair again, and found the beaming landlady waiting to receive us, and a party of our ocean friends in the parlor, we spent a pleasant, home-like evening before starting on a more extensive trip through the north of Scotland.

IV.

RAIN AND RUINS.

THE "IONA"—THREE HUNDRED AND FIFTY-TWO DAYS OF RAIN—KYLES OF BUTE—GENUINE HIGHLANDERS—THE HUNTING SEASON—FINGAL'S CAVE IN A STORM—BIRTHPLACE OF CHRISTIANITY IN SCOTLAND—THE CALEDONIAN CANAL—DRIP FOR DRIP—A BANISHED CLAN—LADS AND LASSIES—A TIRESOME REST—WE DIFFER—ONCE MORE IN THE LOWLANDS.

AT six o'clock one August morning we bade adieu to the smoky city of Glasgow for the last time, and embarked on the pretty little excursion steamer "Iona," to go up the western coast of Scotland.

As we had been told on first entering this country that during the previous year there had been only thirteen days on which it did not rain, of course we were well provided with water-proofs, rubbers, and damp anticipations.

As we passed down the narrow, coffee-colored Clyde, we could hear a constant chink, chink of tools, and we counted more than a hundred large ocean steamers being built. They were in every stage of progress, from the mere iron frame-work to the finished vessel, all painted and ready to be launched.

We next saw the green fields, and the cattle browsing under the trees; then grand old Dumbarton Rock; then—the rain. The shores became more and more distant as we floated out into the Firth of Clyde, and, finally, they disappeared on one side, so we could look far out to sea. We passed the Isle of Arran, and then wound through the Kyles of Bute (or "Beauty," as they should have been called). The Crinan Canal, through which our course lay, separates a long, narrow peninsula from the main land of Argyle. Although the canal is only nine miles in length, it has a succession of fifteen locks, and the process of raising us from one to another was so slow, that many of the gentlemen left the steamer and walked to the end of the canal, which enabled them to see more of the country.

We who remained on the boat were amused watching the little Scotch children who brought pails of fresh milk, which they distributed to the passengers at a penny a glass. There were no houses in sight, and the children had run down from the hills in their Scotch plaids and bare feet, like so many little Highlanders, armed with milk-pails, and springing up from the heather like Roderick Dhu's soldiers.

We saw a man standing near one of the locks, who recalled vividly to mind the famous Rob Roy. He wore the entire costume—kilt, jacket, scarf, cap, short leggings, which left the knees bare, and even the heavy leathern purse suspended from his belt, while he had the remarkably long arms, and sandy red hair, characteristic of that hero. A lad of about twelve years, evidently his son, was with him, clothed in the same plaid, and gazing at the steamer and its passengers with open-mouthed wonder. They had guns, and were undoubtedly on a hunting expedition. These were some of the few genuine Highlanders, so clad, that we saw during our stay in Scotland. They wore their costume with a natural ease and grace that showed it to be their every-day attire.

We happened to be in the hunting regions on the "twelfth of August," the opening of the shooting season, and the Highlands were overrun with Englishmen, many of whom had donned the picturesque garments of the country for the occasion; but it was impossible to mistake their nationality.

After issuing from the Crinan Canal, it was not long before we reached Oban, a Scotch watering-place, beautifully situated around a semicircular bay, dotted with islands, and surrounded by mountains. There are several old ruined castles, covered with moss and ivy, in the neighborhood. Just beyond a short point that encloses the bay on the north, an arm of the Atlantic reaching inland, has been stretched across Scotland from lake to lake until it shakes hands with the North Sea at Inverness; this is the great Caledonian Canal.

We took up our abode for a short time at Oban. The morning of the day that we had set apart for circumnavigating the island of Mull, which was dimly visible from my window, we awoke to find the sun and the clouds struggling for the supremacy. By the time the little steamer "Chevalier" was ready to leave the pier, there were not more than four or five gentlemen and one lady, besides Uncle and myself, who were willing to venture. When we had shot out of the bay and were fairly out to sea, in addition to the heavy rain-storm that had now come upon us in all its fury, a fierce wind struck us, and the brave little vessel was tossed about on the waves, and rolled from side to side like a toy. We had a choice of two evils: if we stayed down in the small cabin of the steamer, we would become sea-sick, for the ports had to be closed to keep out the waves, making the air very close; if we sat on the deck, we would certainly be drenched. We preferred the latter alternative. The lady passenger and myself sat together near the smoke-stack, our chairs lashed to the railing of the hatchway, and covered up to our necks with an immense piece of canvas. In spite of the umbrellas we held over our heads, our hair and the feathers on my hat were like wet strings, the water trickling down from the ends of them as if they were water-spouts, and the rims of our hats were gutters on a roof.

At length the island of Staffa came in sight; but though the rain had almost ceased, the captain said he was afraid we could not land. It was decided that we should try it in a row-boat. Accordingly, the boat was let down over the side of the vessel, and the steps lowered by which we slowly and cautiously descended. The little boat was dancing up and down as if it were on red-hot coals, and had feelings. When I stood at the bottom of the ladder, with one foot extended, about to step into it, lo! it sank into the "trough of the sea" far beneath me; almost instantly a great wave washed over my feet, and dizzy and startled, I looked upward, to see the row-boat dancing above me, higher than the deck of the steamer. Thus a see-saw was continued for several minutes, for when the boat went down, the ladder went up, and *vice versa*. As they rested on a level for a few seconds at a time, we were dragged hastily into the boat, one after another. Once started, we hoped our difficulties were at an end, but the water washed in on us, and a great piece of slimy, yellow sea-weed flopped into the boat. It would be as much as our lives were worth to attempt to row into Fingal's Cave on such a day, but we were determined to see it, so we landed on the opposite side of the island where the rocks were not so precipitous, and walked a mile through the tall, wet grass to the cave.

We then ascended a hill, and when on the summit, found ourselves standing over a precipice, the waves foaming and dashing up into the crevices of the rocks at the base, and near at hand a frail, little wooden stairway leading over the ledges, by which we descended. The only way I can describe the peculiar formation of the rocks we then scrambled over is, by suggesting the idea of octagonal or many-sided columns, about two

FINGAL'S CAVE.

feet in diameter, placed close together and broken off at irregular heights. The cave is very high, and has the same formation, except that the broken columns are hanging overhead as well as lying under-foot. It extends back into the hill more than two hundred feet, and each wave of the ocean rushes in and dashes half-way up the cave at the back. The wavering rope by which we clung, the dangerous, slippery rocks we trod on, the gloomy grandeur of the cave, and the deafening roar of the waters inspired a feeling of awe and sublimity, and it was with a sensation of relief that we emerged into the daylight.

Soon after leaving Staffa, we landed on the island of Iona, the birth-place of Christianity in Scotland, where all the inhabitants turned out to see us, and offered sea-shells and ocean treasures of all kinds for sale. Then they took us to see the ruins of the oldest cathedral in Scotland, and the nunnery founded by St. Colomba. We saw the burial-places of several of the early Scotch kings, and of a great many Highland chiefs and ecclesiastics, with rough inscriptions, and odd old carvings of warriors and bishops.

On returning to the steamer, we took our places under the canvas again, and prepared for several hours more in the rain. The island of Mull was in sight all the while, and its innumerable tiny mountain-rills, swollen by the rains, came pouring over the cliffs into the sea, making so many cataracts; from the distance at which we saw them, they appeared like white ribbons streaming over the rocks.

The next time we left Oban, it was to go through the Caledonian Canal, and unlike our last expedition, it was undertaken on a sunshiny day. The scenery in this part of Scotland is more like Switzerland than that of any other country. There is an endless play of sunlight and shadow on the mountains, and every old castle we pass awakens some historic or romantic interest.

At one place, we land to take a ride through Glencoe. We sit on the top of a coach with two dozen other tourists, the driver cracks his whip, and we jog merrily on. We enjoy the bright landscape a few minutes, and pass the great slate quarries, near which entire villages are built of slate, even to the fences, and then, down comes a shower, and up go twenty-six umbrellas. Uncle says to the lady beside him:

"Madam, I fear my umbrella is dripping on you."

"Never mind," she replies, "I see the water from mine is dropping down your niece's neck."

"And here is a perfect stream of water from somebody's umbrella running down my back;" "and mine!" "and mine!" says one after another.

Everybody's umbrella is dripping on somebody else, making it even all around. We conclude that, under the circumstances, the best thing we can do is to laugh, and we all share the merriment as well as the drenching. The shower ceases for a moment, and down come twenty-six umbrellas. They are all handed to the gentlemen sitting at the ends of the seats, who hold them over the sides of the coach, letting the water run off on to the road. If we should happen to pass through a dusty city just at this moment, we would serve the purpose of a first-class "sprinkling wagon." During the half-hour's ride through the glen, I count ten separate showers, before and after each of which, the umbrellas go up and down simultaneously. At a turn in the valley, the guide points out to us a small dark hole, or a cave near the summit of a mountain, where, he says, a hermit once lived. I should think that when he once got up there, he could never have come down again without breaking his neck, so he may have been a hermit by necessity. I tire of counting showers, so I do not know how many we have on the way back to the steamer. There is one man in the party whose pockets are filled with "tracts," printed in the Gaelic dialect, which he distributes at the little Highland villages

EDINBURGH CASTLE AND SCOTT MONUMENT.

Face p. 36.

through which we pass. We are soon once more on the canal.

We stop for a night at the foot of Ben Nevis, the highest peak in Scotland, hoping for an opportunity to ascend, but he wears such a heavy night-cap of mist and cloud, that there is little chance of his uncovering his bald head for a week or more. So we continue our journey, passing from one beautiful lake into another. The shores of Loch Oich particularly interest us as being the country of the MacDonalds of Glengarry. One chieftain of this clan, whose castle we saw, an unfortunate adherent of the Pretender, was the prototype of Fergus MacIvor, of Scott's Waverley, and Flora MacDonald, his sister, was the original of Flora Mac-Ivor. Driven by poverty and the encroachments of the great landholders of Scotland, this clan emigrated in a body to Canada. It is said that the scene of their departure was heart-rending. They were obliged to tear themselves away from their own beautiful country, every spot of which was endeared to them by their ancient traditions. These people, who were all Catholics, have formed quite a settlement of their own in Canada. Uncle says that he once met their chief in New York.

As we neared the end of our journey, a party of young people came on board, who had been out in the woods on a picnic. They were the real Scotch "lads and lassies," and right "bonnie" ones they were. They danced old-fashioned country dances on the deck, talked very broad Scotch, and sang ballads. They amused us all the way to Inverness, which is at the termination of the Caledonian Canal.

From there we came southward through the beautiful Pass of Killicrankie and the Perthshire Highlands. This long and uninteresting ride gave us a rest from sight-seeing, which was quite refreshing for the moment, and enabled us to appreciate more fully the adventures awaiting us in Edinburgh and the Lowlands.

We had seen so many castles and mountains during the past few weeks that we began to feel tired of them —yes, actually tired of them. Uncle and I quite naturally did not always agree as to how they should be regarded. For instance, when we stood on the top of a mountain he would like to study the geography of the country, and to fix definitely in his mind where each mountain and valley was situated; while I was perfectly indifferent as to which was Ben Voirlich and which Glen Artney, if the whole scene was beautiful and imposing. Then in visiting an old ruin he would enjoy wading through the mud and rubbish to examine how thick the walls were, how many guns such a castle had, and like details; while to me it was much more enjoyable and picturesque to look at from a distance, with its ivy-grown battlements and towers standing out against the sky, or with a dark mountain in the background. Fortunately we could both be satisfied. First he would look at it from my point of view, then I would join him in entering into particulars. I soon found, too, that his way was very interesting.

Americans meet us at every step. Some one told me that eighty-five thousand had come over since the year began.

Our ladies do not lose their reputation for carrying large trunks. The other day, as a very heavy one was rolled on to the coach, making every one inside start at the sudden thump! an English lady sitting by me exclaimed:

"Gracious! that must belong to an American lady."

Of course it was not my modest valise. It is certain, however, that if the English ladies are sensible as to quantity in dress, they are quite insensible as to taste. Even old ladies wear the most remarkable contrasts in color.

But, in the meantime, Uncle and I are hastening towards our destination. We stop a few hours at Perth, where we walk through the old "South Inch" or common. We reach Edinburgh at nightfall, and after much difficulty in finding accommodation, we are received into a crowded hotel, where Uncle is obliged to sleep on a couch in one of the parlors, while a small bath-room is fitted up for my inconvenience.

V.

EDINBURGH AND THE HOME OF SCOTT.

HEART OF MID-LOTHIAN—MEMORIES OF MARY, QUEEN OF SCOTS—EDINBURGH CASTLE—ABBOTSFORD—SIR WALTER SCOTT'S STUDY—HIS COLLECTION OF ANTIQUITIES—HIS TOMB—MELROSE ABBEY.

HERE, at Edinburgh, we found two letters from the other side of the Atlantic. How welcome they were! We had been travelling a whole month and not even a line had reached us to say whether, at home, they were all alive or not. We had changed our route and missed our letters.

Although in travelling it is pleasant to meet agreeable people, it seems that we must always part with them just as we begin to know them well and like them. It is but a variation, you see, of the old story—Hinda's "dear gazelle." We have sometimes been fortunate, however, in meeting the same people at different places. The English lady and her nephew who travelled with us in the region of Ben Lomond and Loch Katrine, happened to be here in the same hotel. Indeed, so friendly had our intercourse become, that, although we had never been formally introduced, they urged us most cordially, when they were leaving, to visit them at their homestead, near London, when we should reach that city One night while we were at Edinburgh, these friends proposed, at about nine o'clock, that we should go to the top of Calton Hill, a steep, rocky eminence near the center of the city, promising

HOLYROOD PALACE.

Face p. 40.

us a spectacle such as could not be seen anywhere else. When we reached the summit there was, indeed, a remarkable sight before us and beneath us—the glimmering lights of the city stretching out on every side until they mingled with the stars. We had quite a dispute in regard to some of them, as to which were earthly and which heavenly lights. One of them we finally

EDINBURGH CASTLE.

decided to be the revolving light of a lighthouse on an island far off in the Firth of Forth, for, on watching it more closely, we saw that it kept disappearing and returning. We recognized Prince's street—that great, broad thoroughfare—by the long range of lamps on either side, extending in a straight line from the distant suburbs to the very foot of the hill, there making one crooked turn and then continuing out to Holyrood. Looking across the valley through which the railroad tracks now run, we could count, by the tiers of lighted windows, houses of nine and ten stories on the opposite hill.

We managed to see the principal objects of interest in Edinburgh in spite of the weather, which was gloomy enough to send one's spirits below zero. The only way to manage in Scotland is to brave wind, rain, and fog, hoping it will clear up before you have gone far, for it brightens very quickly when the sun can once get a peep at you. We drove through all the old parts of the city, and took great delight in hunting up the scenes of "The Heart of Mid-Lothian." We found them too; the Grass Market, Cow-gate, the course of the great riot, Jeannie Dean's Cottage, and (will you believe it?) even the old Muscat's Cairn. A large heart inlaid among the pave-stones right in the middle of a street, marks the place where the old Tolbooth or Prison stood, after which the novel is named.

We wandered through gloomy old Holyrood Palace, with its beautiful little ruined chapel and imposing courts, every portion of which is haunted with sad memories and incidents of the life of Queen Mary of Scots. So vividly do these quiet old walls recall the scenes, that in passing from room to room, one starts and fancies that the spirits of her persecutors and her friends are either peering from behind the faded tapestry, or rising from the blood-stains on the floor; while one is seized with an almost irresistible impulse to draw aside the time-worn, embroidered trappings of her stately bed, expecting to behold the same lovely form that once lay there seeking troubled snatches of repose when surrounded by attendants among whom this hapless

THE OLD TOLBOOTH.

Face p. 42.

young queen scarce knew which to trust and which to dread.

It was the same sad story that followed us through Edinburgh Castle; it was a portrait of the same beautiful face that looked down upon us from its walls—proud, yet bewitching, the delicate mouth seeming now to smile sweetly and sadly, now to curl scornfully, but always enchaining our admiration. In another room we saw the ancient regalia of Scotland—a golden crown, sceptre, and sword—the cause of so much misery and bloodshed; but now when the Scots have no longer a king of their own to wear it, an iron-barred case and armed sentinels guard it as a mere curiosity.

Upon the ramparts stands old "Mons Meg," the famous large cannon that has made its mark, and a deadly one, no doubt, in the annals of Scotland. It is only a step from the door of the beautiful little chapel of St. Margaret, the one quiet, holy spot in the midst of all these warlike surroundings.

Although we had despaired of pleasant weather to ascend Salisbury Crags and Arthur's Seat, we would have been loth to leave this interesting city, had it not been for the delightful place toward which we now turned our steps—the home and haunts of Scott. On the cars we met two very agreeable ladies from Louisville, Ky., so the time passed pleasantly until we reached Melrose. There they took a carriage with us, and we drove together to Abbotsford, about three miles west of the village. We passed the Eildon Hills, three large, rounded elevations that really look as if they might once have formed a single mountain, and suggested the words of the old monk at the wizard's grave, in the "Lay of the Last Minstrel:"

> "And, stranger, I could name to thee
> The words that cleft Eildon hills in three,
> And bridled the Tweed with a curb of stone."

Abbotsford is a handsome building, with turrets and towers, just such a place as you might imagine Sir Wal-

ABBOTSFORD.

ter Scott's residence to be; it had a quiet, hospitable air about it, and although the gardens were a little stiff and prim, they were relieved by the old stone walls, almost covered with ivy and holly, which enclosed the grounds. The place is still occupied by a descendant of the family, but visitors enter at a side door, and a guide conducts them through Sir Walter's private apartments. A stream of people were entering the gates all the time, and while we were waiting for the party that was already up-stairs to come down, we had an opportunity of buying a few photographs of the place, which were displayed, with boxes, paper-cutters, and various mementoes, in the little room or vestibule where we stood.

'We were first shown the study where Scott composed and wrote; his desk and chair are there, also a case containing his walking-sticks, pipes, and the last suit of clothes he wore. About half-way between the ceiling and floor, around three sides of the room, is a small wire balcony, with steps ascending to it in one corner, and a door opening from it into his bed-room. Above this balcony the walls are lined with books, while below it there is a handsome wainscoting; and an inlaid chest or cabinet stands near the broad, low window. In a little circular tower-room opening off the study is preserved a cast of the skull of Sir Walter Scott, taken after death, but it suggested an idea so repulsive, that I did not wish to see it. Uncle, who examined it with unusual interest, said it displayed to great advantage the fine development of the forehead and intellectual faculties of the great author.

The study is a small, cozy room, but the adjoining library is very large, with magnificent woodwork. It contains a number of costly presents from kings and nobles. Among others, a handsome set of ebony furniture, exquisitely carved, from George the Fourth. The paintings are also very fine; there are portraits of Sir Walter's two daughters, both noble-looking women, and of his eldest son, who was a soldier, and measured six feet four inches in height. The last is a full-length oil-painting, and reaches from the mantel almost to the ceiling, which is exceedingly high. Before we fully realized what we were doing, the guide had pointed out, and we were looking at, a painting of the head of Mary, Queen of Scots, lying on a silver charger the day after her execution. The guide told us that this picture was never allowed to be copied. It is said to be a very good likeness, but I did not wait to examine the features; a glance is sufficient to give one a shock that is long remembered. The rooms we then passed through are stored with antiquities and curiosities of every description. One would think there is scarcely a hero or a battle of which there is not some memorial in this collection. Rob Roy's gun and purse, Napoleon's writing case, whole suits of armor found on battle-fields, instruments of torture, specimens of architecture, a pen-and-ink sketch of Queen Elizabeth dancing the Highland-fling at the age of sixty, and curious articles from all parts of the globe, that would take the lifetime of such a man as Walter Scott to collect. We could almost imagine ourselves his guests, and that he was showing us through those elegant apartments himself, and telling anecdotes of each object as he pointed it out and gave its history. A week would not be long enough to see everything; but others were waiting for the guide, so we were obliged to be satisfied with a passing glimpse, and hasten down.

Dryburgh Abbey, two miles east of the village, is an interesting ruin, containing the tombs of Sir Walter Scott and several of his family.

Melrose Abbey is too beautiful in its decay, and delicate in its tracery-work, to be described by a less skillful pen than that which traced the exquisite description

Dryburgh Abbey.

Face p. 46.

of it in the "Lay of the Last Minstrel." As I sat on Sir Walter Scott's favorite seat of fallen stones near those pillars which he calls "bundles of lances which garlands had bound," and looking towards the east oriel, how could I help quoting those beautiful lines referring to that very window, and composed, no doubt, while seated on these very stones!

> "Thou wouldst have thought some fairy's hand
> 'Twixt poplars straight the osier wand
> In many a freakish knot had twined;
> Then framed a spell, when the work was done,
> And changed the willow wreaths to stone."

VI.

THREE CITIES OF IRELAND.

THE IRISH COAST—JAUNTING-CARS—A WILD IRISHMAN—DUBLIN—
ACROSS THE COUNTRY—LOST IN LIMERICK.

FROM Melrose we travelled through the "border country" to Newcastle, then over again to Dumfries, where Burns is buried, and, finally, to a little Scotch port whence we sailed for Ireland. After three hours on the steamer we came in sight of Belfast. I have a special kindly feeling toward the Irish coast, owing, probably, to the fact that it was the first land we saw after crossing the broad Atlantic, on our way to Glasgow. How we strained our eyes to see the first gray outline of a something lying like a cloud against the horizon, and how we sat watching it for hours, while it grew into the semblance of mountains, then the valleys and the nearer hills appeared, and soon the jagged cliffs were visible, hanging over the water. We saw the froth of the waves as they dashed up the crevices, but the roaring sound was deadened by the nearer rippling of the water around the ship. With something of awe we passed the Giant's Causeway, and as the rocks were pointed out to us where vessels had been wrecked a short time before, we said to ourselves with a secure, contented feeling, and with a new meaning, "Distance lends enchantment to the view." And then, as we passed longingly the white cottages up the hill-sides, and the green, green grass, we were not sorry that our

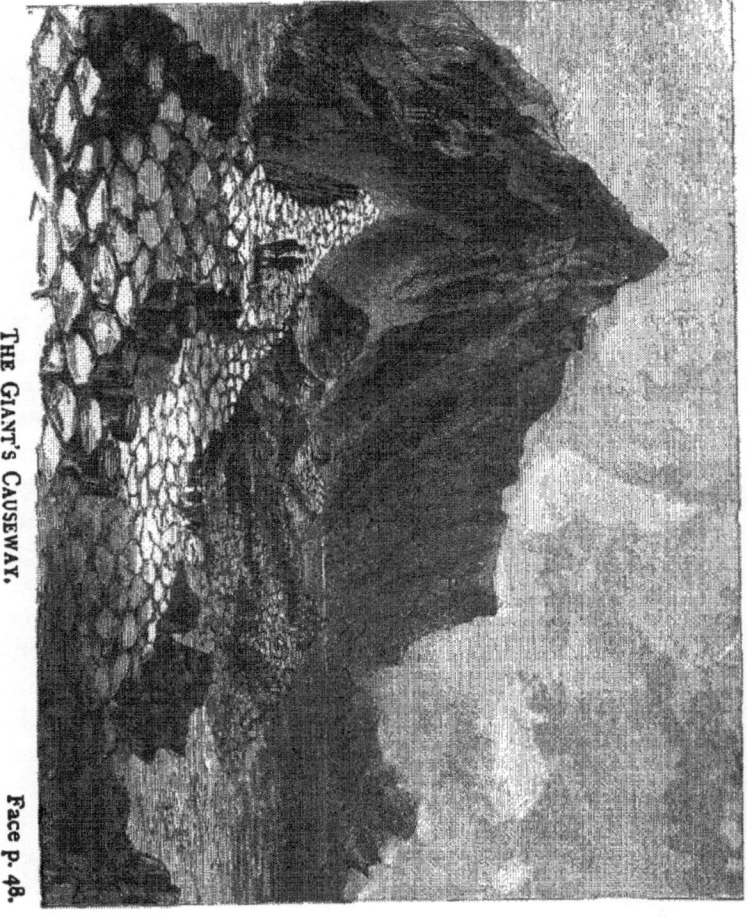

The Giant's Causeway.

Face p. 48.

ocean trip was nearly over. We naturally thought of that view of the northern coast as we approached Ireland, this time from the east.

When we reached Belfast, our minds were wholly engrossed with the jaunting-cars. There they stood, drawn up in line, and waiting to be hired. We immediately determined upon a ride. The vehicle seemed to me to consist of three steps on each side. The lowest one is for the feet, the next is to sit on, and the highest one to lean against. A person sits on each side of the car, and thus they ride, sideways, with their faces and feet toward the houses, and back to back. A small iron arm, or railing, is at each end of the middle step, or seat, and it is generally in great requisition by novices in this style of travelling as a preventive against sliding off.

We merely intimated to our driver at Belfast that we were in a hurry to reach the other depot, when with a "whoop," and a crack of his whip, he dashed off at full speed, and we clung to the railing for dear life. He raced us through those streets like a madman, scattering the heavy wagons and carriages right and left, every now and then uttering a peculiar cry that seemed to clear the way for us. We had found a "wild Irishman" the very first thing. He cut round the corners in a startling manner, just grazing the lamp-post each time, and once, when my umbrella happened to be sticking out, it nearly upset a gentleman who was standing on the curbstone. We alighted at the depot in a marvelously short while, and found we had some time to look around at the city; but all that I can say of it is, that I saw nothing to distinguish it particularly from the ordinary run of modern cities.

From Belfast we were soon spinning along on the express train toward Dublin. Here we engaged rooms in a hotel on beautiful Sackville street, the pride of an Irishman's heart; but it rained so hard while we were

DUBLIN (from Phœnix Park.)

there that we scarcely had a glimpse of the statue on top of the tall column that stands in the centre of the street. We drove round to see the city and its sights in a jaunting-car, guided by the driver, who was lively, intelligent, and entertaining, which can not be said of the English hackmen, who seemed generally as stupid as blocks, and ignorant of all that was not directly connected with their driving. This reminds me of a story I heard of how an Irishman "chated" a Yankee. A lady, whom we met, told us that when she had arrived at the depot in Dublin, or it may have been one of the other Irish cities, she went to the carriage stand, and asked a jaunting-car man to drive her to a hotel which she named. He looked at her a moment with an odd twinkle in his eye, but then helped her politely into the car and started off. After driving ten or fifteen minutes, he stopped before the door of the hotel, received his pay, and drove away. The next day, when preparing to continue her journey, she told the hotel-clerk to order a carriage to take her to the depot. "You do not need a carriage, madam, the depot is just next door." She then appreciated the little game that had been played on her by the jaunting-car man. We afterward found these tricks upon travellers to be of very common occurrence, and we were more than once the victims.

The ride on the railway from Dublin to Limerick was very interesting, because so characteristic of "ould Ireland." We passed ancient round towers, built in the time of the Druids (?), acres of potato-fields, miles of bog, and piles of peat ready to be burned when the cold weather came.

In spite of its mud, the Shannon is a fine river, and Limerick, with its fragments of ancient wall, an interesting city in some respects, though I have unpleasant recollections connected with it. We happened to lose our way in some of the back streets, and before we found it again, we wandered through scenes of human wretchedness and poverty that would make one's heart sick.

VII.

KILLARNEY AND BLARNEY.

AMONG THE LAKES OF KILLARNEY—COTTAGE OF KATE KEARNEY—GAP OF DUNLOE—"OLD WEIR BRIDGE"—MUCKROSS ABBEY—A SUDDEN SQUALL—"BOOTS"—THE BLARNEY STONE!

AFTER leaving Limerick, our next stopping-place was Killarney, and one could not but think it a pity that here, so much ground was left wild for sports and pleasure while those poor people we had seen in Limerick were, perhaps, starving for want of a place to plant their potatoes.

One morning we started from the hotel on an excursion round the lakes. The first part of the trip was in a jaunting-car, on a beautiful winding road, past several picturesque ruins, with glimpses of the Lower Lake through the foliage. The latter is wonderfully green and delicate, distinguished by a certain freshness due to the frequent rain, which gives to the island its emerald hue. After riding some time, a dark cut opened between the mountains, and the guide told us that it was the Gap of Dunloe. All this time, a woman was running after us with a basket of bogwood jewelry, and begging Uncle to buy some. "Ah!" she said, in her most winning tones, panting between the words, as she tried to keep up with the car, "sure ye'll take them home to yer dear lady." Uncle told her that he had no "dear lady" at home; but she persevered until her good-natured entreaties were irresistible. While we were still in motion, the bogwood was thrown into the jaunting-car and the silver was thrown out to the woman, who gathered it up with a beaming smile, and wafted us a grateful "God bless ye!" as we disappeared round a curve in the road.

Horses were awaiting us at the entrance to the Gap, and we mounted them at the door of the cottage of the famous "Kate Kearney, who lived on the Lakes of Killarney." We were told that the young girl who brought us a drink of "Mountain Dew" and fresh milk, was her namesake and lineal descendant. The beverage she offered was not whiskey — O, no!—only the dew that falls on the mountains in the night-time. Kate Kearney would not be guilty of distilling whiskey unlawfully, and thus avoiding the tax, so you see it was only "mountain dew" after all.

At different points on the way through the Gap, boys fired off guns so that we could hear the echoes of the explosion repeated again and again. Sometimes the guide blew a blast of his bugle, making the whole gorge ring with the music, and once, he held a long conversation with "Paddy Burke," who, he informed us, inhabited the opposite rocks. "Paddy," he said, "are you very well?" "Very well," said Paddy. After further parley concerning his wife and children, the guide said, "Let's sing a duet." "Sing a duet," assented Paddy, and they sang a rousing chorus, but Paddy did not keep good time; he invariably came in a little late at the end of each line, repeating the last word several times. "Good-bye, Paddy," said the guide, "and good luck to you!" "Good luck to you," said Paddy, "Luck to you," murmured a voice on the other side, "To you," said Paddy, faintly, and we rode on.

We skirted the borders of Serpent Lake, a gloomy

pool, where, according to the guide's story, the devil, in the form of a "sarpint," was once outwitted in some way, by St. Patrick, who locked him up in a box, which, if I remember rightly, he threw into the lake.

From a high point in the Gap we looked down on the Black Valley, lying in deep shadow at the feet of the Purple Mountains and McGillicuddy's Reeks, like an ink-spot on the bright landscape.

Ross Castle.

On emerging from the Gap of Dunloe, we dismounted from the horses, and walked a short distance through a grove, when we found ourselves standing on the shore of the Upper Lake of Killarney. A row-boat, with a basket of lunch, had been sent from the hotel to meet us, and we were soon rowing down the Upper Lake, which winds here and there, so that we often wondered where we would next turn. The characteristic beauty of these lakes is the remarkably rich foliage that covers the mountains, especially an oddly-shaped one, which has an eagle's nest perched on a cliff overhanging the water, whence it takes its name.

We passed under several moss-grown bridges before we reached the "Old Weir Bridge," under which the waters of the Middle Lake flow into Lough Leane, or the Lower Lake. There are fierce rapids and a strong current under the bridge, so the men drew in their oars, and we darted through the dark arch and far out into the lake, with a rapidity that nearly took our breath away. We passed safely, though the warning old song says, "Shoot not the Old Weir, for death may be there." We stopped a short time on the lovely little Island of Innisfallen, with its crown of ruins and its store of legends, and then rowed rapidly towards the hotel, for the oarsmen were anxious to get to the races that afternoon, and they made the little boat fairly skip over the water.

Muckross Abbey is, I think, the most beautiful ruin in the neighborhood of Killarney. It stands as an ornament in the grounds of Mr. Herbert, one of the principal land-holders in this part of Ireland. A giant tree is growing in the centre of the cloister, spreading a dense shade over this entire portion of the ruin, and making it gloomier and more secluded than ever.

In exploring these old castles and abbeys, we noticed how the ivy, that destroyer of new, and preserver of old buildings, winds itself in and out, crunching the mortar and grasping the stones with an iron grip, supporting the building to which, as a tiny vine, it fastened its tendrils; and now, as if in gratitude, it throws its beautiful green mantle over the flaws and defects of the old structure, and thus it will continue to protect and adorn it

"Till the walls shall crumble to ruin
And moulder in dust away."

Is not the ivy on a ruin like a child clinging to its mother until able to support itself, when, in its turn, embracing and upholding the now tottering form of the mother, it supports her with its strong arms till death claims her?

From Muckross Abbey we drove through the surrounding grounds, which are laid out in beautiful landscape gardening. The family mansion is built in the real old English style, with a broad, stately avenue of trees leading to it, and a lawn like velvet. While we were standing there, "mi lady," in a long riding suit, rode rapidly by with a party of gentlemen and two or three dogs. They were evidently off for a hunting expedition, and all seemed in high spirits. The picture was complete. We have all seen it in imagination.

A few miles beyond, we saw Torc Cascade, a perfect gem of its kind, and had a beautiful view from Torc Mountain, which we ascended. We stood just above the falls, and an old gentleman, who took care to choose a very safe spot from which to enjoy the beauties of the lakes which lay beneath us, was dreadfully concerned lest I, who was more adventurous, should fall over the precipice.

As we were returning to our hotel on the lake, a sudden squall and rain-shower came up, nearly overturning the boat, and taking Uncle's beautiful, blue cotton umbrella from his hand. The men rowed very hard to save it, but before we could reach it, it sank, with a melancholy flop, beneath the angry waves, and one small parasol was all that was left to shelter us. Uncle had an especial attachment to this particular blue cotton umbrella, and I had an especial aversion to it. When he bewails its sad fate, I try to comfort him with the assurance that the famous O'Donahue, who dwells at the bottom of the lake, and makes midnight journeys on a fleet, white horse, will take good care of it, and when the day comes on which rains shall cease in Ireland, he will probably return it, having no further use for it himself.

The morning we were to leave Killarney, I remember to have heard, while preparing for breakfast, an incessant ringing of bells, and impatient jerking of bellropes, while visions flitted before me of gentlemen in their shirt-sleeves, peering from behind doors, and roaring after poor, bewildered "Boots," who ran about with a scared face, holding odd boots and shoes in his hands, and exclaiming, "Och! thin have patience, sirs. A bowld young gintleman of the Navy has been changing all thim chalk marks the night as was on the boots, an' I can't tell whose is whose an' what's which, no more 'n these boots can git mated an' fly to the right doors all aloun by thimselves."

He was more puzzled than the Irishman who brought two odd boots to his master's room, and said, "Plaze yer honor! thim two don't match, an' what's sthranger, thir's two more jist like 'em down stairs in the same fix."

When order was finally restored at the hotel, which was a very large one, and the guests were started for the depot, we had to drive very fast, and then nearly lost the train, for we had all been delayed by the young officer's prank.

When we reached Cork, our first act was to ride out to Blarney, plod through the mud, and ascend the Castle. From the top there was a fine view, and under the building were some horrible dungeons, which we visited by torch-light—but what do views and dungeons amount to, when there hung the veritable Blarney Stone, suspended a hundred and fifty feet from the ground. In order

3*

to kiss it, Uncle lay flat on the wall with his face downward, and, at the risk of his life, stretched himself across a space at least four feet wide. While he was performing this difficult feat, a party of Irishmen spied him from below, and gave him a tremendous cheer.

IRISH JAUNTING-CAR.

VIII.

ENGLAND.

NORTH WALES—CHESTER FROM THE WALLS—A LABYRINTH OF RAILROADS—THE GREAT CATHEDRALS—WITCHERY OF YORK, SOLEMNITY OF PETERBOROUGH, AND GRANDEUR OF ELY MINSTERS—THE "DARK AGES"— CAMBRIDGE AND OXFORD —"GREAT TOM"— KENILWORTH AND QUEEN BESS—DESOLATION—" WHERE ARE THEY ?"—STRATFORD-ON-AVON—SHAKESPEARE FROM HIS CRADLE TO HIS GRAVE—INN OF THE RED HORSE—SOUVENIRS OF WASHINGTON IRVING.

FAREWELL, Ireland! with a glimpse of your beauty, a glimpse of your misery, and a glimpse of your fun, we are off—bound for England, your haughty step-sister, who lies there in her glory, while you, poor Erin, sit among the cinders. But we will remember that they are the cinders of your former glory—your bravery, your science, and your learning—whose bright gleams lit up the darkest corners of Europe long before the first spark of England's fame had been kindled.

America can sympathize with you, Ireland, in your present condition. She knows, from experience, what it is to be subject to the sway of England. But though, like saucy children, we spilt her tea and broke loose from her apron-strings one bright Fourth of July, we can not forget that she is our mother-country, and we love to visit her. On, then, little steamer. Three cheers for Old England! There she lies. But no; it is her little brother Wales that she has sent out to welcome us.

We land at Holyhead, jump into the railway carriages, and, in an instant, we are spinning across North

Wales. The nearer scenery, rocks, castles, towns, bridges, and tunnels flash past in confused succession; but raising our eyes to the southward, we see the distant, misty, chalky peaks of the Snowdon range, looking quietly down upon us as we rattle on, very much as a lady watches a fly crawling round the bottom of her skirts; while to the northward the sea is rippling gently in the sunshine and playing among the crevices in the rocks, equally regardless of the important fact that the great Irish mail-train is on its way to London.

At Chester we step out of our compartment and let the train whiz off, while we turn to look around us. The plan of Chester is very unique. It is surrounded by a massive high wall in excellent preservation, which is believed to have been built by the Romans. Four principal streets lead from four great gateways, and meet in the centre of the city, forming a cross. In these streets are the "Rows," a name given to long galleries or piazzas in the second stories of the buildings, which project over the sidewalks, and contain all the principal shops. This is certainly a curious old city. Not only are the shops up-stairs, but the favorite promenade of the inhabitants is up-stairs too—on top of the walls. As we "circum-promenaded" the city in this novel manner, we had a splendid opportunity of seeing the interesting places. There is the beautiful cathedral with its high tower, all built of red sandstone, and further on, the site of the old castle, which has given place to a county-gaol. Just outside of the city, at the foot of the wall, is the race-course, and beyond, the River Dee, crossed by a great iron railroad bridge, while in the distance is the country-seat of the Marquis of Westminster.

We continued our walk, which now led us through the thickly-populated parts of the city, where high houses, built close to the wall on both sides, shut out the view till we reached the gate from which we had started, and stood over it watching the carts and carriages as they rumbled in and out. We then descended to the street by a flight of stone steps, wishing that every city could be seen with as much ease.

From Chester our route lay along one of the great thoroughfares of England—through the busy, buzzing, whirring, manufacturing districts, whose two great centres are Manchester and Leeds. Railroads intersect this portion of the country like the veins in a grape-leaf, but Manchester is the principal focus towards which, after much winding and interlacing, they all converge like the spokes of a wheel. If you wish to travel through this labyrinth with any comfort or pleasure, trust in Providence, but don't try to study the railroad maps. Sunday overtook us at Leeds, and one would think that a spell had been cast over the city, so noiseless, so hushed did it seem, so contrasted to the busy scene of yesterday.

During the next week we visited four of the great English Cathedrals, York, Lincoln, Peterborough, and Ely. Each one seemed the largest, the grandest, and the most beautiful while we stood within its walls, and it was not until we had escaped from the magic influence of its presence, that we recovered the faculty of criticising and comparing.

When we reached York, we obtained glimpses of the Cathedral towers over the house-tops, and I was roused to the highest pitch of enthusiasm before we saw the building. "To the cathedral! to the cathedral!" was the cry. Uncle could take it more coolly—he had seen Old World churches before; and he tried to interest me in the things we were passing—the old walls, a bridge, a ruined abbey, historical spots—but I scarce saw them.

Those towers, with their slender, pointing fingers, floating against the clouds, had bewitched me. My thoughts bounded on, round every corner, far in advance of our footsteps, till, finally, we reached an open square, and

YORK MINSTER.

there it stood—the great Minster, crouched among its three towers. Yes, it actually rests on solid ground, and our eyes and thoughts quickly mount up from doorway to arch; from arch to niche, each with its carved saint; from niche to window, with tall, slender mullions interlacing at the top like a forest of pine-trees; from gargoyle to cornice; and thus up, up, up, through a maze of beauty, to the tips of the tiny spires on the tower-tops, which still point higher, higher, till they pierce the clouds and the sunshine, and seem to leave us at the very gates of Paradise.

But as we intend to visit the Cathedral and not Paradise, we descend to earth once more, and pass under the massive, arched door-way. Here again we find but the carrying out of the same grand design. A forest of branching columns, birds stopped in the midst of their song, flowers plucked in their bloom, angels arrested in their flight, saints surrounded by their glory, rainbows caught before they faded—all these have been held fast for hundreds of years in the carved stone and stained glass. But surely man alone could not have done all this—God and His angels must have helped him!

York Cathedral had scarcely faded from our sight, when Lincoln rose before us. This Minster stands on a hill, and presents an imposing appearance as we near the city. It also has three towers, but the façade, though marvelously rich in statuary and mouldings, is less graceful and pleasing than that of York.

Peterborough Cathedral, which we next visited, did not resemble either of the previous ones. The façade consists principally of three immense, high, deep, Gothic arches that throw heavy, gloomy shadows against the wall. A shady old grave-yard, with broken slabs and illegible inscriptions, surrounds the church, and the whole scene is peaceful, quiet, solemn in the extreme. As we approached from a side street, chatting gaily, the wind among the trees seemed to say, "Hush!" and with voices subdued to a whisper, we passed within the shadow of the central arch and entered the Cathedral. We stopped a moment to examine the slabs which cover the remains of Catherine of Arragon, and Mary, Queen of Scots. It is fit, though strange, that they should lie here together—both so royal, so wronged. The body of the old sexton who buried these two celebrated queens, one fifty years after the other, also lies under the church, and on the wall there is a picture of him with a spade in his hand, and under it a quaint inscription in rhyme. It is said that at the time of the Reformation, when these old churches were being destroyed, Henry VIII. was induced to spare this one of Peterborough, as a fitting monument to his Queen. It is even now in excellent preservation.

Ely Minster was another revelation of beauty, though of a very different style of architecture—the old Norman. Imagine a tall, white column, at least ten or twelve feet in diameter (equal to a California tree!), then place fourteen or fifteen in a row on either side of the building, connected by great, heavy arches; think of three tiers of these colonnades, arch resting upon column, column upon arch, till they reach the roof of the building. This is the nave. Nothing could be more simple, or grand. Then if we pass under the old Norman dome and step into the choir, the contrast is so great that it dazzles and confuses, for instead of the plain, heavy mouldings of the Norman style, there is a maze of sculpture and tracery resembling lace-work or ivory-carving. This part of the original Cathedral had been crushed by the fall of the central tower, and rebuilt in the Gothic style as late as the fifteenth century.

But greater changes than those of mere construction have taken place in these old minsters within the last few centuries. The old saints and angels, at least those of them who have escaped the hoofs of Cromwell's horses and the hands of his more destructive soldiers

Ely Cathedral

seem to look down from their niches in dumb amazement at the new order of things. Instead of the grand old Gregorian chant that used to roll through the lofty arches, the clouds of incense that curled up the pillars, the learned old monk; who lined the choir, the richly-vested priest, the file of altar-boys, and the crowd of kneeling worshippers which filled the great nave—there are now a few cushioned pews and a desk or pulpit in some distant corner of the mighty cathedral, where a choice number of elegantly-dressed ladies and gentlemen assemble once a week to attend the Church of England service, while down the whole length of the nave the rich colors of the old stained windows fall in unbroken lines on the bare floor.

The more I see of the works of the middle centuries, the stranger it seems that they should be called "Dark Ages." Our inventions and discoveries may be great, but their ideas were grand. We may have the light of science, but they had the light of inspiration. The greatest artists of the present day can not grasp the divine as did the Old Masters. The greatest specimens of architecture they build now can carry one's thoughts no higher than the topmost pinnacle. No! it requires the Faith of the "Dark Ages" to picture a Man-God, or to form those grand old cathedral designs; to band together thousands of the most skillful workmen; to inspire each one to do his best, even though his work was hidden in some lofty niche or dark corner from the eyes of all but God and His angels; to harmonize the work of so many brains and hands into one grand whole; and, finally, to have breathed into it that wonderful power of raising the mind at once from the contemplation of the wonderful structure to the very feet of Him for whose dwelling-place it was intended!

But to turn from the great cathedrals to the great universities, Cambridge and Oxford. The latter is, of course, the most interesting of the two, and on a much larger scale. In fact, it may be called a little government in itself—a republic in miniature. It consists of nineteen colleges and six halls, each of which forms a distinct establishment, with its own students and teachers, and its own revenues and regulations; but they are all united under the University government, at whose head is a chancellor, vice-chancellor, and other officers, whose duty it is to preserve law and order, call convocations and courts, license taverns, impose punishments, and expel delinquents. Each college has been founded by some distinguished man, beginning with Alfred the Great—the George Washington of this republic of learning; and each has its own particular history and associations. Brazenose College derives its name, oddly enough, from an old brass nose which used to serve as a knocker on one of the doors. Christ Church College, founded by Cardinal Wolsey, is built in a very classical and imposing style. Some of this learned information about Oxford I got out of a book (as you may perhaps have guessed), but no book could give me an idea of the beautiful walks we took through the grounds of St. John's College, and from Christ Church down to the river and the racing-boats, through a splendid broad avenue of trees. Uncle went out several times without me to see Magdalen, Wadhams, and some of the other colleges.

"Where have you been, Uncle?" I asked, one afternoon, as he entered my room.

"To see 'Great Tom.'"

"Who is he," I asked again, "and why do you look so tired?"

"I gave the old monster a great pounding," he said, taking no notice of my questions. "Didn't you hear what a noise he made?"

"No," I answered, very much puzzled; "I have heard nothing but a great bell ringing very spasmodically."

"That is just it," laughed Uncle. "It was I who 'boned' it—the famous bell of Christ Church College, that weighs seventeen thousand pounds."

"No wonder you are tired; but how did it happen?"

"Well, when I mounted the tower, the old sexton was just going to ring the bell, when he saw me looking on with great interest, and proffered me the honor of 'boning the Great Tom.' I accepted, and "—

"Poor Tom, it seems, went into spasms," I added.

On arriving at Kenilworth, a pouring rain served to dampen our bright anticipations. After a genuine roast-beef dinner, however, at the old-fashioned inn, we felt courageous enough to defy the weather. After getting out of the omnibus at the castle, I had reason to envy Queen Bess the use of Sir Walter Raleigh's cloak, for no doubt we plodded ankle deep through the very puddle across which she stepped so daintily.

At the immense gate, flanked with heavy towers, which is now used as a dwelling-house, we were met by an old man who pointed out the path to the castle. I often wonder how they find so many antique specimens of humanity to watch, like visible Lares and Penates, over the fate of the hundreds of old ruins in the British Isles. They are always gray and tottering like the castles. Whenever I meet one of them, I think of the old family steward of whom we so often read— who has outlived his generation and his master's glory, but who still lingers on till his life crumbles away with the last wall.

Following the directions of the ancient of Kenilworth, we soon found ourselves standing in front of the entire ruin, with its great towers and broken walls surrounding an open court, which we entered. After ascending one of the corner towers by a crumbling stairway, in each step of which a large hole was worn,

Kenilworth Castle.

Face p. 68.

we mounted the highest of the fallen stones, and saw the outside walls lying around us, apparently without any regular design, making a great variety of angles, at each of which was a tower that suggested some separate story of history or romance. In one direction was a long, narrow causeway leading to the tilting-ground.

We then hastened to explore the nearer ruins. As we approached the grand old Banquet Hall where "Queen Bess" so often presided in person, visions rose before us of great feasts and merry times, but when we stood in one of the beautifully-moulded windows and looked to see the table and the guests, we were startled to find ourselves gazing meditatively into—the cellar! for it has no floor; and on raising our eyes to the ceiling, we were blinded by the pelting rain. We sought shelter in a little bay-window, almost the only thing with a roof, and with the aid of a plan of the building, we studied out of the *debris* around us, the position of the throne-room, the little ante-room adjoining, and many others, for every stone in this castle seems stored with associations. But it is with a melancholy interest that we linger amid all this desolation:

> "Where are the high-born dames, and where
>   Their gay attire and jewelled hair,
>   And odors sweet?
>   Where are the gentle knights that came
>   To kneel, and breathe love's ardent flame,
>   Low at their feet?
>
> "Where is the song of Troubadour?
>   Where are the lute and gay tambour
>   They loved of yore?
>   Where is the mazy dance of old,
>   The flowing robes, inwrought with gold,
>   The dancers wore?

✴ ✴ ✴ ✴ ✴ ✴ ✴

> "The countless gifts, the stately walls,
>   The royal palaces, and halls,
>   All filled with gold;
>   Plate with armorial bearings wrought,
>   Chambers with ample treasures fraught
>   Of wealth untold.
>
> "The noble steeds and harness bright,
>   The gallant lord, and stalwart knight,
>   In rich array.
>   Where shall we seek them now? Alas!
>   Like the bright dewdrops on the grass,
>   They passed away.
>
> * * * * * * *
>
> "O world! so few the years we live,
>   Would that the life which thou dost give
>   Were life indeed!
>   Alas! thy sorrows fall so fast,
>   Our happiest hour is when at last
>   The soul is freed."

From Kenilworth a carriage and horses, with a stupid driver, conveyed us to Warwick, where we had to be satisfied with an outside view of the castle, from the bridge near by, for the family were then occupying it. But we did see Guy's Cliff, where the penitent old earl lived so many years as a hermit, and lingered in its romantic neighborhood with great interest, for we had found a queer little book telling us The Wonderful History of Guy, Earl of Warwick, and his Doleful Lady.

After driving a few miles further we came in sight of Stratford-on-Avon. Before reaching it we passed Sir Thomas Lucy's park, where Shakespeare shot the deer. It was so well stocked that I thought one could hardly be missed. Perhaps Shakespeare thought so too.

The house in which the "Immortal Poet" was born

is a curious old structure, with the beams and rafters all exposed. It has been very carefully preserved, and serves as a kind of Shakesperian reliquary—that is, it is filled with curious old documents and all kinds of articles connected with the life of Shakespeare and his family, even relics of the crab-tree under which he slept one night when he was "off on a spree."

Of course we visited the grammar-school which Shakespeare attended as a boy. The house in which

WARWICK CASTLE.

he lived after he was married, and in which he died, called "New Place," has been pulled down, but the garden remains very much as he himself arranged it. The old gentleman who showed us through the grounds offered us some mulberries from a tree which Shakespeare planted, or rather from a descendant of the old tree, which latter died some time ago. We next directed our steps towards Trinity Church, which is situated in a quiet spot near the river. Here Shakespeare and his family are buried; and on a wall of the church is the monumental bust of him, erected by his daughter. At some little distance from the town we passed the meadows across which he used to go courting to Ann Hathaway's cottage.

I think it was very considerate in Shakespeare to be born, live, die, and go courting all in the same place— it is so pleasant and convenient for tourists!

The entire town of Stratford is a real quaint old English place, and so is the inn of the "Red Horse," where we stopped. It is not built like most of the houses, with the upper story projecting over the under one, but an archway runs through the building from the street to the court-yard. From this arch doors open into the dining-room on one side, and the hall on the other, from which access is had to the stairs and the rooms on the first floor.

I noticed on the door of one of these rooms, a brass plate with the words, "Washington Irving's Parlor." The landlady invited us in to see it, and explained to us that our honored countryman, Washington Irving, had stayed a long time at the "Red Horse" during a visit to England, and had written parts of his Sketch Book in that little parlor. His table was there, and the arm-chair he had used stood in the corner, with a brass plate attached, upon which his name was engraved.

While we were examining various articles in the room and looking at the pictures, among them a portrait of George Washington, the landlady left the room and returned with something carefully tied up in a cloth-case. She said that it was another relic of Washington Irving, and, as we stood expectantly waiting, she drew out a small, black poker, turned at one end.

"He used it to stir the fire on cold evenings," she said.

This little incident shows how highly they value such things in the "Old World," and how they happen to have so many curious and interesting articles that have belonged to distinguished men. Who knows how many people will visit Stratford-on-Avon in the far future, to see Washington Irving's poker!

SHAKESPEARE'S TOMB.

IX.

LONDON.

VISIONARY COMPANIONS—"THE GOLDEN CROSS"—PANORAMIC PICTURES—WESTMINSTER ABBEY—HOUSES OF PARLIAMENT—BEWILDERING COLLECTIONS—AN ARTIST'S GENEROSITY.

THE night we spied the lights of "London town" in the distance, for the first time, I thought of the scene in Oliver Twist, where Noah Claypole and his bride are travelling on foot towards the great metropolis. I seemed to see Charlotte, exhausted by the heavy load which she was forced to carry, seated on a stone and asking how much further they must go, while her long-legged lord and master stood, pointing his thumb over his shoulder towards a cluster of bright specks stretching far along the horizon, and gruffly answered, "Those are the lights of London ; come along, Charlotte, will yer." There they were, twinkling in the far, far distance, and leaving Mr. Claypole and lady to trudge along in the dark, we whizzed into the midst of the brightness, and were soon trotted about the city in a cab, though as ignorant as they as to where we should "rest our weary limbs." After going to all the hotels mentioned in the guide-book, and being met at each one with the same greeting, "No room," we returned to the depot in despair, thinking that London was not very large after all, since it could not accommodate two poor, tired travellers. We were almost tempted to leave on the next train, when there, at the very spot

LONDON BRIDGE.

Face p 74

from which we had started, we saw a large gilt sign—
"Hotel of the Golden Cross."

"Is it a good place to stop?" we asked the driver, but with a secret determination to "stop" there, whatever might be his answer.

"Tol'rable," was the reply, and that expressed it exactly.

Its principal attraction was in being only "round the corner" from Trafalgar Square and Charing Cross, quite a landmark in the city. Whenever we lost our way—a daily occurrence—in the mazes of crooked little streets which take a different name every few blocks, we would ask every other straggler we met which was the way to Charing Cross, and thus we soon found ourselves on familiar ground.

I always think of London as a series of vivid pictures—a shifting panorama; not as other cities, in which we laid out a plan of sight-seeing, and went to a certain number of places each day.

One picture is of a massive stone gateway, the entrance to a beautiful park. It consists of a large arch, through which handsome equipages and gayly-dressed people are passing, and two smaller arches at the side, under each of which is a magnificent, manly figure, in gorgeous uniform, with glittering steel helmet and sword, mounted on a jet-black steed. "What life-like statues!" I was on the point of saying, when one of the horses began prancing, and the rider reined him in, making him stand once more under the arch. Then I was told that these were some of the famous Horse Guards.

Now I remember a beautiful ride to Hyde Park, Rotten Row, St. James, and Buckingham Palace. We passed the gilded monument to Prince Albert, and the curious-looking exhibition hall for the industrial arts which he patronized.

Every one bears in mind some picture of Westminster, and can imagine how we lingered around it with affectionate veneration. It is, in itself, a monument to the great of the nation; while in it each great man has a monument to himself. We forget there is a present while we stand within its walls; and the moment we leave them, the mighty structure seems to have vanished away into the past, and we believe we have not seen it for years. Even when we look on the spot and on the chair where Queen Victoria was crowned, it is difficult to convince ourselves that the coronation did not take

WATER LILY—ZOOLOGICAL GARDENS.

place several hundred years ago—nothing could have happened in Westminster Abbey later than that!

The next picture of my mental panorama is the Parliament House—a marvellous structure, with a tower so high that the immense building looks dwarfish beside it. In the open square in front is a noble bronze statue of Richard, Cœur de Lion. The interior of the Parliament buildings consists of broad halls, with portraits and statues of England's great statesmen, stained glass windows, hundreds of doors opening, I should think, into everywhere; and, with all this, a miserable little cramped room for the House of Commons. A funny old woman, who talked very fast, showed us which was Gladstone's seat, and those of the other leading mem-

HOUSE OF PARLIAMENT.

bers; where they stood when they made speeches, and how they voted.

The British Museum is a very bewildering picture to

look at, or even to think about. We wandered through halls of stuffed animals, wild and tame, halls of birds, halls of minerals, halls of fossils, halls of skeletons, and halls of antiquities—Greek, Roman, Persian, and Egyptian. We wandered till our heads ached, till our limbs ached, till we ached all over, till we were ready to drop. Then we left, glad to free ourselves from the bewildering maze, yet sorry that we could not stay and see more of its wonders.

If I did not see enough of London, it was partly because our stay was short, for we dared not linger long at the North, lest we should fail to arrive in season at Switzerland; but another reason was, that full half the time we were there, I sat in my room at the Golden Cross, with a severe cold caught among the fossils and stuffed monsters of the Museum.

Our visit to the Museum made us rather dread the National Art Gallery, which we knew would be equally trying. But profiting by our former experience, we did not attempt to see everything, but passed rapidly through most of the rooms, only stopping occasionally to admire some master-piece. I was delighted with a graceful picture, by Murillo, representing the Child Jesus at about eight or ten years of age, standing between the Blessed Virgin and Saint Joseph, with some angels, if I remember rightly, floating above them. The design was simple, but beautifully carried out.

One of the distinguishing features of this gallery, is the collection of Turner's paintings, which, as we had been reading Ruskin, we were particularly anxious to see. Besides being scattered here and there through the gallery, there is a large room entirely devoted to them. I believe Turner had some defect in his eyesight during the latter part of his life. We noticed that his last pictures were blurred, and that many of them had very noticeable distortions of figure and atmospheric effects, that were not only singular, but startling. Some of them looked, to my uncultivated eye, as if the colors on his palette had been very much mixed up, and his brush had danced over the canvas at its own free will. I have heard that Turner took pleasure in trying to imitate the styles of different famous artists, showing that he could excel in all. There was an example of this in a room where two very similar large pictures hung side by side, one entitled the "Rise of Carthage," and the other, the "Fall of Carthage." One was by Turner, the other by Claude Lorraine. Each represented a portion of the city on the banks of the river, but in the first, the buildings were still in process of erection, and the sun was just rising on the scene, while in the last, the buildings were in ruins, and lighted up by the last beams of the setting sun. As far as we could judge, they were of equal merit. Ruskin speaks very highly of Turner's generosity. At one time, when a picture of the latter was exhibited in the Royal Academy, the contrast of colors destroyed the effect of the production of a young artist which hung beside it. Turner seeing that the young man was distressed about it, daubed his own painting over with a coating of dark paint, which he left on it, much to the detriment of his own interests, until the other picture was removed or sold.

X.

THE TOWER.

THE THAMES—THE TOWER OF LONDON—TRAITOR'S GATE—SPECTRES—BLOODY TOWER—THE LITTLE PRINCES—"THE BLOCK"—THE HORSE ARMORY—TROPHIES—ST. PAUL'S—DOVER AND THE CHANNEL—LEAVING THE BRITISH ISLES.

BUT my panorama is shifting rapidly, and now I can see the Thames. We have wandered down to the docks, past grand old Somerset Palace, and stand among the crowd waiting for the little wherry. It puffs up to us; a throng pours out and we crowd in, and again it plows through the muddy waters. We pass under bridge after bridge, and watch the smoke rising from hundreds of chimneys, while, asserting itself above every other tower and steeple, St. Paul's stands in bold relief against the murky sky.

Finally, we arrive at the famous London Bridge. We land, and walk through queer, narrow alleys and byways, between very tall houses, our noses telling us, all the while, that we are among the fish-markets.

We wander on round more corners, dodging through the carts and vehicles that crowd the narrow streets, till the Tower of London rises before us and everything else is forgotten.

How we shudder as we pass under the first dark gate, guarded by frowning towers, and see the teeth of that fearful portcullis grinning down at us as we cross the broad moat. At our right is the Traitor's Gate, whose name tells its own story. Under its dreaded portals have they all passed, never to return—those murdered, often martyred, victims of power and passion, whose spectres seem even now to be issuing forth and crossing the bridge in a shadowy line through the foggy air. We follow them and stand for a moment under the Bloody Tower. I can almost see two little white faces peering at us from the square grating—the ill-fated Royal Princes; here they were murdered. At the same grated window appears another face; 'tis a gray-

THE TOWER OF LONDON.

haired old man—Fisher, Bishop of Rochester. He is giving the last blessing to "the gifted, the excellent, the beloved, and brilliant Sir Thomas More, Lord Chancellor," who is passing on his way to execution.

We follow on after the gloomy procession, and when we arrive in the open square we tremble lest we shall see the block, the headless body, and the bloody axe. We are soon relieved. There is only a plot of green grass and a jabbering old raven hopping about. I thought it might be the embodied spirit of all the dark deeds that were hissing through our memories.

The office of wardens and guides to the Tower of London is bestowed as an honor and reward on veterans who have done good service to the country. They are called "Extraordinary Yeomen of the Guard," and have a very peculiar uniform. They wear a long belted tunic of red and gold, on the breast of which is embroidered a crown, with the rose. the shamrock, and the thistle, emblematic of England, Ireland, and Scotland. To this may be added knee-breeches, long stockings, and old-fashioned pumps, with bright rosettes of red and gold. They wear broad, low beaver hats, and a great ruff around the neck. A sword hangs at the belt, and on grand occasions they carry a long, odd mace. They are called "beef-eaters," being a corruption of *buffetier*.

The warden who accompanied us was a large, fine-looking man, who wore his gorgeous uniform with quite an air, and was very pompous in his manner of speaking, as if well aware of the responsibility and honor of his position. As we entered the main central building, he said, "Ladies and gentlemen, this is the White Tower, one hundred and sixteen feet by ninety-six. Its height is ninety-two feet, and the external walls are fifteen feet in thickness."

He led the way up a winding stair, and through a great many large halls. Stopping in one of these, he said, in a loud voice, that all the party might hear, "Queen Elizabeth's Armory." Then pointing to a cell formed in the thickness of the wall, he added, "Sir Walter Raleigh's prison; here he wrote his 'History of the World.'"

In the centre of the room was a large, darkly-stained block, showing the very indentures made by the axe when it severed the necks of its victims.

"Perhaps poor little Lady Jane Grey knelt by that very block," said one of the party, musingly, "and laid her pretty head there to be cut off with that ugly axe. It may be that her blood made those dark patches in the wood."

"Ay!" broke in another, "and I dare say, the blood of some good old Jesuit is mingled with it!"

"I wonder if Mary, Queen of Scots, was beheaded on that same block?" added a third.

The warden, who, up to this time, had been listening with a condescending smile to these surmises, now spoke. "No," he said, in a deep, decided voice, straightening himself up to his full height, and awing the whole party to silence by his appearance of superior knowledge; "Queen Mary of Scots was never in the Tower, she was executed at Fotheringay Castle. You will notice at the end of the room a figure of Queen Elizabeth, life-size, mounted on a carved horse. She is attended by her page, and on either side is an officer of the household in armor. On the wall behind the Queen is a painting of the old Cathedral of St. Paul. Fronting the Queen you see a knight of her period in close armor, in his hand a tilting lance." Thus he continued, pointing out the various articles in the rooms, and explaining all about them.

In conducting us to the Tower Chapel, he stopped suddenly on a short pair of stairs, and startled us by saying abruptly, "The bones of the little princes who were smothered in the Tower by order of Richard III., were found under these steps." Without waiting for further parley, he strided on.

The Horse Armory contains figures of a great many armed kings and knights on horseback. It is the most interesting room of all, showing the varieties of armor that were used in the different periods of English History. We saw the complete suit made for Henry VIII.

when he was eighteen years old, from which we concluded that he must have been a slight, well-formed young man at that time. We also saw the armor made for him after he became old and stout, which we thought could easily accommodate two ordinary-sized men within its mighty compass. It was very interesting to see the miniature suits of armor made for the different kings of England when they were little boys. As all this actual, historical armor, is not hung on the walls, as is generally the case, but is put on life-size wooden figures of the individuals who originally wore them, and as the figures are mounted on horses, also in armor, and often hold their lance or sword in the attitude of battle, the whole effect is very impressive.

One floor of the White Tower is used for the modern armory, and contains an incredible number of fire-arms all in beautiful order. The walls and ceilings are ornamented with pistols and swords artistically arranged in the form of stars, crosses, and various geometrical figures.

It would be impossible to remember half of what one sees in the Tower of London. There are trophies of almost every British hero since the days of William the Conqueror. The most modern relics I saw, were the guns taken by General Wolfe at the siege of Quebec, and also the cloak in which he died.

When we left the Tower, we took one of the cabs which we found waiting outside the gates, and drove to Saint Paul's Cathedral. We were not very much impressed with the appearance of the interior. Its grandest aspect is when seen from a distance, towering over all the steeples and smoking chimneys of the mighty city. Thus we saw it as we left London for Dover.

The next day, we took passage across the channel to Ostend. While the little vessel pitched uneasily about on the choppy sea, and the other passengers deserted the deck, and lay below in all the misery of seasickness, Uncle and I sat comfortably under the shelter of a deck cabin, and let the spray dash around us and over us while we talked over what we had seen in the British Isles, and what we still expected to see on the Continent.

Now that we had been through England, Ireland, and Scotland, we were struck with the differences between these three countries that lie so close together. Each has its own peculiar features. Scotland has its rocky, barren moors, and purple, heath-clad mountains with wooded glens and valleys between, each containing a loch or chain of lochs. Ireland has its bogs and its steep sea-coast, cut into a thousand caves and crevices by the waves; its potato and cabbage-fields, marked off with dark-green hedges, making them look like patch-work laid out on the hill-sides; also its old castles and round towers in every picturesque spot on the island. And, lastly, England, which is like one vast park, with stately avenues of trees leading to old family homesteads.

"But," said Uncle, after we had enumerated all these peculiarities, "there is one thing common to all three countries. Can you guess what it is?"

"Rain!" I answered promptly.

We now turn our thoughts towards the Continent, but with rather heavy hearts, for we have had a great disappointment in not finding letters from home.

"I am sure they have written to us, Uncle; but where are the letters wandering, that we can not catch them!"

"You mean that they can not catch us," he said. "No wonder! we never know one day where we shall go the next. And to my mind this is the only true way to travel."

XL

BELGIUM.

MISUNDERSTANDINGS AND MISTAKES—DESPERATION OF A BOSTONIAN—BRUGES AND ITS BELFRY—A VOICE IN THE DARK—ROMANTIC FLANDERS—GHENT—"MARKET-DAY"—THE GRAND BÉGUINAGE—ANTWERP ART—EAU DE COLOGNE—AND O, THE CATHEDRAL!

SINCE we landed on the Continent we have had our full share of funny experiences with French and German. In fact, at our very first meal on this side of the Channel, we asked for *dessert*, and they brought us eggs *(des œufs)*. Fortunately, laughing, the language of fun, is common to all nations, and with a small amount of good nature one can have a great deal of amusement here among these lively foreigners. It is generally, however, at the expense of our own countrymen. The other day a Boston gentleman was sitting near us at table, and after waiting nearly half an hour for some apple-sauce, the gravity of the whole party was considerably ruffled when the waiter appeared with a small piece of dry toast, smiling triumphantly upon his fellow-waiters who had given up all hope of understanding the Bostonian's order. A friend of the latter, after trying every other means in vain, to make them understand that he wanted some eggs, finally struck up a "cock-a-doodle-do!" This had the desired effect, and several waiters, with their faces buried in their white aprons, darted out at different doors to bring him what he wanted.

What amuses me most is, when we are a little late at

a railroad station, where nothing is spoken but German, and it is almost impossible to make the ticket-man understand where we want to go, or how many tickets we need, or indeed, anything at all. I enjoy the confusion and flurry. Once Uncle got between a French and a German porter; one of them had the two valises, and the other had grabbed up his shawl and umbrella. They both started for the train, but in different directions, each calling after him in a different language to follow, and he answering both in English. The whistle, and rush for the train, and Uncle heated and excited, starting first after one of them and then the other, struck me so comically that I was still laughing heartily, when the train emerged from the depot, and the bright daylight flooded in through the windows of the narrow compartments. There we sat just opposite each other, Uncle still out of breath, and provoked at having to pay both porters what neither deserved; while our bundles, thrown in pell-mell at the last moment, were scattered, some on the seats, some on the floor. Wasn't I a cruel giggler to sit there enjoying his discomfiture, while I had only to look on, and be taken care of? But all at once the ridiculous side of the performance seemed to come over Uncle, and he joined in my merriment.

As the sound of foreign languages becomes familiar to our ears, and we see the desperate attempts of other tourists, our courage increases, we venture to speak French openly, and Uncle even tries German and Italian. But how well I remember the uncomfortable feeling I had when we first landed at Ostend from Dover! The sound of strange words buzzing in our ears, the French and German signs over the shop-doors, and the foreign newspapers we picked up, all inspired me with a certain uneasy dread of opening my mouth. We walked out in the afternoon to take a look at Ostend, and, for the first time, I saw a herald passing through the streets, and stopping at each corner to blow a horn, and proclaim something in a loud voice.

"What is he saying, Uncle?" I asked. "Let's listen. Here he comes."

"Citoyens!" said Uncle, repeating what the herald said, as he caught a word here and there among the rolling of r's. "Chien—perdu—ses oreilles sont—what? It's all bur-r-r-r—"

"O," said I, "it's the old story—'where, O where, has my little dog gone?' This is one way of advertising lost articles. See, there he goes to the next corner. What a commotion he makes in these quiet streets!"

We reached Bruges, from Ostend, that same evening. The next morning we went to Mass in the Cathedral of St. Sauveur, which contains many fine paintings by artists of the old Flemish school, especially one of the Crucifixion, the most beautiful I have ever seen. Over the rood-screen is a splendid statue of "Dieu le Père." We ascended the famous Belfry of Bruges, mounting over four hundred feet by a dark, winding stairway, and holding on by a strong rope which hung down from the top of the tower. "Where are you, Nell?" said Uncle, as he came stumbling up in the dark.

"Way ahead of you," I said, "but all out of breath. I'll sit on this step till you catch up."

"Look out!" he said, as his head came on a level with my feet, "I hear footsteps above you."

"What a treat it is to hear a little English!" said a cheery, deep voice coming down through the darkness.

I jumped up, and as the owner of the voice crossed a ray of light which fell through a chink in the wall, I caught a glimpse of a gray beard, a smile just above it, and the outlines of a coat and pantaloons.

"Are we nearly to the top?" I asked.

"O, not half!" he said, laughing.

"Suppose we go back, Uncle!"

"What!" he said, "give up already?"

"O no," I answered quickly, "I just wanted to see if you were tired."

"That's all, is it? Then we will go on up and hear the chimes."

"You will not want to hear them twice," said the pleasant voice, now moving downwards; "don't come down too fast." The voice was now becoming fainter as it descended.

"Did you let go the rope on purpose?" we called down to him.

"Yes—struck bottom—wish you joy!" The words died away, and we climbed higher and higher, till we had left the streets of the town four hundred feet beneath us. If you want to look at this famous old town from a historic point of view, mount the old Belfry. When you stand down there in the streets it is the Bruges of to-day you see, but up here in the airy region of the birds, you look down on the red tiled roofs at your feet and the little towns and hamlets scattered here and there over the broad landscape, through the hazy atmosphere of history and romance that hovers round the old Belfry. It is the Flanders of old that you see, the land of Maximilian and Mary, of those bold foresters, famous weavers, and brilliant pageants that we love to read about.

When the chime of forty-eight bells rang in our ears we hastened down to the market-place, convinced that they sounded much sweeter in the distance.

In the Church of Notre Dame is a statue of the Blessed Virgin and Child ascribed to Michael Angelo. In the hospital adjoining are some celebrated paintings on wood, by Memling, and one or two by Vandyck, and Albert Durer.

We left Bruges in the afternoon and arrived at Ghent about six o'clock. Here a commissionaire, a long enough name for a guide, showed us around the city. We visited many ancient and historical buildings, and the open square called the Marché du Vendredi, where all the famous city riots took place. It is still used as a market-place, and as the next day would be Friday, the square was covered with frames and stalls to be used on the morrow. It is a curious sight to pass through one of these towns on a market day. The people from the neighboring districts are there with vegetables, dry-goods, leather, crockery, and all kinds of small merchandise. They occupy the middle of the wide streets and squares, leaving only a narrow passage on each side for wagons and carriages to pass. Women with babies in their arms, and children running under the horses' feet ; dog-carts full of cabbages and carrots, driven by little boys, who yell at the top of their voices, and crack their whips, while the dogs bark ; little Dutch women with white caps and short petticoats, buying and selling, chattering and quarrelling : some carrying heavy baskets and bundles on their heads, and others sitting on the ground counting their profits and scolding their children—make, altogether, as lively a scene as one is likely to find anywhere.

While we were at Ghent we went to see the Béguines, a strange kind of religious order peculiar to Belgium, where there are several of these Béguinages, or places where they live. The order was, I believe, founded by Charlemagne's sister, from whom they take their name. They do not live in community like other nuns, but they dwell either alone, or one or two together, in little brick houses with gardens. There are regular streets of these, and the whole is surrounded by a high wall, making a perfect little city. These semi-nuns can, I hear, invite each other to tea, and each receives her own visitors and friends, and keeps her own house. They have a superior, and occupy themselves with works of charity and religious exercises, but their rules are not many. There are seven hundred of them in this Grand Béguinage at Ghent, and it is really like a town within a town. We visited in one of the streets, a little chapel or shrine that had been erected in honor of a Béguine who was considered to be a saint. It contains a number of old crutches, silver offerings, and wax tapers, attesting the miracles wrought through her intercession. There is quite a large church near the centre of the enclosure, and the bell was just ringing for Benediction as we approached it. The Béguines were coming out of their houses in all directions and moving towards the church. They wear black habits, and short, thick, white veils, which end in a point behind, about half way to the waist. I noticed that each one, as she came out of her gate, put on her head a piece of cloth folded square, making it look something like the head-dress of an Italian peasant. I wondered what they were for, especially as they were constantly slipping around and had to be straightened every once in a while. But when we reached the door of the church I saw that each one, as she entered, unfolded the mysterious article and threw it over her head. It turned out to be simply a long white veil, enveloping the figure. When these seven hundred noiseless inhabitants of this curious city were all seated, they filled the whole church, and looked, in the thickening twilight, like a vast flock of sheep. Uncle and I knelt in the back of the church, and when Benediction was over, we slipped quietly out with our guide and hastened to the hotel.

We reached Antwerp at eleven o'clock the next morning, and went directly to the cathedral, where we found a Mass going on. After twelve the great pictures were unveiled. Rubens' "Descent from the Cross" is exquisite. I was agreeably disappointed, for I did not like his other pictures that I had seen; there was something so coarse about them. But this one is wonderful. He has shown us the body of a God even in the mangled corpse they are loosening from the cross. He has depicted the grand dignity of the mother of God in the sorrowing figure that stands beneath it. And he has given us a picture of men in such violent exertion, that we almost see the quivering of their sinews and muscles. To be sure, Mary Magdalene who, fearful lest they will let fall the body of her Saviour, rises on her knees and stretches out her delicate hand to support it, loses something of her charm when we learn that Rubens painted her not from an ideal of the saint, but from his own wife. However, we must admit that that outstretched hand and arm is worthy of the beautiful penitent.

The "Raising of the Cross" and the "Assumption," both in the cathedral of Antwerp, are very fine, but not like the other. I do not think any one man could paint two pictures equal to that "Descent." There were at least half a dozen artists making copies of it on the spot, and it was quite interesting to watch them.

As we were bound for the Rhine, we travelled to Aix-la-Chapelle, and then on to Cologne, where one of the first things we did was to buy some Eau de Cologne at one of the numerous Johann Maria Farina's, each of whom sells "the only veritable article."

Then we visited the Church of St. Ursula and the Eleven Thousand Virgins (more or less). The walls are lined with bones and relics. The "golden chamber" contains the remains of Saint Ursula and her bridegroom, with the most notable of her companions, and the skull of the Pope who was massacred by the Huns at the same period.

By this time it was getting dusk, and we had not yet been to our hotel, for we had sent our baggage on before us from the depot, while we turned aside to take a stroll through the city. We now hastened our steps in order to reach our night quarters before dark. On the way we passed that great pile of stone and mortar which is known as one of the famous cathedrals of Europe, and which has been so long tinkered at, but never completed. How many human lives it resembles! Beautifully, heroically begun, but, alas! the grand design never carried out.

XII.

UP THE RHINE.

THE FIRST GLIMPSE—PLEASURE-SEEKERS—SUNDAY AT KÖNIGSWINTER—THE WAY WE WALK—LEGENDS OF THE DRACHENFELS—AN ISLAND NUNNERY—ROMANCE OF ROLANDSECK—THIRTY-THREE RUINS—SUNSET ON THE RHINE—OUT OF DREAMLAND—MAYENCE CATHEDRAL—CHARMS OF HEIDELBERG—FOOLED—LAGER IN RUINS.

WHEN I awoke the next morning from a sound sleep, and remembered that I was in the city of Cologne, I rushed eagerly to the window to get a glimpse of the Rhine, that enchanting river, that region of water-nymphs, of robber-barons, and of impregnable castles—"castles in the air," actually, for as we floated past them on the water, they seemed far above the reach of mortals, perched, as they were, on the dizzy heights of the German mountains.

That first view, however, was only of steamboats and wharves, of a flat country and a muddy stream, of a dirty town, and an unfinished cathedral towering over all.

"The river Rhine doth wash Cologne,
But what shall wash the river Rhine?"

So thought we as we embarked on that stream, but such reflections soon vanished as the hills began to surround us, casting an endless variety of light and shade on the rapid waters now becoming clear and transparent as we left behind the busy thrift and turmoil, dirt and enterprise of the "Low Countries."

Strange to say, there were none of our own countrymen among the pleasure-seekers who filled the little

RHEINFELS.

Face p. 94.

steamer; they were principally Germans. This did not prove as unfortunate as might have been expected. Uncle was soon engaged in conversation with a gentleman who could speak French, and we learned from him that his daughter had been studying English, and would be pleased with the opportunity of speaking it with me. This young lady, with her father and two little brothers, were travelling to their home, which was further up the Rhine. Living on its very banks, and frequently travelling back and forth on the river steamers, they were familiar with every spot, and the stories and legends they told in connection with the ruins we were passing, made the trip doubly interesting.

The accounts we had heard of the way in which some tourists torture themselves with guide-books, while they lose all the best of the scenery, made us appreciate still more our good fortune in meeting with such agreeable informers. It is a very common occurrence on the Rhine steamers to see an English or American tourist plodding through a large volume of "Bradshaw," containing a very dry history and description of each castle, in very fine print. Suddenly a head emerges from the red covers of the book, and this seeker of pleasure and information asks which is Godesberg, or further on, the Rheinfels. "Rheinfels!" says some one standing near, "we passed that long ago; there is Hocheim just in front." Scarcely stopping to look at it, down goes the head again to see what Bradshaw has to say about Hocheim.

Our first stopping-place on the Rhine was Königswinter, and we found it such an attractive spot, that we determined to stay several days and visit the neighboring ruins. As the next day was Sunday, we went to Mass in the little village church, and then we strolled along the river banks until we found same shady seats near the water's edge. Here we sat and watched the country people as they came from the church, and crossed to the opposite bank on a little ferry-boat which was anchored in the middle of the river by a long chain, and moved from one side to the other, simply by the force of the current. Following the crowd we crossed over too, and walked in the direction of Godesberg Castle, which had been looming up before us all the morning. The airy, intangible Godesberg we had seen from Königswinter, seemed now to be transformed to a steep, rocky hill, and a winding stair, to be mounted step by step. But we stood at last on top of the stone tower, and behold! the Rhine glistened here and there through the landscape, from Cologne, whose steeples and whose smoke could be seen nearly thirty miles to the northward, to where its windings are lost to view among the mountains which break up the southern horizon. The beautiful plain at our feet resembled mosaic work, and the villages scattered through the valley of the river, seemed to me like clusters of toy houses and fairy dwellings.

"Which is Königswinter, Uncle?" I asked.

"Just over there at the foot of the Drachenfels, that mountain with the sharp-cut outlines and the ruined castle on the topmost peak—"

"Yes, I see that, and all those other mountains beyond, but I don't see why they call them the 'seven mountains' when there are eight, nine, ten—any number you please, clustered together. But what about the village?"

"Why, don't you see it over there with the queer church tower? And, by the way, we must hurry back, for I want to make a sketch of that pretty little altar we saw this morning."

"If that little thing down by the river is the village

STOLZENFELS.

Face p. 96.

of Königswinter, I hope it will grow before we get there, or we might step on it by mistake."

Uncle was about to protest against such an exaggeration, but I ran down the steps of the tower before he had a chance, and was fairly on my way down the hill, when he overtook me. Uncle always walks so fast and takes such long steps that it is often hard for me to keep up with him, but I make it even by running up and down all the hills we come to, and then sitting on a stone to rest while he, breathing hard, comes tramping slowly after me. In the cities, however, where it would be too undignified to run, his long strides have a great advantage over my little short steps; especially when, with some interesting object in view, he happens to forget all about me, until turning suddenly around at a street corner, he is surprised to find that I am trudging along half a square or so behind him.

We recrossed the Rhine on the little ferry-boat, and, armed with pencil and paper, started for the church. While we were there the vesper-bell rang, and when the congregation had assembled they said the rosary and litanies in German. Then they all sang. Nothing can be sweeter than the singing in some of these country churches.

Our interest now turned towards the Drachenfels, or Dragon's Rock, which we next ascended. There is a dreadful cavern in one side of this mountain, the mouth of which can be seen from the river. According to the legend it was once inhabited by a horrible monster, whom the people of the country worshipped, although he was a constant terror to them—rushing down on the plain and devouring whole flocks, sometimes even human beings.

It happened in those days that a beautiful Christian maiden visited this region, and tried to convert the people from idolatry. They would not listen to her, but on the contrary, determined that she should be offered to the dragon. Accordingly, she was bound to a tree not far from the cave, while a great crowd of people from miles around, were collected on the cliffs above to watch the result.

There was a moment of suspense, then the dragon darted toward her, lashing the ground with his tail and spitting fire, as dragons always do. The maiden looking calmly up to Heaven and calling aloud on the God of the Christians, had already begun to feel the deadly breath of the monster, when he slipped and fell. In an instant he was dashed down the precipitous side of the mountain, his hideous, scaly body cut and gashed by the jagged rocks, and with a terrific howl he sank beneath the dark waters of the Rhine. That howl was the death-knell of idolatry. For a moment all was still. Then the shout of triumph that arose from the lofty heights above, was a fit herald of the Christianity which was to follow.

The young girl, now regarded as a deliverer, was betrothed and married to a neighboring baron, who built, on the summit of the dragon's mountain, the castle which can still be seen for miles in every direction. A long line of powerful barons were descended from this union, and the story of the last of the family is quite as romantic as that of the first.

In the time of Charlemagne, Prince Roland, a favorite warrior and courtier of the great ruler, was travelling through the valley of the Rhine, and chanced to be belated when in sight of the castle of the Drachenfels. He made his way to the summit of the mountain and was hospitably received by the old baron, whom he recognized as one who had fought with him in battle. They soon became great friends, and Prince Roland

RHEINSTEIN.

Face p. 98.

was urged from day to day to remain at the castle. His willingness to accept the baron's hospitality was, however, chiefly owing to the charms of his only and beautiful daughter, who, the Prince had reason to believe, requited his affection. The old baron approved of his suit, and all was sunshine for the happy pair.

But alack! a messenger came speeding over the hills with the intelligence that Charlemagne was going to war, and Prince Roland must accompany him.

With great grief and promises of everlasting constancy the lovers parted. Long and dreary were the weeks and months to the remaining inmates of the castle. Secluded as they were from the rest of the kingdom, they heard only vague rumors of the war from stragglers and chance travellers. At last came the news of some great battle, in which Prince Roland had been killed.

His lady-love, when the first passion of her grief was over, determined to spend the remainder of her life in a cloister. Much sought after by the young barons of the country around, she continued to refuse all their offers, and founded a convent on a pretty little island in the river, which lies but a short distance above the Drachenfels and near the opposite bank. Here she made a vow of perpetual virginity.

In the meantime Prince Roland, who had not been killed, but only desperately wounded, slowly recovered, and still true to his first love, he turned his steed in the direction of the Rhine, expecting to find on his arrival a beautiful bride and a happy home. What was his sorrow and dismay on reaching the castle to find it dark and deserted, for he learned that the old baron had died, and the fate of his daughter had been sealed for life, during his absence!

Directly overhanging the island with the nunnery—

which is only separated from the shore by a narrow channel of water—is a very high, rocky cliff, thickly wooded on the top, and terraced up the sides with vineyards. I remember what a time we had scrambling up among the grape-vines, and how long we wandered through the woods that crown the summit, before we discovered the single crumbling arch that stood out against the sky so prominently from below. This one picturesque fragment is all that remains of Rolandseck, the castle that Prince Roland built, and where he used to sit at the window watching the movements of the nuns in the garden far beneath, until he saw her whose form his lover's eye could detect even at that distance.

Thus he spent year after year, and grew to be an old man, served by a faithful attendant. One day he missed a familiar form at her accustomed occupations in the grounds of the convent—a funeral procession, with lighted tapers and solemn tread, wound among the trees, and faint cadences of a hymn ascended to the castle.

At the usual hour the old servant went to call his master, but his eyes were fixed and glassy and his hands were cold. Still seated in his accustomed place at the window, he had died with the last echoes of the song among the rocks, and he was buried under the pine trees on the cliff.

As I sat in the arch of the old ruin, the bright sunshine streaming over the vineyards, the wind sighing among the pines; across the river the rugged outline of the Drachenfels, with its castle and its gloomy cave in sight; and far beneath, the quiet little convent where the nuns were walking in the garden, and the Rhine running swiftly past, now glistening in the sun, now blackened by the shadow of a mountain, its banks dotted with quaint little villages; I thought of the

OBERWESEL.

Face p. 100.

story till it mingled with the landscape. I was startled from my musings by the whistle of a little steamboat as it touched the landing below, and we hastened down the hill, wondering how the time had slipped away.

Then we glided on and on, further up among the vine-clad hills, each with its crown of fabled ruins. Thirty-three crumbling castles, and a number of walled towns, we counted that one afternoon. Then we saw the rock of the Lurlei, or Syren, who enticed a young baron, by her wonderful song, to the very edge of a frowning precipice, and then disappeared in the waves, leaving him to roam over the hills distracted, where he is still heard at night shrieking, and calling her by name. There, too, is the place where the "seven sisters" embarked and were never heard of again; and here we passed the old tower standing on an island in the water, where the cruel Bishop of Bingen, together with the grain he had hoarded so avariciously, was devoured by rats and mice. It is still called the "Mouse Tower."

Just as we landed at the town of Bingen—"Bingen on the Rhine"—the sun went down behind the hills in a flood of golden glory, and the river, the vineyards, the town, and the tower, looked gorgeous and magical in the glowing light.

Here seemed to end the glories of the Rhine. The poetry of this river of ruins is all among its mountains. When we awoke the next morning and embarked for Mayence, we seemed to have left behind the dreamland in which we had been wandering for the last few days, and this part of the journey was not very interesting.

The cathedral at Mayence is rich, and full of fine old monuments. There is a tablet to the memory of Fastrada, the wife of Charlemagne, and a beautiful monument to Frauenlob (the woman-praiser), so called on account of the poems he wrote on female virtue. This tribute to his memory was, I believe, erected by the ladies of the city.

We left Mayence by rail and reached Heidelberg in the evening, where we slept on feather beds for the first time. The next morning we went shopping, and with a mixture of English, French, and German, managed to buy some warm clothing for our winter campaign. Then we took a delightful drive along the hill on which the castle is situated. The views were very fine, and the castle itself the largest and grandest we had seen. With the assistance of a guide we went all over this wonderful ruin, even to the cellar, where the great Wine Tun is to be seen. I had often seen pictures of it, and now we really walked over the top of it, ascending by a pair of stairs on one side and descending on the other. It holds seven or eight hundred hogsheads of wine, and they tell us that in the days of the old Count Palatines they used to fill it with Rhine wine every few months. In the same room is a statue of a famous jester who lived in the castle, and near it is a clock which he invented to fool people. I was requested to wind it up by pulling a ring, when, to my amazement, the thing flew open and a fox's tail popped in my face. When I looked up it was to find the statue of the jester grinning complacently at my discomfiture. Fooled by a fool! How they all laughed at me. This city of Heidelberg must be a delightful place in which to spend one's time. The castle is a perfect study in itself, to say nothing of the beautiful walks and drives over the hills, and that splendid view of the broad plain, across which the Rhine glitters like a band of silver.

It is strange that these Germans have so great a fondness for lager-beer and the beauties of nature, which they seem to enjoy most together. No scene along the

Rhine would be complete in my recollection, without a party of sturdy Germans seated among the ruins, clinking their glasses, and roaring at the top of their voices, in tones not unmusical, some thrilling drinking song, making the mouldering old walls ring again with the sounds of revelry that filled them hundreds of years ago.

RUINS OF THE DRACHENFELS.

XIII.

NUREMBERG AND MUNICH.

IN BAVARIA — ANTIQUE CHARMS OF NUREMBERG — MODERN ART OF MUNICH — A DANCE ON A SCRUBBING-BRUSH — PALACE OF THE KING — THE ROYAL CHAPEL — PORCELAIN PICTURES — BEAUTY ON THE WALLS — THE GLYPTOTHEK — COLORED STATUES AND STAINED GLASS — A GIANTESS — A WARRIOR — FROM MUNICH TO ULM.

WE next spent a day at Wurzburg, where we took a look at the great bridge which crosses the Main, and then went on to Nuremberg. It took us some time to see this quaintest of towns. We visited several old churches, and also the castle, from which we could look down on the queer roofs and turrets of the houses. Then we walked some distance on the walls, and went to see the old Council-House, which contains some fine frescoes and historical relics. Everything in the city is antique and curious. It does, truly, take one back to ancient times. Uncle says, "See Nuremberg and die!"

And now we journeyed toward Munich, a place where one learns a great deal about modern art. Clustered into that city from all parts, one finds painting, sculpture, and architecture of the nineteenth century, which interest and please, even in the presence of great works of the past. Indeed, we tired ourselves nearly to death during the few days we spent there, in our eagerness not to lose one of the beautiful works of our own day, to be seen in that "City of Art."

Why, even the "salle à manger" of the hotel was

quite a little gem. The wainscoting, the panelling of
the doors, and all the wood-work, were finely carved

THE WALLS AND MOAT—NUREMBERG.

with figures, flowers, and fruit, while the pillars and the
walls were prettily frescoed, and the floor was of in-

laid wood. One morning when we came down to breakfast late, and all the other guests had retired, I was much amused at the novel way in which a man was polishing the floor. He was in his stocking-feet with a scrubbing-brush strapped to one foot. This foot he slid along from side to side, the other hopping after it, and thus he performed quite a fancy dance around the tables and pillars, lifting the chairs out of his way as he glided on, without ceasing the rapid zigzag motion. It was quite as lively as a jig.

Our hotel was not more than a block from the Botanical Gardens, so they were naturally among the first sights to be seen. They were very large, and of course we could not see near as much of them as we wished, for that would take weeks instead of hours. The most interesting thing to me was the collection of tropical plants. There was a full-grown palm-tree enclosed in an immense dome-like green-house, together with cactuses, banana plants, and a great variety of rarities which I stood gazing at in wonder, always keeping at a respectful distance, not daring to touch them, much less to pluck one of their leaves. I little dreamed that in a few months I would be in their native regions, walking through groves of them and picking as much of their fruit as I liked.

One of our most interesting visits at Munich was to the Royal Palace. The King of Bavaria was in the country, and strangers were allowed to go through it during his absence. There was such a number of outer courts and inner courts, and long corridors with many twistings and turnings, through which the guide conducted us, that I have not a very connected idea of the building. I know that one of the beauties they showed in the way of art, was the Royal chapel. The king's private chaplain, a venerable, white-haired priest, unlocked the door for us, and let us in. It is small and rather dark on first entering—the only light coming through one or two very richly-stained glass windows. The ground-work of the entire chapel, both ceiling and walls, is of solid gilt, on which are exquisite frescoes representing religious subjects, painted by modern German artists, whom the courtly old chaplain seemed to name with appreciative pride, as he called our attention to their beautiful productions.

This was only a glimpse of what was to follow. We were conducted through a long corridor, hung with portraits of the kings and queens of Bavaria; then through whole suits of apartments, in room after room, where each wall was a beautiful fresco with life-size figures, representing some scene in history; while each floor was a marvel of inlaid work, sometimes of precious woods, then again of marbles. The furniture was in keeping—luxurious chairs and divans of gilt, cushioned with satin and velvet of different colors; mosaic tables, where each tint in the flowers and leaves showed us some new variety of rare marble; chests and cabinets studded with amethysts, rubies, and other precious stones; and great, old-fashioned beds, curtained with silk and satin. Richest of all was the throne-room. It is still quite dazzling, though dimmed with the tarnish of many years. A small reception-room adjoining it is a most peculiar work of art. The walls are entirely concealed by small pictures, representing both Christian and mythological subjects, minutely painted on porcelain, each picture being about ten inches square, and all set in a delicate frame-work of gilt, reaching from ceiling to floor. Some of them are copies of famous paintings, others are originals, and we became so interested in them that we stooped down to see the lowest ones, and raised on tiptoe to examine those above our heads, finding them all done with equal care. But we had to leave them before we were half satisfied, for the janitor came around clinking his keys to remind us that our time was limited. As we entered a large room, hung with oil-paintings of Bavarian battle scenes, we heard drums beating outside, and presently a whole band struck up a stirring march. We all hurried to the windows just in time to see a large body of Bavarian soldiers moving along the broad, magnificent street in front of the palace. They had been ordered to another part of the country and were just beginning the march. It was a splendid sight, and it seemed to me as if we had before us the heroes of those battle scenes on the walls.

The next two rooms were filled with portraits of beautiful women, most of which were painted during the reign of the old monarch, father to the present king. It is said that whenever he particularly admired the beauty of some woman, no matter to what country or condition in life she belonged, he employed one of the best artists of the times to paint her portrait and place it in the palace. In this way it happened that he had a most remarkable collection of striking faces. One of them haunts me still. It is that of a pretty young peasant girl, wearing a coquettish little white bonnet, and carrying a prayer-book and rosary, evidently on her way to church. Her eyes are cast down very modestly, almost concealed by her long lashes, but for all that there is a marvelous deal of frolic and mischief there, that seems to be trying very hard to get the better of the piety. One can not help exclaiming, "Isn't she a little rogue!"

Munich reminded me somewhat of Washington, on

account of the number and magnificence of its public buildings, which are principally of white marble. Besides the Hall of Fame for receiving the busts of celebrated Bavarians, and numerous other large establishments, there are the Glyptothek and the Pinakoteck, built in imitation of old Greek architecture, and containing splendid collections of paintings and ancient statuary. Near them is a triumphal arch, looking as clean and white as I imagine some of those in Rome looked a thousand years ago. There is a great obelisk in the centre of the square, made of cannon which the Bavarians captured from the Russians in 1812.

After spending a few hours among the old gods and goddesses of the Glyptothek, we went from this quiet region of paganism and the past, to the large and busy establishment of Meyer's, a centre of modern, Christian art, from which colored statuary and church ornaments are sent to all parts of Christendom. This does not, I believe, fall into the ordinary routine of sight-seeing, but Uncle wished to order some statues for his altar, and Mr. Meyer took us over the whole establishment. We went through several large rooms in which men and boys of all ages were painting the statues. When we passed one that pleased us we would ask for what place it was intended. There were several for Great Britain and Russia, but more had been ordered for the United States than any other country. Among other things, they were making a very elaborately-carved altar for a church in New Orleans.

An establishment of this kind is interesting to see, but dry to write about. For instance, while there one can watch the artists working in the damp clay, each touch he gives it changing the whole expression of the face, sometimes imparting a new grace or characteristic feature, then again, by some unlucky stroke spoiling what was already there. Indeed, though only stopping to watch him a moment, one becomes almost as intent upon the work as the artist himself, and turns away with reluctance.

Those who have statues made here send a drawing or sketch of what they wish to order, and from this the clay model is made. A plaster cast is then prepared, from which the wooden statue is carved. When this is completed it goes to another part of the building and is colored. Thus it undergoes five different transformations before it is finished and ready to be sent to its destination.

We visited one room where a man was at work on a wooden statue, eight feet high, a copy of Guido Reni's magnificent "St. Michael," the original of which is in the church of the Capuchins at Rome. The workman was just giving it a few finishing touches, and chipping away at the devil's horns when we entered. The figure was supported horizontally on two blocks, so that he could work with more ease. As he continued hammering rapidly, making the tiny chips fly here and there, I thought how one little slip of the chisel would destroy that beautiful production of so many hours and days of close attention and labor. Each scale of the archangel's armor, and each lace of the sandals was carved with wonderful minuteness. While we were examining it, Mr. Meyer called several men and had the statue placed upright, so that we could enjoy the full effect. I had often seen engravings of this famous conception, but how tame they were compared with the life-like figure before us!

Every one has heard of the beautiful stained glass of Munich. I remember that one of the windows in the Cathedral at Albany is from there. Of course we visited this great factory, too, which was founded and supported by the late king—a great patron of art, by the way, and to whom Munich is principally indebted for her present preëminence in that line.

After some delay in hunting up the janitor and unlocking doors, we were finally allowed to enter, and were shown into an apartment where we saw a large window just completed and joined together, which was about to be sent to England. Then we were led into a darkened room where they had an arrangement something like a stereoscope, filled with stained glass pictures, placed in such a way that the light fell through them as it would through a window. I had not the least idea that stained glass could be made so exquisitely beautiful. It was impossible to see where it was joined, though each design consisted of many separate pieces. There were fine representations of natural scenery, especially of mountains, cascades, and snow-scenes among the Tyrolean Alps; copies of some of Raphael's principal madonnas; and a quantity of miscellaneous subjects. They were indeed as perfect as oil paintings, and, in addition, had the peculiar soft light that is only seen through stained glass.

Many of the prominent German artists have assisted in adorning the various churches of Munich with sculpture and painting, but we were particularly pleased with the Frauenkirche, a curious old cathedral, into which—drawn by some unaccountable attraction—we nearly always happened to stray before the day was over. We found it a real rest, after the hurry and excitement of sight-seeing, to sit or kneel for awhile in the dark, silent old *kirche* which at this time in the evening was generally deserted, except that now and then a peasant or day-laborer on his way home would step in to say a short prayer before some favorite shrine.

On Sunday we went to High Mass in the Cathedral, and were just seated, when I heard an unusual noise in the back of the church, and a heavy tramp, tramp, tramp, of feet. On looking round I was startled to see a body of soldiers, in full uniform, marching up the middle aisle. What could it mean, I thought. My mind at once reverted to Pope Gregory and Thomas à Becket, and with my imagination still picturing bloody scenes, and priests dragged irreverently from the altar, I looked hurriedly around at the congregation. When I saw they were unconcernedly saying their prayers, and that the soldiers marched quietly up to the altar and took their places, and finally, that at the consecration and elevation, they made a military salute and remained reverently on their knees, I came to the conclusion that it must be an ordinary and peaceable spectacle. Moreover, being by this time rather ashamed of my little scare, I resolved to keep it to myself. So when, after Mass, Uncle alluded to the soldiers I quietly said:

"Why, yes, it was a very pretty sight. I suppose they do that every Sunday!"

The great wonder of Munich is the colossal statue of Bavaria by Schwanthaler, which stands in the Theresian Meadow just outside the city. From a distance it appeared to be of the natural human height, but as we came nearer and nearer, it kept growing and growing, just as those mysterious people do in ghost-stories, until at last we found ourselves standing under a great giantess, holding a wreath of laurel high above her head, and with a lion crouched at her feet. The statue is made of bronze, sixty-four feet high, and if you take the granite pedestal into consideration (which is quite necessary if you try to ascend this gigantic lady), the top of her head is a hundred and twenty or thirty feet from the ground. We found it comparatively easy to mount inside of her by a little winding iron staircase, as long as we were under her skirts, but we had to stoop a little when we reached the waist, and it was really quite a feat to get through the neck. Once safely in her head, there were comfortable seats for eight persons, and a pleasant look-out over the city from a little hole near the ear. But it is time we were saying good-bye to Bavaria.

When we were leaving the hotel for the cars a military gentleman entered, and as we saw all the attendants bowing very low, and paying him particular attention, while we were left to take care of ourselves, we ventured to ask who the distinguished individual might be? We were told that he was the commander-in-chief of the Bavarian forces, who had won a great reputation during the late Franco-Prussian war!

As the train left the depot we caught a glimpse of the gloomy waters of the River Iser, and as my mind was still dwelling on warlike scenes, those old lines so familiar to every school-boy, about the battle of Hohenlinden, which was fought near here, kept coming back to me again and again, until the very train, as it jolted and rumbled along towards Ulm, seemed to be mumbling over the words to a rattling, jogging tune, always keeping to the one verse:

"And dark as winter was the flow
 Of Iser rolling rapidly."

XIV.

SUMMIT-GAZING.

SWITZERLAND AND THE TYROLEAN ALPS—A LEGEND OF LAKE CONSTANCE—GERMAN ROOFS AND SWISS COTTAGES—A PECULIAR INTRODUCTION—ZURICH AT NIGHT—MOUNTAINS IN THE AIR.

> "Girt round with rugged mountains
> The fair Lake Constance lies;
> In her blue heart reflected
> Shine back the starry skies,
> And watching each white cloudlet
> Float silently and slow,
> You think a piece of Heaven
> Lies on our earth below."

THOSE beautiful lines were continually in my mind during the two or three hours we spent in crossing Lake Constance. A lunch was brought to us on the deck of the little steamer, and we sat there watching with interest the Swiss shore of the lake which we were approaching. I had always looked up to Switzerland in my dreams as something entirely beyond my reach; here, to be sure, I was looking up to it, and its lofty mountains, but in a real, not an ideal sense. To our left were the Tyrolean Alps, and overhanging the lake in that direction was Bregenz, "that quaint city," about which Adelaide Proctor tells a thrilling legend.

It is of a Tyrol maiden who has fled from her home to toil in the Swiss valleys, and as the years pass, she ceases to think of her native country or language save in her prayers, and the songs she sings to the children around her. She hears rumors of a war with Austria, but she thinks little of it, until one night, when a large party of men are gathered for a feast in the house, and she hears them drink to " the downfall of an accursed land ; " they tell how Bregenz, the enemy's stronghold, will be attacked that night, while the unsuspecting inhabitants are sleeping soundly. This rouses all the maiden's love of country. She thinks of her native hills, of the battlements and towers of her own beautiful town, and the faces of her friends. The men around her are no longer kind masters, but her enemies—the bitter enemies of her country. She hesitates not a moment, but speeds to the stables where the white charger who feeds from her hand, is standing in his stall. She mounts him, and swiftly as the wind they dash through the darkness. As they pass village after village she hears the clocks strike "nine!" "ten!" "eleven!" and still they rush madly on, and still she cries, "Faster! faster!" At last she hears the roaring waters of the Rhine, and the horse, frightened, starts back—but he knows the voice that is urging him forward in agonized tones, and he plunges in. The current is fierce and rapid, but he struggles through and staggers up the opposite bank. She sees the lights of home far above; they gallop up the heights, and reach the gate of the city as the clock strikes twelve. Her task is done, the sentinels are roused, and Bregenz defies the army that marches against her.

This was three hundred years ago, but there is still an old gateway in the town with a carving of the maiden's ride. A warden paces up and down all night, calling out the hours as they pass, and

> "When midnight pauses in the skies
> He calls the maiden's name!"

From Lake Constance we went by train to Zurich. I was struck with the difference between this, my first ride in Switzerland, and the ride of the day before in Germany. They were both beautiful and picturesque as could be, but there is a difference even in one's very sensations in the two countries. Those solid little German villages, where the houses, with heavy red-tiled roofs reaching nearly to the ground, are clustered around the country church, with its quaint, straight, square tower, and where the neighboring hills and valleys seem to drink in the sunshine—give you a real snug, cosy, sleepy feeling as if this world was such a comfortable place. On the other hand, those airy little Swiss cottages, with their light wooden balconies, scattered over the valleys and up the hill-sides, while the sunbeams fairly dance over the mountain peaks, and on the haystacks, and the peasants singing at their work—inspire you with a light-hearted, happy feeling, that leads you to imagine that you too could dance up the mountains, over the clouds, and, indeed, right into Heaven.

We reached Zurich late in the afternoon, and as it was a delightful day, we walked out on a little exploring expedition through the grounds of the hotel. We found that they extended to the very shores of the lake, and we remained close to the water's edge watching the sun sink slowly behind the mountains. As I stood there I began to write words in the gravel with the end of my parasol, when all at once I heard, " O, you are English!" from a voice just behind me. I turned suddenly, and there stood a pleasant-looking old English gentleman, who, like ourselves, had come to see the sunset. He drew a puzzle on the gravel walk and asked me if I could decipher it. I just happened to guess it immediately, and he said:

"You are as smart as a little Yankee!"

"I am one," I answered.

He had supposed at first that we were his own countrymen, but nevertheless we were mutually pleased with this opportunity of using our mother-tongue.

That night Uncle and I took a walk through the city of Zurich. The banks of the river on which it is situated are very steep, and the city is built right up house above house, so that from the river we could count every building on the hill. We were walking along a broad level street, that was close to the water, when I saw a pair of public stairs leading up between two stores, and proposed that we should find out where they went. On reaching the top, we were on what would be, in any ordinary town, the roofs of the houses, but in this case it was the back yard or court of a great church that towered up before us. We wandered around, and down several pairs of stairs, expecting to find our way to the river again, but they all ended abruptly at private doors, until at last we found ourselves on the street in front of the great church; we followed its winding course down the hill, between tall houses, where each story projected farther out, until they almost met overhead. It brought us finally to a very wide bridge, lined on both sides with small stands of fruit and nicknacks. When we were half-way across, we noticed that the lights reflected from the city made the river so bright that we could follow its course for some distance among the hills. Looking in the other direction, the rippling reflection widened out into the lake, which was dotted with the colored lights of the little steamers, and just at the mouth of the river was a small island with a grove of trees, connected with the gardens of the hotel by a narrow bridge. We had visited it during our afternoon ramble, and it was also the place from which we embarked when we left the city.

I remember what a dispute arose among the passengers the day we went down Lake Zurich. There were mountains all around us, but from the end of the lake towards which we were steering, rose quite a high range. Over their summits the clouds extended up some distance, and, strange to say, a succession of peaks were to be seen above the clouds, suspended, as it were, in the sky, and having no connection with the peaks below, except a close resemblance in form. Their outlines were distinctly marked against the clear blue sky, but they had a strange, chalky, light appearance, as if they could be blown away by a breath. Some of the passengers said they were merely unusual forms taken by the clouds; others insisted that they were a reflection of the peaks below—a species of *Fata Morgana*. A few old Alp frequenters, among them our friend of the gravel acquaintance, ventured to assert that they were real mountains, but their idea was laughed down as ridiculous. While the dispute was hottest, the wind, by a strange freak, dispersed the clouds almost in an instant, and we had before us one of the mighty ranges of Switzerland, beside which our mountains of the lake shore were mere hillocks.

XV.

SWISS VALLEYS.

ENTHUSIASTIC TOURISTS—RAGATZ AND CHUR—A FRENCH LANDLADY, SWISS MAID, AND GERMAN DOCTOR—LUCERNE—MY WINDOW—THE RIGI—THE LAKE — WILLIAM TELL — WASHERWOMEN OF GENEVA— MOUNT BLANC.

FROM the foot of Lake Zurich we took the railroad carriages for Ragatz and Chur. This journey is among my most vivid recollections of Switzerland, for we were following the courses of the valleys and streams through that wonderful range of mountains that we had seen from the lake. We twisted ourselves into every possible position to see the snow-capped summits directly above us, and our fellow-travellers—English, French, and German—became so excited over the scenery, that they would call out to each other, for though the language might not be understood, the gestures were unmistakable, and they would rush from one side of the car to the other, even dropping down on the floor to get a sight from the car-windows of the very tip-top of the mountains. The enthusiasm seemed contagious; there were haughty Englishmen, stolid Germans, fashionable young ladies, and confirmed dandies equally forgetful of appearances. Indeed, as we passed peak after peak, now clustered together, now opening and showing beautiful valleys between, or dark, shaded chasms, the jagged rocks taking new shapes and hues every instant, it was like watching a grand and ever-varying kaleidoscope.

We travelled for some time along the shores of Lake Wallenstatt. It lies between perpendicular walls of rock rising out of the water from two to three thousand feet, and here and there, where the land slopes a little at the top, one can see the villages, and the cattle grazing far above.

A cold caught from the mountain breezes on the lakes, and our constant summit-gazing, had given me a horrid " stiff neck," so I had to let Uncle go without me to see the remarkable gorge at Ragatz, and by the time we reached Chur (that queer little town, nestled in the bottom of a great mountain bowl, with a few cracks in it for people to come through), I was in a condition to be laid up for four or five days. We just happened on the cosiest inn we had found anywhere, and the most kind-hearted and talkative landlady you can imagine.

She rubbed me, steamed me, dosed me, and talked French so fast that I could not begin to keep pace with her. She gave a long account of a trip she had taken through Russia, interspersed with pious exclamations; and told how she had visited her daughter in Africa, who, by the way, spoke English, and had left " Uncle Tom's Cabin " in the house. The landlady's attempts to pronounce the title of this book were very funny, but I was delighted to find something I could read. The chambermaid who waited on me was a Swiss girl. Our ideas were communicated by means of four words, and such gestures as could be made with a stiff neck. " Monsieur " was understood to mean my Uncle, " Madame," the landlady, " Fraulein " was either the chambermaid or myself, and " Yah ! " had to do for everything else in creation. I was attended by an old doctor whose French was about on a par with mine, and in spite of his German and my American accent, we man-

THE SPLUGEN PASS.   Face p. 120.

aged to talk together better than any of the others. Such a sickness was very funny, but I should not like to go through it again.

We had started for Chur with the intention of crossing the Splugen Pass, but we retraced our steps and went to Lucerne instead.

One of the first things we did here was to walk through the old covered bridge, with the quaint pictures of the "Dance of Death." How prettily Longfellow describes it in the "Golden Legend," in a conversation between Prince Henry and Elsie, as they ride through it!

Lucerne is a perfect gem for an artist; just such crooked streets and irregular houses, with little turrets and lattices, as they love to paint. There is also a more modern part of the town, with magnificent hotels—finer than any I had seen since I left the United States—and also handsome stores, in whose windows were exhibited many beautiful carvings in wood. One subject was copied over and over again, representing a grief-stricken lion lying with one paw resting on a shield, other weapons being scattered around. We were told that they were taken from the monument erected in honor of the Swiss Guards who were shot down while defending Marie Antoinette in the Tuilleries. With the aid of a small boy we found the original in some public gardens. It is cut in the centre of a solid sheet of rock that forms one bank of a pond or fountain, and must be over fifty feet high. It is beautifully executed, though one can not but wonder how the sculptor ever managed to carve it in such a place.

On our way back to the hotel we were hunting for guide-books and maps, when we happened to see a translation of Schiller's "Tragedy of William Tell." It was just what we wanted, and made the trip on the Lake of Lucerne much more interesting.

After our experiences at Chur, Uncle had a mortal dread of stiff necks, and would not allow me to ascend the Rigi with him. So after taking an early breakfast with me at our Lucerne hotel, he started off alone, and left me standing at the dining-room window. The Rigi was in full view, and, like all "forbidden fruit," looked very inviting. The rosy tints of the rising sun were skipping from point to point, gradually lighting up the whole mountain. I watched them till they whitened into broad daylight, then went to my room, and with a Tauchnitz volume for company, sat down by the window. Whenever I raised my eyes from the book they rested on a bewitching scene: the picturesque streets of the town, the old bridge, and the lake twining herself around and seeming to clasp the bases of the mountains, whose glaciers glisten in the sun, while

"Overhead,
Shaking his cloudy tresses loose in air,
Rises Pilatus, with his windy pines."

Towards evening I began to feel lonely, and the sudden recollection that this was my fifteenth birthday only increased my despondency. "What a forlorn birthday," I thought; "I wonder if anybody at home remembers it!—I suppose not, though, since I nearly forgot it myself." After a solitary supper, I came back to my window. The full moon had risen, and the scene was more beautiful than ever. This fact, in connection with my melancholy and sentimental mood, caused me to pencil the following lines, which, in a great flurry, I thrust into my table-drawer as I heard Uncle's ringing rap at the door. Now, however (to introduce them in approved style), "at the earnest solicitation of many friends, I present them to the public:"

O moon! triumphant, lovely, bright,
Thou, maiden ruler of the night,
Art gentler than the king of day ;
O'er toil he reigns—o'er rest thy sway.

O lofty mountains! grand and high,
Your snow-peaks tow'ring towards the sky—
Submissive at your queen you gaze,
Wrapt in a soft and silvery maze.

O lovely lake! deep, dreamy, blue,—
Fear not, for thou hast sentinels who,
Like brothers, guard thy still retreat
Whilst thou art sleeping at their feet.

The moon, now glancing at thy rest,
Finds her own beauties on thy breast.
This must be dreamland. 'Tis not real,
'Tis but some fanciful ideal.

But no! God made yon moonlit heights
To tempt our souls to higher flights,—
Borne up from earth on fancy's wings,
To contemplate sublimer things.

Uncle was very tired after his expedition to the Rigi, but he gave me a funny account of his sensations on being jogged up the mountain in a small car, with the engine pushing from behind. Besides the two ordinary rails there was a cog-wheel under the centre of the car, so that, as he expressed it, they were boosted up by a succession of bunks. Of course from the summit he had a fine view of the lake and the glaciers.

He wanted to meet an early boat in order to reach Lucerne before dark, and determined not to wait for the steam-car, but to walk down. He looked at his map to find a short route, but as mountains and maps do not often agree, he found he had chosen one of the longest. The Rigi is covered with pebbles, and very steep, so it was down, down, down, and slip, slip, slip, until he had worn holes through the toes of his boots, and was stiff all over the next morning. He said he envied a young man who passed him on the way with a long Alpine staff, with which he tripped down and swung himself over the hollows and ruts with the greatest ease.

We had a delightful trip on Lucerne, the lovely "Lake of the Four Forest Cantons." The main part of it is in the form of a cross, and when we reached a certain point we saw four arms branching off in different directions, and at the extreme end of each was a town. Behind us was the city of Lucerne, which we had just left; to the east could be seen Küssnacht, where Tell killed the tyrant, Gessler; to the west, the end of the arm is tipped with Alpnach, a starting-point for crossing one of the passes of the mountains; and we were steaming on towards Brunnen, a little town that is quaintest of the quaint.

At this last point the lake gives another very unexpected twist off among the mountains, rather spoiling the symmetry of the cross. The spot is noted as being the place where William Tell crossed during a terrible storm, when no other would venture in a boat, in order to save a co-patriot from the pursuit of his enemies. The shore here juts boldly into the lake, and standing out from the point is a solitary rock, having naturally a shape resembling a monument, and by looking through an opera-glass, the name "Schiller" can be read on it. What a beautiful idea!—that his monument should stand in the very lake whose legends he has immortalized.

It would be impossible to tell of all the places around Lake Lucerne which are connected with the life and achievements of the great Swiss hero. At Altdorf, the southern extremity of the lake, a statue

LUCERNE.

Face p. 124.

marks the precise spot where Tell stood when he split the apple. It represents him at the moment after he had made the famous shot—in the mountaineer's costume—with his cross-bow falling from his hand and his face raised to Heaven, as if with a fervent "Thank God!" he had not killed his boy. A fountain now plays upon the spot where stood the tree, the apple, and the boy.

By following up the valley from Altdorf we arrive at Tell's birthplace, and were we to continue still further we would reach the great St. Gothard Pass across the Alps.

From Lake Lucerne we went by way of Bern to the beautiful city of Geneva. Here, among other things, we were interested in the sheds along the banks of the river, under which merry-looking washerwomen were dashing the clothes energetically into the water and slapping them on boards, while they chattered like magpies. From one of the large bridges that cross the Rhone here, we took a little steamer to go up Lake Geneva, from which we had glimpses of Mount Blanc.

XVI.

UPS AND DOWNS.

"LETTERS FROM ABROAD"—AN ADVENTURE—MARTIGNY; ITS STRANGE MUSIC — VALLEY OF THE RHONE — ACROSS THE SIMPLON BY MOONLIGHT, DAYLIGHT, AND LIGHTNING —"WHERE THE RIVER RUNS"— THE GORGE—IN SAFETY—THE STORM RAGES.

SOMETIMES after a day of travel or sight-seeing, when I would sit down in the evening to write home, and scribble away till my candle burned out, or my fingers were stiff, I would go to bed and dream of the Kenwood ladies who spent so much time trying to teach me the art of letter-writing. Madam D—— or Madam W—— would rise before me with my last letter in one hand, while with the other she pointed out, one by one, blots, scratches, misspelled words, and, oh misery! she would occasionally read aloud a long, complicated sentence of my own manufacture, and say, with severe brevity, "Parse that!" In the midst of my consternation she would vanish, leaving the uncorrected letter to be sent in the morning mail. Then I thought of the long "letters from abroad" that I used to write at school for compositions, in which the incidents and descriptions were entirely imaginary. Why, I remember when, on two or three pages of foolscap, I gave an account of a trip through England, Norway and Sweden, Russia, Italy, and France, ending with the safe arrival of the travellers in America; and strange as it may now seem, I thought that I had given quite a description of each country. In writing real letters from abroad, however, the difficulty is that we are constantly seeing new wonders and beauties, and meeting at every step with ridiculous or pleasing incidents, so that the mind becomes bewildered with the variety, and our thoughts fly too rapidly from one subject to another in our efforts to describe everything. But what a blessing it is to the reader that we can not do so!

For instance, I would like to say more about Mount Blanc, the strange colors that dye Lake Geneva and the surrounding mountains towards evening, and the people we saw on the steamer, but my thoughts are galloping on to Vevey and I must follow them there.

Our hotel was on the lake shore. Up the hills as far as the ground slopes gently enough to permit, vineyards cover every foot of available land. Uncle and I took a stroll up the mountain a short distance, hoping to obtain a fine view of the lake. We soon found ourselves right among the grapes, following a public road that wound through the vineyards, with high walls on either side. Here and there other roads, also walled in, branched off in different directions. After walking some distance, we saw, on an eminence not far above us, a little tower that looked very inviting and promised a fine prospect. We turned off very confidently into one of the side roads. As we proceeded the walls became lower and lower, and at length ceased altogether, so that we found ourselves following a narrow foot-path among the vines, scrambling over low walls and through cobwebs, until we looked quite rustic and dusty. When we ascended a few stone steps and reached the tower, we saw a gentleman sitting there with a cigar in his mouth and a gun in his hand, apparently enjoying the landscape. Uncle accosted him with a

"Bon jour, monsieur."

He looked surprised, but raised his hat politely, and we expressed our admiration of the beautiful scene before us. Soon the gentleman informed us, with many polite expressions and bows, that he was proprietor of the vineyard and tower, and that we had passed "un grand danger," for the men whom he had appointed to guard the vines, were "très-méchant," and arrested any one found straggling among them. (How glad I was that I had resisted the temptation to pluck some grapes as I was coming up!) "O," said Uncle, jokingly, "in our country a person can go anywhere, just so that he does not look in the windows!"

Our Swiss proprietor seemed, for the moment, to be dumbfounded by this statement, but presently he said, brightening with the idea, "Ah! c'est l'Amerique, n'est ce pas?" "It is a country I have often wished to know more about."

Here was a subject of mutual interest, and we soon became very good friends. During the course of the conversation, he showed us how the tower was built of rough stones, with a little stairway mounting to the roof, and where he kept his gun, which he used to protect the grapes from the flocks of birds that would otherwise destroy them just as they begin to ripen. He pointed out Chillon, and other places of interest on the lake, and finally he told us how to reach the public road by going through his back yard. Then we left him, as we had found him, seated in the little tower, and wondering, perhaps, at the impudence of the Yankees!

The next day we went on the lake as far as Bouveret, passing close by the Castle of Chillon. A few hours' ride in the cars, from which we had a full view of the Dent du Midi, then brought us to Martigny, a little town among the highest of the Alps, at an opening where four beautiful valleys meet. Towards dusk, as I was seated by my window in the tidy, old-fashioned country inn, I heard a tinkle, tinkle, tinkle of bells, seeming to come from every possible direction, and filling the whole air with the sound. I jumped up, listened for a moment, and then ran down to the door of the inn.

"Come, Uncle," I called out as I passed his room, "let's see what it is; quick!" For the sound was so aerial, and scattered, that I feared every minute it would vanish. But no! it was imperceptibly coming nearer, and growing more compact and distinguishable, as we stood out in the road listening attentively.

"Why, Nell, it is the cows coming down from the mountains," said Uncle.

"You surely don't mean to say that cow-bells can make music like this," for I was quite disappointed. "But, at any rate," I added, "they are not at all like those old creaking, clanking concerns that they use at home. I wish they would import some of these."

"See!" said he, "they are beginning to enter the village. You know these Swiss herds often have a leader, one of the cows who is considered to be the most beautiful, the best trained, and who wears the sweetest-sounding bell."

"If there is one here, we must find her out by that last sign then, for it is beginning to get dark. Listen, here she comes; and now I can see her. Yes, I think it must be the leader. How proudly she steps along, as if she were queen of all creation! And look! there is no end to the herd that is gathering in from all directions."

"Come," said Uncle, "we had better go in."

All during supper the cows kept coming, coming, and it was at least an hour before the tinkling music died away. Then all was quiet until the next morning, when I awoke to hear the same melodious sounds ringing through the valley, as the herd started off once more for the mountains.

Cascade — Alps.

We followed up the valley of the Rhone as far as Brieg, most of the way by *diligence*. The scenery became more and more beautiful as we proceeded, watching for every opportunity to see the great glaciers lying between the peaks and appearing at every opening.

We crossed into Italy by the Simplon Pass, starting from Brieg at three o'clock in the morning with a bright moonlight. Although it was damp and uncomfortable at that early hour, the ride was enchanting, for the moonbeams cast a witchery over the dark, indistinct outlines of the mountains with snow-white peaks appearing here and there, while a deep and gloomy chasm lay beneath us. Slowly the horses drew the heavy, lumbering coach up the zigzag, though comparatively smooth, road; sometimes going a long distance in a straight line, and then turning back in the same direction, but ever higher and higher, the scene always changing. Sometimes hemmed in by mountains, the snow lying directly around us; then sudden glimpses of the distant glaciers, or the green valley beneath us, with the white cottages and tiled roofs of the village we had left. It was broad daylight long before we reached the summit, where there is a Hospice, kept by the monks of Saint Bernard. But we dared not stop, for a storm was brewing; already we were enveloped in a dense cloud; and before we had descended far on the Italian side, it began to rain heavily.

As the mountain-torrents, rushing down, would wash away the road, tunnels are built under it for them to dash through, or where this can not be done, the road is tunnelled through the rock, leaving the stream, or the avalanche, as it may be, to rush over it. Thus we sometimes heard the water roaring under our feet, then again it was splashing directly over our heads. Everything connected with this wonderful road is constructed with a view to its durability. The telegraph wire is supported for miles by tall, tapering blocks of gray granite, hewn with a care and precision that make them quite ornamental. For the conveniences and comparative safety of this route across the Alps, we are, I believe, indebted to the energy of the great Napoleon. We may well conclude, however, that his object in constructing the road was not altogether the benefit of humanity, for it is said that when the engineer went to him to report the progress of the work, his first question would be, "Le canon quand pourra-t-il passer au Simplon?"

One of the large Italian rivers flowing into Lago Maggiore, begins on the southern side of the mountain in a mere tiny brooklet. We followed its course down through all its windings, watching it gradually increase as countless mountain streams rushed down to meet it; and then saw it, burdened with the waters of all its tributaries, wander restlessly and aimlessly through the valley and the plain, till finally it reached the placid bosom of the lake, and was at rest. I never before studied so interesting a geography lesson!

For some distance the river and the road run side by side through a terrible gorge, grand and wild, dark and narrow. It is only by putting our heads out of the diligence-windows, and looking straight up, that we can see a slender slip of sky between the perpendicular walls of rock. Sometimes the river, out of patience with his bed-fellow, the road, takes boisterous possession of the whole gorge, leaving his peaceable companion to leap over him on bridges, or lie in dark, dripping tunnels, until the wild, willful stream is pleased to make room for the civilized road, and then the one rippling and smiling, the other staid and expressionless, they run on, once more, side by side.

In some places there were masses of snow, that had evidently been avalanches, tumbled over the precipice and blocking the gorge, until the resistless torrent had worn its way through, thus causing the snow to form a natural bridge across the ravine. At intervals we saw where forts and batteries had been cut in the rock about midway between top and bottom. Ugh! the very thought of a battle in such a place is horrible. Yet, as we ride rapidly over the smooth road, we are told that when there was scarce a foot-path here the mighty Hannibal and his army fought their way, step by step, through this awful pass.

It would be impossible to describe the beautiful torrents and cascades that come roaring down at every turn. Their spray constantly spatters the windows of the diligence. So does the rain-storm that has overtaken us near the summit, and which is now increasing every moment in fury.

We soon pass a stone column marking the boundary line of Switzerland. Hurrah! we are in Italy. The shout has scarce died away when the horses are reined in at the Custom-house. What! must our baggage be examined here in the midst of the ravine, in the fury of the storm? There is no help for it, and we are all kept waiting while one man packs up a host of little boxes which the Custom-house officer has tumbled out of his trunk. The driver gets out of all patience, and declares that the bridges will be washed away before we get down the mountain.

We thank God that they are not, but before we reach Baveno we are detained an hour while a tree that has been blown down across the road is chopped away. It is pitch dark and we sit silently crowded together in the motionless diligence. Suddenly, in a ghastly flash of flickering, white lightning I see the pale face and three-cornered hat of the old Curé who sits opposite me, the frightened face of the bride very close to the anxious face of the groom who sits in the far corner, and just as I look up to Uncle, who is next to me, all is dark again. As I sit peering out at the window I discover, by the light of a great many flashes in quick succession, that we are right on the lake-shore. I see a tall, scraggly tree standing out against the water, and even the houses and towers of a village on the opposite shore. I would look more, but Uncle puts his hand over my eyes, saying, "You will ruin them, child."

We reach Baveno at eight o'clock at night, stiff and sleepy, after a ride of fifteen hours. The storm howls all night and all the next day and the day after, and then all the passes of the Alps are snowed up. Verily, we crossed at the "eleventh hour."

XVII.

MILAN AND VERONA.

SOJOURNERS AT LAGO MAGGIORE — FUN OVER TURTLES — MILAN, A SPIDER'S WEB—CATHEDRAL CONTRASTS—TOMB OF SAINT CHARLES BORROMEO—GALLERIA VITTORIO EMMANUELE—A CHRISTIAN CHURCH OF THE EARLY TIMES—ST. AMBROSE AND THEODOSIUS—REVERSED— DA VINCI'S MASTERPIECE — OTHER PICTURES — VERONA — MORE CHURCHES—SCALIGERS—THE AMPHITHEATRE.

WE were charmed with Lago Maggiore. Little Isola Bella, belonging to the great Borromeo family, is as beautiful and strange as a fairy isle. Besides a few fishermen's huts, it contains an immense palace, whose massive stone steps, leading to the entrance, rise out of the lake, and under which is a pebble grotto with Grecian statuary disposed here and there in appropriate nooks. But the principal attraction of the island is its tier of airy, tropical gardens suspended one above another on rustic arches, which are adorned with colossal statues and full of delightful, shady retreats. In one of these we encountered some of the Borromeo family, as we were informed by the old gardener who accompanied us. Our intrusion being accidental, we bowed and passed on. After this we met the children again and again, running through the arches and playing under the trees. I dare say that if we had visited this island three centuries ago, we should have seen the little St. Charles Borromeo amusing himself in the same way with his brother and sisters.

The hotel at Baveno was filled with the pleasantest

kind of people; a jovial old English judge and his handsome lady, with kind-hearted, motherly ways; Americans whom we recognized as former friends; the interesting young honeymoon couple from Ireland who had crossed the Alps with us—not Irish as we Americans are so apt to conceive them—poor, ignorant emigrants, subjects for most of the newspaper jokes—but belonging to the real Irish gentry, whom I remember as some of the most cultured, elegant, and genial people we met anywhere; then there was a very pretty, bright young Scotch girl, who asked me innocently if New York was not on the Red River, and if I had often seen people scalped in America; but the most entertaining character of all was an eccentric old Englishman, whose front teeth were all gone, whose pantaloons always managed to hitch above his gaiters when he sat down, who, as he expressed it, possessed "a competency, in fact, quite a competency," who travelled with a funny Irish valet, and who, to crown all, indulged in a remarkable propensity for buying all kinds of odd trinkets.

One day he came in from a walk, with two turtles which he had bought from an old woman by the roadside, and he was showing us how beautifully they were carved, all in wood.

"Look!" he said admiringly, as he set them down on the piazza, "who would imagine that they are not—," he stopped short, for lo and behold! his supposed carvings began to crawl. O, what a shout of merry laughter rang over the water, as he stood running his hand through his hair till it stood on end, and glaring in bewilderment at the turtles, who were rapidly making for the grass-plot. He caught them, however, and kept them, consoling himself, perhaps, with the reflection that after all mere blocks of carved wood are not as interesting as real live turtles. We travelled through the mountain region around Lake Lugano and Lake Como, with our peculiar friend and his peculiar pets. The last that I saw of him was at the town of Como, striding off for the cars, followed by his grinning valet, and holding in one hand an umbrella and in the other a cigar-box, secured by a shawl-strap, containing the animated carvings squirming in fresh grass.

Our travel, ever since we left Munich, had been through natural scenery; so, for a change, we were not sorry to find ourselves in one of the largest and wealthiest cities of Italy—interesting not only for its antiquity, but as being the capital of Lombardy and the centre of a great arch-diocese that extends even into Switzerland. I speak of Milan. The plan of this city is very singular and convenient. The great Cathedral is the exact centre, from which the streets branch off on every side towards the gates of the city, the cross-streets becoming less and less intricate as the suburbs are neared, thus giving it nearly the form of a spider's web. Our hotel was near the centre, so we always walked first to the Piazza di Domo, or Cathedral Square, and then shaped our course to whatever part of the city we wished to visit. Most of the streets are narrow, as in so many of these foreign cities. They are paved with small round stones, having a strip of smooth flagging about a foot and a half wide close to the houses for people to walk on, and two strips down the centre of the road just far enough apart for the carriage-wheels to roll on. There are no curb-stones, and the streets all slope towards the centre, where the drains are placed.

The first thing to be seen in Milan, is, of course, the cathedral, which I found by frequent visiting improved upon acquaintance. I learned from it, that cathedrals, as well as individuals, may be judged unjustly from outside appearances; that a giddy, showy exterior does not always indicate want of depth and meaning within. All the large cathedrals that I had yet seen, both English and German, had loomed up before us grand, solemn, and majestic. I never imagined that it could be otherwise. But when I first saw Milan Cathedral, I nearly laughed outright.

"Why, Uncle!" I said, "it is like a great toy. But no; it is too white and frosty for that, and looks as if it might melt away—it reminds me of an iceberg."

"It is very easy to perceive, my dear, that you have never seen an iceberg. I hope, for your enlightenment, that we shall meet one on our home voyage."

"So do I, with all my heart. An iceberg and a whale! How I watched for a glimpse of either of them all the way across the Atlantic! But truly, Uncle, don't you think that this cathedral looks like a centre-ornament for a gigantic cake? For instance, a birthday-cake for one of those genii in the 'Arabian Nights?'"

"That will do till you can think of something better. But do genii have birthdays? I ask for information."

Seeing that Uncle was determined to make fun of my similes, I dared not attempt any more, but began to examine the great cathedral in earnest. The whole structure is of white marble, and on the exterior of the building alone, there are over three thousand statues, images each of some individual saint, martyr, or other great personage, and all by celebrated artists, even Michael Angelo, Raphael, and Canova. Pinnacle rises above pinnacle, and buttress succeeds buttress—adorned with myriads of statues, gurgoyles, hideous creatures spouting water from their mouths, and innumerable other designs in which every flower and plant, every leaf and vein, is as minutely and delicately carved as if

MILAN CATHEDRAL. Face p. 138.

intended to be examined with a microscope. (This, however, we discovered later, when we ascended to the roof; now we could appreciate the general effect.) Can you wonder that all this looks like fairy-work? Only it does not fade away, but stands before us as distinctly as ever on the solid foundation on which it has stood for centuries.

On entering the church I was startled by the contrast. Everything is dark, solemn, impressive, and silent. The rich stained glass casts a mellow, soft light through the whole place, while here and there a many-colored sunbeam piercing the gloom, brings out the massive columns and heavy Gothic arches; and at the back of the church, far, far off in the distance—as it seems, and really is—lights are seen burning before the Blessed Sacrament, and the tomb of Saint Charles Borromeo.

The latter is directly in front of the high altar. From the church, no part of the shrine is visible except the handsome bronze railing and magnificent candlesticks, in which candles are continually burning, around a closely-wired opening in the floor, through which may be dimly seen the chapel or tomb in which the body of the saint is preserved. On descending into the crypt and entering this little chapel, we find that its walls are entirely lined with silver, exquisitely worked into representations of different scenes in the saint's life, personifications of his special virtues, and various appropriate emblems. The body is preserved in a case of crystal and silver, enclosed with a thick outer covering, which is let down that we may see the relics. This great bishop, who, during his lifetime, so despised worldly grandeur, so loved the poor—as we are told by the pictures on the wall—is seen through the transparent crystal, lying in state, and clothed in richly embroidered, jeweled vestments and mitre. In fact, I never before saw so much splendor in so small a space. The body is covered, so to speak, with a mass of gold, silver, and precious stones, gifts of the great ones of the earth. The things that I remember most distinctly, are: a cross composed of a dozen or more emeralds as large as good-sized marbles, an offering from Maria Theresa; a beautiful crown of jewels from a French king, who had obtained some great favor through the saint's intercession; and a plain, gold cross from Cardinal Wiseman.

Leaving the damp crypt, we ascended once more into that beautiful interior of the cathedral. There was such a calm, holy, soothing presence in the very atmosphere of the place, that for the moment, every wish, every feeling seemed gratified. Oh! it was hard to tear oneself away; to leave what was almost a paradise upon earth for the noise and commotion of the street, the rattle of wheels, and the discordant cries of the vendors and beggars always hanging around the steps of Italian churches.

But in travelling, one's emotions are constantly being jarred upon. The religious and the profane, the artistic and the ridiculous, are so hopelessly mingled, and are thrust upon us in such quick succession, that if we do not learn to turn our interest and attention rapidly from one to the other, we are apt to lose half of what we see. I wonder if it is not a lack of this happy faculty that makes us so often fail to appreciate certain things, and see in them all that others have seen?

What could be more out of joint than to step from Milan Cathedral into the Galleria Vittorio Emmanuele, a beautiful bazaar, full of gay shops! It is also adorned with some fine modern statues, especially one of Christopher Columbus. The ground-plan of the building is in the form of a cross, each arm terminating in a street, and the roof is all of glass. It is still in the hands of the builders, but one of the four entrances that is completed, presents quite an imposing appearance.

The various churches of Milan are of unusual interest, particularly that of Saint Ambrose. It carries one's thoughts back to the early Christians, having been founded about the third century, on the site of a Roman temple, which was demolished. In the construction of the Christian church, some of the columns and other materials of the old building were used, and even now, strange Pagan animals and devices are seen here and there. The curious old sarcophagus of Stilico, the conqueror of the Huns, stands near the pulpit.

This church has all the old divisions which we read of as belonging to the primitive ages of the faith. We first enter a square enclosure surrounded by high walls and columns, but open at the top. This was the place for the catechumens and penitents, who were excluded from all participation in the more sacred mysteries. Traversing this court we reach the entrance to the church, part of the ancient door being still preserved, where the undaunted Saint Ambrose met the Emperor Theodosius, and after solemnly rebuking him for the barbarous massacre of his subjects in Illyricum, resolutely refused to admit him into the church until he had done penance. And it was there on the rough pavement of that outer court that the great Emperor of the East, in penitential garb, prostrated himself, weeping and imploring the prayers of the faithful as they passed in and out. These, touched by the sight of their sovereign in such deep humiliation, joined their entreaties with his that his punishment might be remitted. This the saintly Bishop refused to do until the Emperor had repealed all the unjust laws that he had decreed in haste or passion. Then, and not till then, did he again attempt to enter the sacred portals.

How vividly the whole scene is pictured before us as the heavy door swings open. But lo! a casual word caught from the conversation of those who are issuing forth, and it is no longer an emperor expelled by a bishop that we see, but a pope thrust out by a king. As we stand on the soil of this same Italy—the scene of the great modern drama of Pius IX. and Victor Emmanuel, which is being enacted before our very eyes, and whose closing scene is looked forward to with deep interest by the whole Christian world — how strange, how far, far back in the past, seems that old story of Saint Ambrose and the Emperor Theodosius! However, the old church stands open before us and we enter. First, there is a large open space comprising the main part of the building, which was intended for the faithful in general. Beyond, the floor is raised, thus marking the boundary of the sanctuary. On this low platform the officiating priest said Mass with his face toward the people, and, consequently, standing behind the altar. It was in those days that the altar consisted of a flat table with no tabernacle, and the blessed sacrament was suspended from the ceiling in a silver dove. Farther back still than this platform, and raised yet higher, is the apse, occupying the far end of the basilica. In this semicircular place the ecclesiastics sat, and at the back of the semicircle is still seen the solid white marble chair of Saint Ambrose. This is the oldest episcopal chair in existence, except that of St. Peter at Rome. The present altar of the church, which stands on the centre platform I mentioned, is plated with pure gold about the thickness of a silver dollar, enamelled in different colors, and set with hundreds of precious stones—diamonds, emeralds, opals, amethysts, rubies, and sapphires. It is really dazzling and was all the gift of one prince to the tomb of Saint Ambrose, who is buried beneath it.

San Lorenzo is an old pagan temple that without any alteration has been converted into a church. It has a round, dome-like shape; and a circle of fluted columns standing out some distance from the wall gives it the form of a large rotunda church with smaller chapels all around.

In the refectory of an old convent we found Leonardo da Vinci's celebrated "Last Supper." Though very much defaced and injured, the expression of our Lord's face is wonderful. It combines gentleness, love, grief, manliness, and divinity so perfectly that one could almost believe that it had been painted by an angel, or at least by an inspired man. The face and position of each disciple is intended to show some especial trait of character. It is very sad to see such a magnificent fresco falling to pieces and becoming more and more difficult to decipher, while so many unsightly productions now in existence will probably be glaring at the world in undimmed distinctness for ages to come.

In the Brera Gallery we saw paintings by many of the old masters—among others, Raphael's "Marriage of the Blessed Virgin," in which Uncle and I were both disappointed. He said that the necks of the virgins looked gawky and wooden; that the disappointed lover breaking his blossomless rod across his knee, resembled a circus clown, and, in a word, criticised it unmercifully. We thought, however, that the conception of the picture was very fine, and that some of the faces were beautiful. I told Uncle that I only wished Raphael had not painted it until he had perfected himself in drawing and coloring as he did afterwards, at which wise little remark he might, perhaps, have laughed in his sleeve had he not become at that moment intent on a "Martyrdom of St. Stephen," by Daniele Crespi, and I, just for the sake of asserting my independence, I suppose, gave it a mere glance and then became very enthusiastic over a little "Saint John the Baptist," by Poussin. Of the innumerable statues and paintings in this gallery, to which we could give but a hurried admiration, it would be worse than useless even to speak.

We have seen nearly everything of note in Verona. Uncle is quite disgusted with it in reality, having formed, in imagination, a very exalted opinion of its beauty and picturesqueness from Ruskin's high-flown description. (I do not mean to complain of Ruskin in general, for, between rusty-brown covers he was one of our favorite travelling companions.) We visited a number of churches, quaint old buildings each and all, but not of particular interest. In one of them is a picture of the "Assumption," by Titian; also some fine frescoes, and the tomb of Saint Agatha.

The house of the Capulets, where Juliet lived and loved, is shown; I must say that it did not look very, very romantic, with damp clothes hanging out to dry all around it; and of course *the very tomb* is pointed out, at which Romeo and Juliet completed the famous tragedy.

This reminds me of our absurd visit to the tombs of the Scaligers. We were told again and again to be sure and see them, that they were one of the sights of Verona. What they could be, we had not the slightest idea. After a great jumbling of keys and confusion of ideas, we were guided into what appeared to be a marble yard, or something of the kind, where stood a cluster of pointed, Gothic, arched, not very large indescribables, each surmounted by a figure. "What do they mean? which is which? haven't they some story? who are these scalawags?" for this was as near as we could possibly come to the sound of the name. To all these questions, reiterated with great emphasis, the guide only looked blank, and the woman of the premises shook her keys.

"Tombs!" said he, stolidly.

"Scaligers!" said she, pointing.

This was all we could possibly extort from them.

"Come, Nell," said Uncle at last, despairing of further information, "let us leave these interesting people to rest in peace. We know that they, he, she or it, are or is dead and buried, and that is more than we knew before."

Verona is wonderfully fortified with walls, moats, and earthworks; there is also the old Roman castle and bridge to visit. The great amphitheatre, though, is best worth seeing. There it stands (what is left of it), with the openings through which the gladiators and the lions bounded into the arena; the prisons where they were kept, the royal balcony, the music stand, the tiers of marble seats, the galleries and arches—everything; and it needed but little imagination to fill up what was wanting, in order to have before us the whole thrilling spectacle just as it appeared in the days of pagan Rome.

XVIII.

A WEEK IN VENICE.

THE GRANDE CANALE AT SUNSET—THE "STARS AND STRIPES"—THE PIAZZETTA—SCENES ON THE GREAT PIAZZA DI SAN MARCO—VENICE AT NIGHT—THE BRAVO—THE LIDO.

WHEN we had left Padua far behind, and were rapidly approaching the sea, the land became more and more flat and marshy, until at last we found ourselves riding out into the open Lagoon, as the bay or enclosure of Venice is called. The railroad is built on a narrow bridge or viaduct. Here we caught the first glimpse of the "floating city," and it was certainly very beautiful, with the spires and domes of its ninety churches rising above the houses, and seeming to have sprung out of the waves, for not a particle of land was to be seen. We went whirling into the depot, and for a few minutes we might have thought ourselves in any other city. There was the same rush and bustle, running after the baggage, and general confusion. But the instant we passed out at the depot door, and saw the steps descending to the water, we realized that we were in Venice. Numerous floating cabs and omnibuses, or, in other words, gondolas, were in waiting, and after some preliminary attempts to make ourselves understood in bad German and worse Italian—these being the only languages spoken—we were comfortably stowed away with our valises in a pretty little gondola, having directed the gondolier to take us to the Piazza San

Marco by way of the "Grande Canale." This principal channel winds through the city in the shape of an S,

VENICE.

dividing it into two distinct parts, and I have heard it called the "Broadway of Venice."

When the gondoliér dipped his oar in the water, our little craft began to glide along as swiftly and noiselessly as a phantom boat, a mere shadow on the water. It was just at sunset, and such a sunset I have never seen elsewhere. The whole sky, from horizon to zenith, was a mass of light, fleecy, golden cloudlets; they produced a remarkable effect that I will always associate with my first gondola-ride in Venice. A strange golden glow seemed to spread over everything. Each turn in the Grande Canale showed us new wonders in architecture; old palaces and churches whose marble fronts, now discolored by age, were elaborately carved into beautiful flowers, hideous faces, or lovely little cherubs. Indeed, if I could describe them as they really are, those who have not seen them might think that I was drawing upon my imagination; I can hardly believe myself that it was not all a dream—those gorgeous vistas that opened before us, as we glided on in the glowing light. When we neared the great square or piazza, the buildings we saw were even more rich and beautiful. Then the inner harbor opened before us, where the flags of many countries were floating over the ships which lay at anchor. It is strange what a thrill one feels at sight of the "Stars and Stripes" in a foreign land—almost like a message from home.

On one side of us was the great dome of Santa Maria della Salute, built in performance of a vow made during a great plague in the city; but the eye turns from this, and the beautiful island of San Giorgio, the ships, the bay, and the sunset, to dwell on the great centre of everything in Venice, the Doge's Palace, a marvel of beauty. Just across a small canal is the prison, a gloomy, solemn, yet graceful structure; and there high above the water, connecting the two, is the lovely little covered bridge—the world-renowned "Bridge of Sighs."

You could not but feel the appropriateness of the name after having seen the dreadful little dark cells prepared for the many prisoners who crossed it never to return.

The Piazzetta contains two tall columns, on one of which is a curious old statue of St. Theodore, ancient patron of the city; and on the other is the famous "Winged Lion," who, with his defiant attitude and fierce eyes, might well terrify any unwelcome intruders. Passing through this small square, we stood on one end of the great Piazza. It is paved with large flag-stones, greenish-blue and white, arranged in different figures like mosaic-work. It is enclosed on three sides by the old and the new Procuratie, or palace of the magistrates, now turned into public libraries, galleries, and private dwellings. It was in a part of these buildings that our hotel was situated, and there was always something lively and interesting to be seen from the windows. When the clock in the Campanile struck two, at which time we generally took dinner, the pigeons, who are thought by the Venetians to bring good luck to their city, would flock to the Piazza in countless numbers to be fed. Then a curly-headed little boy, sometimes a young girl, would throw handfuls of grain to them. Uncle and I often coaxed dozens of them to the window where we sat, by scattering crumbs on the sill. How tame they were, and how well they knew the sound of their dinner-bell!

In the evening, when we sat at the same window, eating our supper, the scene would be very different. The pigeons had all gone to roost, and the people now began to gather from all quarters to enjoy the air and a walk, on the only large spot of open ground in Venice. In a short time the vast square would be covered with a shifting mass of promenading humanity. A band of music played in the centre of the square, in the midst of a circle of gaslights; then all around the edge, as if in defiance of the massive, frowning buildings above them, were the most brilliant shops of beautiful pictures, delicately-wrought vases, and glass-ware, for which Venice is so noted, rare jewelry of every kind, and, in fact, everything most exquisite and bright, for the stores of heavier and coarser goods are confined to the strange little narrow passage-ways that are called streets, though in many places scarcely wide enough for two persons to walk abreast. By means of these and three hundred bridges, you can go to nearly every part of Venice without a gondola, but if not familiar with them, it often happens that you find yourself in the court-yard of a house, and must retrace your steps to find some other way; these paths are so intricate, that it is impossible to go more than a few yards without twisting about in the most outlandish fashion. As there are no carriage-wheels or horse's hoofs heard in this strangest of cities, it has a characteristic quiet, only broken by the mingling of voices, the clatter of feet on the pavement, or the shrill calls of the gondoliers as they turn each corner.

To be out in a gondola at night—this exceeds all. There is a strange witchery about Venice at all times, but in the evening it seems ablaze with hundreds of lights, each one reflected far out in the water; the glittering steel prows of the phantom-like gondolas (all except the prow is black) appear, flash in the light, and vanish as they glide swiftly and noiselessly along; the dark outline of the buildings, the dizzy height of the Campanile can be traced on the deep blue of the Italian sky, dotted with stars apparently so near, that at a little distance on the water, they seem to mingle with the lights of the city, which appears itself to be suspended in air.

THE RIALTO.

Face p. 150.

The Cathedral of San Marco I will not attempt to describe, for I have already exhausted my adjectives and superlatives. Its general appearance, with its five domes and countless pinnacles, suggests the idea of an old Oriental mosque. One can not pass unnoticed its four gilt horses that have been such travellers, having been carried by different conquerors from the East to Venice, to Rome, to Paris, and are at last resting, or rather prancing, in their old place over the door of San Marco.

We read Cooper's "Bravo" while we were in Venice, and it was just the kind of a story to attach a mysterious interest to everything we saw. When we crossed the Piazzetta in the evening, I imagined I saw Jacopo's pale face near the tall columns. When we visited the Doge's Palace, the scenes of the story were constantly before me; peering into the cells, I seemed to see the old father stretched on the floor; in their darkened room the awful Council of Three were sitting in solemn conclave; and midway on the Bridge of Sighs, we were encountered by the jailor's daughter, coming timidly forth with the Bravo. When we went over to the Lido, and saw the Adriatic, and the long, narrow stretches of sand that separate it from the Lagoon, I thought of Jacopo's expedition to the bleak old Jewish cemetery out there, the steel blades flashing in the moonlight, and the return to Venice in the dark. But then again, gorgeous pictures of the marriage of the Adriatic would chase from our thoughts such gloomy scenes.

On our way back from the Lido, Uncle changed places awhile with the gondolier, but he found that the motion of the one long oar in propelling the gondola was very different from any rowing or sculling he had ever done, and I laughed to see the way he made the little craft spin round and round on the water. After five or ten minutes of great exertion on his part, we were still in the same spot, and there is no telling how long we might have remained there, whirling around on the quiet water, had not the gondolier once more taken the oar, and with a few graceful strokes, sent us skimming swiftly toward the city.

XIX.

ART.

A DREARY SCENE — BOLOGNA — A PILGRIMAGE CHURCH — OPINIONS ABOUT PICTURES — GUIDO RENI'S MATER DOLOROSA — A RIDE THROUGH THE TUNNELS.

OUR week in Venice was like a beautiful dream—more fanciful and fairy-like than any picture of the imagination—from which we did not fully awake until we found ourselves once more on the cars rolling over the flat campagna towards Bologna. After we caught the last glimpses of the Tyrolean Alps in the distance, it was a long ride on the dreary plain, stretching towards the horizon on every side without a break. It was covered with scrubby little mulberry trees, the last yellow and forlorn vestiges of grape-vines clinging to their trunks, instead of the graceful festoons of luxuriant leaves and dark purple or golden grapes that adorned them in the summer months, reaching from one tree to another and almost touching the grass between. The busy silk-worms were at work among the mulberries.

Bologna is a curious place, and noted for other things besides sausages. The houses are built out over the pavements, supported by rows of pillars and arches, making a succession of beautiful colonnades with long vistas through them. We found them useful as well as ornamental, for in spite of a rainy day we could walk around to the different "sights" with comparative comfort, only raising our umbrellas at the crossings.

By the way, one hears so much of "sunny Italy," yet we have found it almost as rainy as Scotland; except the week we spent in Venice, where we had a real, deep blue Italian sky, fleecy, snow-white clouds and a strange, soft sunlight. But to return to Bologna. There are two old leaning towers in the central square of the city that look as if they might tumble down on the heads of the market people below at any moment. There were several churches of interest, but principally the Pilgrimage Church of St. Luke. It is on the top of a small mountain at a short distance from the town. Leading to the summit is a long zigzag colonnade erected by different pious persons for the convenience of pilgrims. There were stations of the Passion, and other holy pictures frescoed on the walls, at intervals, in a rude manner, and much defaced, but they evidently inspired as much devotion as if they were masterpieces, for as we slowly ascended, puffing and blowing at a great rate, and wondering at each new turn if we were nearly up, we saw a number of persons making the pilgrimage and stopping to say a few prayers at each shrine. The church (when you get there) is quite pretty; it has a dome in the centre, and being perched on the very top of a hill, it can be seen at a great distance; from it we had a fine view of the Apennines. We saw the famous Madonna di San Luca, believed to have been painted by the Evangelist himself, and for which the church and the pilgrimage were built. All that remains of the picture are the faces of the Blessed Virgin and Child, whose expressions are very sweet; they are carefully enshrined in a case rich with precious gems, as are all of these miraculous pictures and images, for every one who obtains an especial blessing brings some present, from a tin heart or plain gold ring to the costliest diamond crown.

The picture gallery at Bologna was grand. There was Raphael's great "Saint Cecilia." I have not seen any other picture of his that I think can compare with this; it seems to express so much more feeling and inspiration than most of his saints and madonnas, which, as Uncle says, are beautiful, but not inspiring. Raphael's designs are exquisitely graceful and charming, and there is a wonderful richness and softness about his paintings that we never see in the copies; otherwise these copies, and even the engravings (good ones, of course), give one a very accurate idea of the originals. But now that I come to think of it, I should not wonder if all this sounded rather ridiculous and presumptuous from me; but never mind! I will just give my own opinions, and they can be taken for what they are worth. Then I hear enough from the conversations of artists and others "that know," to learn something about what is, and what is not, the right thing. It is generally understood that everybody who comes to Italy begins to talk about Art. Why, you couldn't help it if you tried! and I often enjoy listening to the discussions of tourists at the *table d'hôte*, when they have just come from some gallery and are very enthusiastic and animated, or at least interested. Some of them take all their ideas from the guide-books—these speak with the perfect assurance of saying what is proper; others have no ideas at all about the pictures; these seem to consider a visit to one of the larger galleries like a long and tedious journey by rail, to be accomplished in such a length of time, with certain necessary stoppages, not for "refreshments," however, O no! but to be bored with another of those everlasting madonnas or Saint Sebastians; finally, there is another class, who have their own individual impressions and tell you frankly what they think about the old masters. These are much the most entertaining, even though they do sometimes say things that would shock some of our learned artist friends.

Michael Angelo is always noble and grand, but we have not yet seen all of his masterpieces; guide-books, travellers, and artists all agree about him; one can not feel anything but admiration for his great works, he was such an overpowering genius. His wonderful boldness is seen in the many unfinished statues that he has left behind him; he scarcely ever waited to make a clay model, but dashed into the marble, where one sees great deep chippings, apparently growing more careful as the figure began to shape itself. He is said to have hammered at the stone with wonderful rapidity, pieces of marble flying here and there, as if the great conceptions of his mind could not wait for the slow development of the hard material with which he labored.

We find it very interesting to trace the different schools of art, each having its peculiar characteristics. For instance, there are Rubens and the other Flemish artists, noted for the great strength and muscle displayed in their paintings. They seemed to take pleasure in showing the human body in exertion, pushing, pulling, lifting, straining. The Venetian artists painted the most beautiful garments of velvet, satin, and other rich materials. The folds of the splendid robes of those old doges, popes, and symbolical figures which they were so fond of representing, are marvellously natural and graceful. The Bologna school was very pious, and certainly there is something grand and inspiring about Guido Reni that I have not found in any one else, except Leonardo da Vinci. I hear so much of the pre-Raphaelite painters, their beautiful expressions, but to me the dreadful disproportions of the figures, and the eyes—sometimes mere slits under the hair—give such a painful sensation in looking at them, that it destroys for me all the beauty of the idea. Of course they are very valuable as showing what wonderful progress in drawing and coloring was made in the course of a century or so, even during the lifetime of Raphael himself. The " Marriage of the Blessed Virgin," one of his early pictures which we saw at Milan, painted, no doubt, while he was still under the influence of his master, Perugino, before his own genius began fully to assert itself, belongs to an entirely different period and style of art from his later Madonnas. I can not see the use of praising and making so much of these early pictures in which you have to look at so much that is frightful with the little that is meritorious, when there are such painters as Guido Reni, Andrea del Sarto, Fra Bartolomeo, and others, in whose works are united with a spiritual expression, beautiful forms, graceful and noble designs.

It seems to me that nothing shows more forcibly the master-stroke, than the power that one picture often has of drawing and confining one's attention in a room full of the works of famous artists.

In the gallery at Bologna, besides his Crucifixion and many others, there is a large picture by Guido, reaching from the floor to the ceiling. The lower part of it consists of a number of saints, patrons of the city, I believe. I did not pay much attention to these, but the upper half of it was sublime. It represented the Blessed Virgin standing behind the dead body of our Lord. It was very simple, but with a wonderful something about it. The body lay on a low bier, with a weeping angel at either end; the livid hue of the flesh sent a chill through me; one arm had fallen over the side of the bier onto the ground, thus exposing the five wounds.

But that grand, noble, sorrowful figure of Mater Dolorosa! it was so solemn, so lonely, yet all nature seemed to sympathize with her grief—the dark outline of the rocks, and the lowering, gray clouds, showing pale streaks of blue here and there. The face was not, in the ordinary sense of the word, beautiful, but care-worn and marked with suffering. It seemed as if her grief were too holy and heart-rending for any but angel eyes to witness; but there it was, traced on the canvas with such marvellous truth, to be appreciated or carelessly glanced at, by any who visited this gallery.

Between Bologna and Florence we crossed the central range of the Apennines, and although it was only a ride of a few hours, we went through more than fifty tunnels, and on our way up toward the summit of the pass, we crossed the same river, or rather stream, about twenty times, or more. A vast amount of labor must have been expended on this road, for it was a succession of viaducts, bridges, and tunnels the entire distance.

I was very much amused with Uncle's attempts to read a book. He had hardly commenced when we dashed into a long tunnel, pitch-dark, of course. When we came out he would try again, and by the time he had found his place, in we would go again. After this had been going on for some time, he finally shut the book in despair.

The scenery was very picturesque and wild, an agreeable contrast to our last trip, and as we often find English or American travellers in the compartment with us, these railway rides are sometimes very pleasant. We have formed a number of acquaintances in this way, and it is delightful to meet them over and over again where we least expect it.

Florence.

Face p. 159.

XX.

CITIES OF ART.

FLORENCE — AMERICAN STUDIOS — THE UFFIZI — SAN MARCO—PISA—PERUGIA—AN AMUSING BOOK—ITALIAN FOUNTAINS—PERUGINO—ASSISI.

WHEN we arrived at Florence, the first thing we did after getting settled at our hotel, was to buy a hand-book and plan of the city, to find out where we were situated. It was in a good central position, within walking distance of all the principal objects of interest. Uncle then found the office of the consul, a family friend. He and his wife left cards for us very soon, and invited us to a social dinner. Some of their relatives were present, and we spent a very pleasant evening. One afternoon Mr. G—— called with his carriage and took us out driving. The drives around Florence are beautiful beyond comparison. We went first to the studios of a number of American artists. Our friend being an amateur sculptor himself, and the consul, it gave us a most favorable opportunity of visiting them. It was very interesting to see the artists at work. They wear a skull-cap and a long, coarse apron when they are moulding the soft clay. We saw the plaster casts from which the employed workmen were chiseling out the marble. It seemed strange to see the figure growing gradually, as it were, out of the solid block, in which little brass pegs were stuck here and there, as guiding points. Then last of all were the finished statues, a great many of which were standing around.

Mr. Mead had just completed a magnificent model of Ethan Allen; it was almost eight feet high, and the fierce, stern features and commanding attitude, with the old revolutionary costume, made it very imposing. I am not quite sure for which city it was intended, but I think it was Boston.

Mr. Hart, of Kentucky, is quite an old gentleman. He showed us the cast of his fine statue of Henry Clay, which, I believe, was unveiled at Louisville a short time ago.

We had also an interesting visit to the studio of Mr. Powers, and might almost believe that his spirit still dwelt there.

The Uffizi is an immense building, where you can wander through room after room lined with the masterpieces of the greatest artists the world has known. We spent two weeks in the city, and had about four days of bright weather; the rest of the time it was rain, rain, rain; but we were only a step from the gallery, and every day we would start out with our umbrellas, pass through the Piazza della Signoria, the open square where the great Dominican preacher, Savonarola, was burned at the stake; then past the old palace of the Medici, with its frowning battlements and towers, looking more like a fortress than a princely mansion. In front of it is a statue of Cosmo, first Duke of Medici, by John of Bologna, and a fountain with a gigantic statue of Neptune over eighteen feet high, with sea-horses, nymphs, tritons, and fauns capering around the basin. Although we had to mount four flights of stairs to reach the gallery, there was compensation for the fatigue in the pleasure of seeing the pictures in a good light. Sometimes it is very annoying to go to a church or palace to see some famous picture and then find it in a dark nook or corner, or worse still, with a flaring light on the canvas.

In the Uffizi there is a small octagonal room that is a perfect little gem. The first thing that meets one's eye on entering is the world-renowned Venus de Medici; we were charmed at once with the wonderful grace expressed in the position, the limbs, the delicately poised head, which is rather smaller than ordinary. She is represented as quite young—I should think, hardly sixteen. There is in the same room the lively dancing faun of Praxiteles, with his pointed, leaf-shaped ears, though this is not the one Hawthorne describes; I saw that one at Rome. There were three other pieces of statuary which were very beautiful; but as Uncle says (and my own impression is the same) in these Greek statues, however delicately the forms and the drapery are carved, the faces are always cold and stony; you can never forget you are looking at marble. It is so different with Michael Angelo, who makes, as it were, living, speaking faces. But no, I should not say that all the Greek statues are expressionless, for here in this very Uffizi is that beautiful, suffering face of Niobe, as she tries to shelter her last child. In the statues of her thirteen other children, who are represented falling under the shots of the arrows, and dying in every possible position, we see only physical suffering. In the figure of Niobe and her child it is not the wondrous grace, or even the touching position, so much as the mental torture expressed in the mother's face, that holds us captive. But to return to the Tribune; there was Raphael's beautiful Madonna of the Goldfinch, and a magnificent portrait by him; a Madonna by Michael Angelo, a fine painting by Rubens (that I did not like), and several others by equally great masters; but what impressed me most forcibly, was a painting by Guercino, representing the Cumæan Sibyl; among the pictures of the old prophets and prophetesses I have seen, there has been no face so wonderfully inspired as this.

I merely mention a few pictures in one of the rooms; this is but a sample of the whole collection. There are in this one-half of the gallery, for I call the Pitti the other half, at least twenty-five rooms, many of them very large, besides three long corridors of ancient statuary. The Uffizi and the Pitti are connected by means of a covered gallery, about half a mile long, passing over the old bridge and through the tops of the houses, twisting and turning in every possible way. In the first part of it are engravings of celebrated pictures by Raphael Morghen, the famous engraver; then came sketches and rough designs in pencil and charcoal, by many of the old masters; they were very interesting, and we spent a long time in looking them over, finding sometimes the artists' first conceptions of what had afterwards been carried out in their celebrated paintings; next beyond these sketches the walls of the passage were covered with tapestry most beautifully wrought by Flemish weavers, from designs by Michael Angelo and Guilio Romano.

We visited the Convent of San Marco, where we saw the rooms of Savonarola, and the cells of the friars, in each of which was a beautiful fresco by Fra Angelico, or Fra Bartolomeo, who lived there themselves. We went also to the Church of St. Croce, which Mr. G—— called the Westminster of Florence, for there were the tombs of Michael Angelo, Raphael Morghen, and many other celebrities. We also saw the remains of Dante's house; and oh! so many things of great interest, that I give up trying to write about them.

From Florence we made a little excursion to Pisa, and saw the beautiful cathedral and the leaning tower, which we ascended, and visited the graveyard, and the Baptistry, which has a wonderful echo, one man's voice sounding like the swell of a whole choir.

STAGE-COACH.

Between Florence and Rome we stopped at Perugia. It is on the very tip-top of a very high hill, one of the Apennines. As we passed along under it, we wondered if the train could possibly ascend it. The railroad did wind about half-way up the ascent, and the rest of the way we had to go in an omnibus.

It was a very zig-zag road but well-paved, and we had beautiful views all the way — first the city, with its queer, old Etruscan and Roman walls; then a turn would show us the long, level plain of Umbria, stretching over fifteen or twenty miles to Assisi, another old Roman town, growing right out of the side of a mountain. The best hotel in Perugia, and the only one, I think, is on the very summit; and a funny, old-fashioned one it is, with low ceilings, frescoed all over with stiff-looking bouquets and sentimental young ladies. The most amusing thing there, however, was an old book of recommendations, in every possible language, of Giovanni Scalchi, one of the waiters who acted as guide for the city. There were prose, poetry, and conundrums, by Americans,

Englishmen, Russians, Frenchmen, and Germans — everybody, in fact, who had visited the place for the last fifteen years, had employed Scalchi, and written about him. The artists made pen-and-ink sketches, the poets extolled him in verse, and the wits made puns and conundrums on his name, his occupation, and everything within ten miles of the city. We enjoyed looking over this curious book very much, and found

BAPTISTRY AT PISA.

some distinguished names in it, also those of several persons whom we knew.

When we visited Nuremberg, I thought that city was quaint enough, but Perugia is still more so. There are all sorts of arches and beams thrown across the streets from one house to another, to prevent them from tumbling down hill, I suppose. Here and there you meet strange, old gateways, beautifully carved, with ancient inscriptions over them—old stairs and streets running down under the houses, donkeys toiling up with great, heavy bags on each side, making them look as broad as they are long; and the country people with goat-skin breeches and colored jackets who drive them flourish a long whip, and shout in a manner peculiar to the Italians, though neither the first nor the last disturbs the donkey's meditations in the least.

There is always a very lively scene at the fountains in Italy, of which every little town has a great number. Very frequently the water runs into an old stone sarcophagus, or else the remains of a Roman bath; at one end you will find a number of women washing clothes and chattering together at a great rate; at the other end the bright-eyed peasants will be watering the dull-eyed donkeys; and perhaps in the centre a market-woman will be washing her cabbages and turnips under the water-spout, and a crowd of girls waiting to fill their jugs, which, by the way, look as if they might be the same ones Rachael used, or the Samaritan woman.

Perugino, the master of Raphael, lived at Perugia, and here you find his masterpieces, among them his "Transfiguration." Uncle and I have been much interested in looking at many pictures by him and his pupils, finding a great similarity in some of the figures and faces, many of them being reproduced again and again, not only by Perugino himself, but by each of his pupils. There is one old man that sometimes represents St. Joseph, then you will find the same face as St. Jerome, or the Eternal Father, or on an old Greek philosopher; there is one young man with very slender limbs and half-closed eyes that is at one time a disappointed suitor, then has wings and personates St.

Michael, and again, leaning on a shield, is supposed to be Alcibiades. We know some of the faces so well that

CATHEDRAL AT PISA.

we recognize them immediately on entering a new gallery.

At Assisi we encountered the works of Giotto and his school at every step. The great two-story-and-crypt Church of St. Francis is fairly lined with them. The houses of this old town cling to one side of the hill on which it is built, like a cluster of toadstools, and I am sure they look quite as useless and dried up.

Scarcely anybody seems to live in them, and as for Uncle and I, we were the only travellers in the town, which can boast of two small hotels, two wheeled vehicles, and two guides. As to these last, we chose the little boy who spoke a little French, and by dint of physical as well as moral suasion, succeeded in driving off his rival, the great man who spoke a great deal of Italian. Now, as we had taken sides with the little guide, we determined to fight his battles all through; so when he advised us to take the frescoed omnibus, we did so, although the man with the rickety carriage, and the big Italian guide, followed us all the way from the station up to the town, pelting us with Italian sentences. A porter now joined them, adding his voice to theirs in praise of the new hotel, but our little guide recommended the old one, so there we hastened. Whole suits of apartments were at our service, but we contented ourselves with the dining-hall, a long, frescoed, carpeted room, with a fireplace, in which we burnt bundle after bundle of faggots, to the surprise of all the household; and two queer little bed-rooms with frescoed bed-posts, which Uncle and I occupied respectively.

The hill above Assisi is crowned with a splendid old ruined castle, where we stood, and sat, and walked for a long time one afternoon, waiting for the sun to set on the vast mountain-girded plain, in the midst of which rose the great church and dome of the Portiuncula. We waited and waited in the wind, but the sun would not go down, until finally we had to go down instead, leaving him lingering, lingering—O so long! just over the verge of the mountains, as if, like a spoiled child, he did so hate to go to bed!

XXI.

CHRISTIAN ROME.

FUMIGATION—THE PANTHEON—ST. PETER'S—THE CURTAIN LIFTED—
AFTER-THOUGHTS — ASCENDING — BIRD'S-EYE VIEW OF THE VATI-
CAN—THREE PICTURES—MANY STATUES—A VISIT TO POPE PIUS IX.—
THE CATACOMBS.

IT was late at night, and we had had a long railroad ride from Assisi, when I was roused from a nap by the whistle of the engine, and I heard the guard roar out "Roma!" We were wide awake in an instant, but had very little time to feel those strange emotions that most people have on entering the "Eternal City."

We soon found ourselves and our baggage in the centre of a large room that was very choky and smoky, where the gentlemen were all making faces and the ladies were holding pocket handkerchiefs to their noses. The cholera was prevailing in Italy, and every one who entered Rome was obliged to submit to the process of being fumigated.

When we were let out into the fresh air we had to pass between a double file of hotel porters gesticulating and snapping their fingers, Italian fashion, before we could find the omnibus we wanted. As we drove through a broad, well-paved street with brilliantly-lighted shops on either side, I asked myself, "Is this Rome or New York?" I was not long, however, in finding an answer. We soon passed an old fountain, then down a dark, narrow street, and through an open square, in the centre of which was a lamp, lighting up two blackened stone horses, nobly carved, and each held by a figure equally discolored. Then we drove up and down more slippery, crooked streets, with here and there little shrines of the Madonna at the corners of the houses, and sometimes votive lamps hanging in front of them. We were surely in Rome, not New York.

We finally stopped in a square, in the centre of which was an old Egyptian obelisk, supported on the back of an elephant. Presently we were escorted into the hotel and up to our rooms through winding passages, where the nooks and corners were filled with pieces of ancient statuary. We were in the old palace of the Conti family, now used as a hotel; but before we had been long there, we would willingly have given up the privilege of dwelling "in marble halls" for a cosy little room with a good Yankee stove, and no cracks under the doors and windows.

But who would mind all the discomforts in the world when Rome was to be seen, and the Pantheon was next door? When we stood within its great round walls, the entire roof of the building rising into a mighty dome, I thought how like a vain boast it must have sounded when Michael Angelo said, "I will lift the Pantheon in the air;" for it seemed difficult to conceive of anything larger or grander, unless, perhaps, the blue vault of Heaven seen through the round opening overhead. But wait! Michael Angelo's embodied conception is within reach, and we hasten towards it with enthusiastic eagerness.

How true it is that we can seldom appreciate at the first glance great works of art, especially in architecture, when all the parts are in perfect proportion; it seems as if the mind had to gradually grow up to them.

We were in Rome a month and visited St. Peter's

CASTLE OF SAN ANGELO.   Face p. 170.

about every third day, yet I saw it over and over again before I began to realize how grand it was. The first time I lifted the heavy curtain and stepped in, I was more surprised than impressed. It was so different from what I expected, and yet I hardly knew what I did expect. It was with an indescribable, unreasonable kind of disappointment that I found my vague ideas of something wonderful put into solid stone—arches, columns, and floor. At the second visit, now that St. Peter's was more substantial in my mind, I began to realize its grandeur in a general way. The third time I examined particulars a little more. To begin, it is true, with a very insignificant object, the holy-water fount being nearest the door, soon attracted our attention; it was supported on each side by a cherub, apparently about the size of an ordinary infant, but when near them we found that they were much larger than full-sized men. When we stood under one of the small side domes it would seem for the moment as large as the central one, though from the outside of the church these smaller domes were entirely hid from view. In this way, by noticing and comparing one thing with another, the separate parts seemed by degrees to fit together, and to grow up into a vast and magnificent whole—the mighty Cathedral of St. Peter—whose lofty design could be ever afterwards grasped and appreciated at a glance, even by the crude capacities of a young truant traveller.

The grand altar, which stands immediately under the dome, is covered with a canopy of bronze and gold, resting on four pillars of the same material. When I was leaving St. Peter's for the last time, I turned at the door to take a farewell view of the church. Looking through, under the canopy, to the far end of the choir I could see the great bronze chair, supported by golden-mitred Popes, which contains the relics of the original chair of St. Peter; and directly over it, the rich-hued afternoon sun was streaming through a circular window, on which was a white dove with outspread wings. From where I stood it seemed as if the Holy Ghost was descending in the midst of a sunbeam.

We obtained permission to visit the crypt under the church, where we saw the tombs of the apostles Peter and Paul, besides those of popes, kings, and other great personages. I remember among the other familiar names, those of Charles the Pretender and his family, of England. We saw a queer old bas-relief there representing Adam asleep and Eve just springing from his side, and a peculiar image of the Creator standing near. There were also a great many pieces of the original church that stood on the spot before the present St. Peter's was built, parts of old mosaics and frescoes, and an old stone image of the saint, from which the bronze one was cast that stands in the church above, and whose toe has been kissed away. Many Americans who have visited Rome during the last fifteen or twenty years will remember with pleasure Dr. S——, a professor in the Propaganda, who, during his long residence among the Romans, has embellished his mother-tongue, which is English, with all the Italian gestures and exclamations. This untiring friend of sight-seers in the great city, kindly obtained for us admission into that transept of St. Peter's which was partitioned off for the use of the last Great Council, and which is still enclosed. He showed us where the Pope, Cardinals, and different bishops were seated, and also the balcony for a few great theologians, and for others who were not, properly speaking, part of the Council.

Even this small part of the church was too large for the human voice to be distinctly heard throughout it, so they were obliged to put up a second and inner partition, making the apartment still smaller; and we could see how, when the Council was over, and the Pope pro-

THE LAST COMMUNION OF ST. JEROME.

claimed from his throne the doctrine of the Infallibility it was caught up from herald to herald until heard by the immense crowd thronging the church.

In a side chapel enclosed with this transept is a monument to one of the Popes, by Canova. The topmost figure of the group represents the Pope kneeling; his head and expression are magnificent. Standing below are symbolical figures, and at the foot of these are two lions facing each other; these last are the masterpieces. One lies with his head resting on his paws, and his eyes shut, the very personification of strength and grandeur—"asleep." The other is "watching;" the eyes distended, seeming fairly to glare at you, the head erect and eager, the paws clutching at the marble he rests on, every muscle strained.

Early one beautiful morning, we ascended the dome of St. Peter's. We went up by an inclined plane, twisting round and round, until we reached the top of the church, when we were obliged to stop and take breath. The roof is like a small city in itself; there are the countless domes of the side chapels, the pavilion which covers the great bell, and the houses of the workmen who are constantly employed to keep everything in repair, besides numerous railings, side roofs, and channels, which must have been constructed with a great deal of care and invention to make the water run off properly. After we had explored sufficiently, we began to ascend between the two shells of the dome, by a broad, easy walk. Presently we turned to one side and entered a door, finding ourselves in the little gallery that runs around the interior of the dome—we were looking down into the church at the Lilliputians walking around and kneeling before the altars. After satisfying our curiosity by examining the gigantic flowers and saints around us, we continued the ascent of the dome, the passage becoming narrower at every step, until we were obliged to lean over to one side as we

The Nile.

walked, for the inner and outer domes were rapidly approaching each other as we neared the summit. The last part was ascended by means of little zigzag stairs. From the cupola, we counted the "seven hills" of Rome, with the Coliseum, the Pantheon, the Castle of St. Angelo, and all the prominent buildings in the city. Beyond we saw the rolling campagna, dotted with the ruins of the Claudian aqueduct, and the tombs along the Via Appia, and still further, the Alban mountains bounded the western horizon. Just beneath us lay the Vatican palace. We could see the entire plan of the building as perfectly as if it had been marked out on a map; its two courts, the queer-shaped corner with the private apartments of the Pope, the library, and the galleries of painting and sculpture. That bird's-eye view helped us afterwards to find our way through its four thousand, four hundred, and twenty-two rooms, though even then it was a bewildering maze.

The Capella Sistina is, of course, the place to study Michael Angelo as a painter; my great attraction for him is, however, as a sculptor. With curious interest I examined his "Last Judgment," crumbling from the walls of the Capella—but spell-bound with admiration I stood before his gigantic conception of "Moses," in the Church of "St. Peter-in-Chains."

Of all the rooms of paintings in the Vatican, there is only one that I will attempt to mention, for it is small enough to dwell clearly in my memory. It contains but three pictures; Raphael's "Transfiguration," "The Madonna di Foligno," and Domenichino's "Last Communion of St. Jerome." These three are a host in themselves; but in a great gallery like this, one becomes too restless and eager to remain long in one spot, thinking that perhaps the next room contains something still more beautiful.

As a matter of course we stopped in our weary wan-

CHRISTIAN ROME. 177

derings through the halls of sculpture, to admire the Laocoon, to discuss the question as to what the Apollo Belvedere is supposed to hold in his left hand, and to

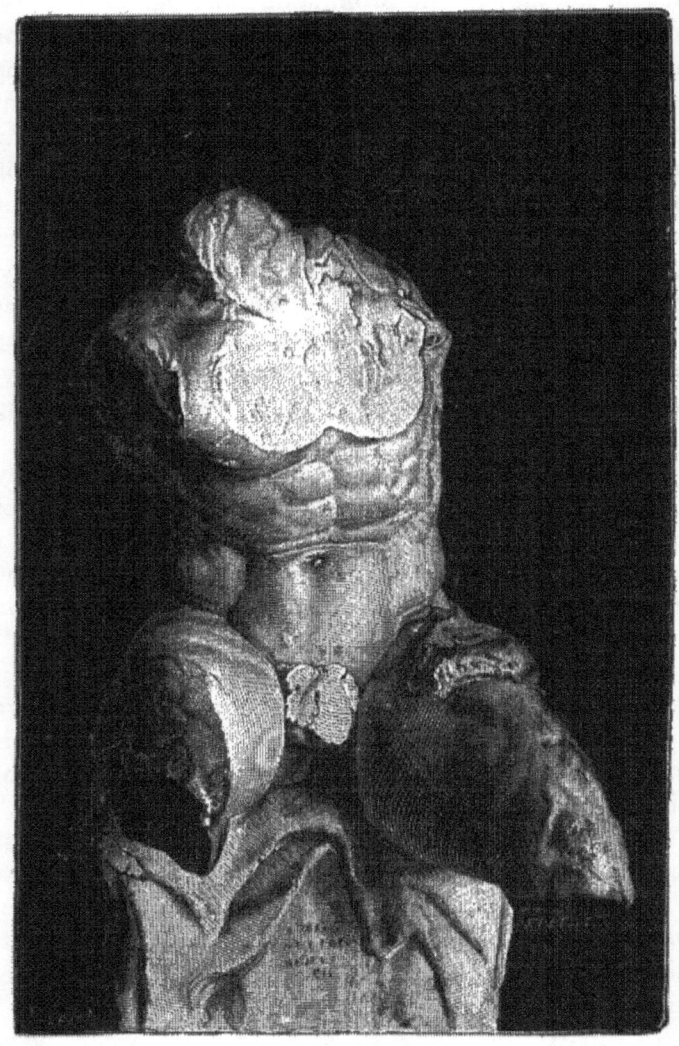

THE TORSO OF HERCULES.

examine and wonder at the Torso of Hercules. But my general impression on leaving the Vatican was, that they had dug up enough old statuary to have completely undermined Rome and the surrounding country. It seemed to me that if they would send a shipload of broken arms and noses to America, where such things never grow (unless, perhaps, an occasional Cardiff Giant!) they would be better appreciated than they are at Rome, where they are as common as stones.

Our visit to the museums on the Capitoline Hill was another treat of the same kind. There was the Dying Gladiator (who must be dreadfully tired of dying), Hawthorne's Marble Fawn, the Capitoline Venus, the colossal old river-personifications, and ever so many other things to interest us, but twice as many more to weary us.

Our visit to the Pope was quite an event in our Roman life. On our way to the Vatican, we stopped for Dr. C——, President of the American College in Rome, who was to accompany us.

Gentlemen go in full-dress, but clergymen are expected to wear cassocks and the large, three-cornered felt hats worn by all the priests on the continent. Ladies dress in black silk and black lace veils, wearing neither hats nor gloves. Etiquette also requires that the carriage and horses should be entirely black.

We drove round to the back of St. Peter's, and then into the court of the palace, through a large gate-way, where stood some of the Pope's "Swiss Guards," with their very peculiar uniform of red and yellow, said to have been designed by Michael Angelo. He must have meant it for a joke! When the carriage stopped before the large double doors, we entered and passed up a broad staircase to the floor above. Chamberlains, clad in crimson satin, ushered us into a room with a marble floor, wood-work handsomely carved, and oil-paintings of religious subjects hanging on the walls.

St. Peter's, Vatican.

Here we were requested to leave our wrappings. We were then shown into a long hall or Loggia, very richly frescoed, and with windows looking down into the court-yard. Several other ladies and gentlemen were also waiting for an audience.

I observed one characteristic of this palace which distinguished it from all others I had seen. Although everything here is costly and durable, artistic and beautiful, there is an utter lack of that luxury almost invariably found in other princely buildings; there are no deeply-cushioned chairs and heavy drapery, no soft rugs or tempting divans, but all seems to indicate the priestly dwelling. I was told by those who had seen the private rooms and offices of the Pope, that they are still more simple and unpretending.

After waiting some time in the Loggia, one of the chamberlains drew aside a curtain at the end of the hall and announced the Holy Father. We all knelt down, and Pius IX. entered, accompanied by his cardinals. He first addressed a lady, whom he appeared to know; he smiled and called her his Canoness, and then they spoke together in a business-like way. Dr. C—— said she was asking some special favor for a charitable institution in which she was interested.

As the Pope approached us, surrounded by all the associations connected with his long and blameless career, his snowy locks blending with his soft, white cassock, and his benignant countenance lighted by his bright Italian eyes, his presence created an impression that must always remain a beautiful and venerable picture in my memory.

He recognized Dr. C—— immediately, and when we had kissed his ring, stood talking with us for several minutes, partly in French and partly in Italian, which our friend translated for us. The Holy Father told us that he was very fond of his American children, and seemed pleased when we showed him the medals and crosses we had brought to be blessed for our friends in the United States. While he was speaking to the others who were waiting to see him, Uncle had

LAOCOON.

quite a long talk with Cardinal Barnabo, who is entrusted with the superintendence of ecclesiastical affairs in America.

The Pope then said a few words to us all, and gave us his benediction. As he was leaving, he turned to me and said, "Addio, cara mia." I understood enough Italian to know what that meant.

Dr. S——, of whom I have already spoken, kindly offered to guide Uncle and me, with three others, through the Catacombs of St. Calixtus. We failed to meet him at the appointed time, and after waiting for us a little while, he had gone on with his other friends. These catacombs are about two miles from Rome, on the Via Appia, and we drove hurriedly out, hoping to overtake him. We stopped, as directed, by a ruined gateway, and walked across a field until we came abruptly to a pair of stairs going down into the ground. At the foot of these we found an old man, left to watch for us, who gave us each a lighted taper, and showed us the way to the other party. We found them in a very small chamber, whose walls and ceiling were covered with rude fresco. By the light of their flickering tapers, we could see how eagerly attentive they were to every word and motion of Dr. S——, who stood in the centre pointing to the queer emblems, gesticulating in a lively manner, and saying, "Do you see that? eh! What do you suppose that means? eh! eh! Let us translate!"

Whether the Doctor expected these questions to be answered or not, it was difficult to say. At any rate, none of the party attempted to do so except myself. When he would call our attention to some rude, almost unintelligible symbol, and turning suddenly round upon us, say,

"There! what's that? eh! eh!"

"A fish!" I would call out excitedly, and then frightened at the sound of my own voice, shrink behind the others.

"Si! si! just so," the Doctor would exclaim delightedly, if I happened to guess right; but woe to me if I made a mistake.

Thus in his odd, but animated way, our learned antiquarian friend told us a great many interesting things about the new excavations that are constantly going on, explained the emblems and frescoes, and gave us his theory about the sand-pits, and the origin of the catacombs. He had made them the study of his life, and was as much at home underground as above. He seemed to know every turn by heart, and, in fact, led us a wild chase through those dark, narrow passages, twisting in every direction, and darting into an opening here and out again there, until we were completely out of breath trying to keep up with him. Had it not been for the gleam of his taper, we would several times have lost track of him completely. Once he stopped suddenly and told us that we were five stories under ground. We had been descending, almost unaware, ever since we started, sometimes by gentle inclinations, and again by odd little stone stairs.

When we came up from the catacombs, it was in an entirely different place from the one where we entered. It was quite dark, the sun had set, and damp, unhealthy vapors were rising from the campagna. The visit was so interesting that we had spent hours instead of minutes, as we supposed, among the early Christians.

XXII.

BEGGARS, BEAUTIES, AND BONES.

"KING OF THE ROMAN BEGGARS"—MORRO—BARBERINI PALACE—BEATRICE CENCI—CHURCH OF THE CAPUCHINS—A GHOSTLY RETREAT.

"BEPPO IS DEAD!" Such was the sad news we heard on inquiring for that worthy. Beppo, "King of the Roman Beggars," is no more. His numerous friends in all parts of the world will be sorry to hear that the crooked, little, old man is no longer seen sitting in state on the steps of the Piazza di Spagna—like some misshapen idol—receiving the offerings of travellers. Beppo kept a bank for the convenience of his mendicant subjects, and rode home every evening on a donkey led by a small boy. "They say" he gave a grand ball occasionally among the ruins of Roman temples. When such an event took place, the beggars from all parts of the city assembled, on the invitation of King Beppo, to have a great jollification.

> "Some in rags,
> Some in tags,
> And some in velvet gowns."

Although we did not see Beppo, there were a number of "models" lounging on the steps of the Piazza di Spagna waiting for the artists to come and engage them to sit for their pictures. We saw the Italian brigands, coquettish peasant girls, and little musicians, all of whose costumes are nearly as familiar to us in

America from pictures, as they are here in reality. We happened to pass them just at lunch time, and I must say the brigands did not look very ferocious or the maidens very bewitching, as they sat munching chunks of sour bread. Others who had satisfied their appetites were playing Morro, the very same game with which the Roman soldiers used to amuse themselves centuries ago. Two men stand opposite to each other with their fists closed. At a given signal they both throw open a certain number of fingers, and at the same instant each guesses what number the other has opened. They play it rapidly and become very expert, telling by the slightest movement of the hand the fingers about to be thrown out. A few baiocchi are always at stake, and an umpire stands by to settle all disputes. The players become very much excited over it, almost jumping at each other as they throw out their fingers, their eyes sparkling, and yelling out, "Due! cinque! quatro!" Their appearance presents an odd mingling of the picturesque and the ridiculous. In spite of their flowing cloaks and handsome faces, they suggest the idea of two fighting cocks just about to attack each other.

Of all the smaller art galleries of Rome, I was most charmed with that of the Barberini palace. Uncle and I were particularly pleased with one large room, the entire ceiling of which was frescoed by Pietro da Cartona. The principal subject was the "Wars of the Gods and Titans," and all of the figures were large. It was a wonderful specimen of fore-shortening; indeed you could scarcely believe that their gigantic limbs did not stand out from the ceiling—like carvings or sculpture.

The room adjoining this contained statuary, and it was there that I saw, for the first time, a veiled figure in marble. I had not thought it possible that the features of the face could be so distinctly represented through a veil; this appears to fall loosely and gracefully over the head and shoulders. We were both diverted from this work of art by a still more attractive one—"Diana Asleep." Imagine a beautiful woman, light and graceful, with a small crescent glistening in her hair, a short, girded tunic, and sandals laced almost

BEATRICE CENCI. BY GUIDO.

to the perfectly-formed knee, who has been chasing the deer through the moonlit forest with her bow and arrow and her hounds, and who, exhausted, throws herself down on a little knoll of grass, with one arm thrown gracefully over her head, and falls asleep. All this is to be seen, and more too, in that exquisite production of Bernini. As I stood gazing and gazing at it, I could almost see it breathe, and it led my thoughts a wilder chase than the lovely goddess herself could have ever run.

The Barberini picture gallery is very small and choice, but, of course, the great gem is Guido's "Beatrice Cenci," of which we see so many copies. It is only the head of a young girl looking over her shoulder, and wearing a large white turban, with a few stray brown curls escaping from under it. But O, such a sad face! it followed me for days; wherever I went I could see those touchingly weary young eyes, longing for pity and sympathy, and yet seeming to shrink from one as if in dread of a harsh look. I could never pass the old Cenci palace without imagining I saw the beautiful Beatrice leaning over the stone balcony, or sitting in some of those dark windows. Afterward it seemed like a profanation to have painted some of those copies that stared at us from the shop windows. Sometimes the white turban and brown curls belonged to the face of a mischievous coquette, then again it was a red-eyed child-face, that suggested no more than a tumble downstairs, perhaps, and a cry after it.

A magnificent portrait of the mother of Beatrice Cenci hung near that of the daughter. It was one of those very dark pictures, the light falling only upon one cheek, all the rest in shadow. There was a great resemblance in their features, but Beatrice's sorrowful face was in striking contrast to her mother's bright, cheerful expression; it made me think that the daughter, too, seemed more capable of smiles than tears, if her life had been more natural.

Not very far from the Barberini palace is the church and convent of the Capuchin Friars. On entering the church we were met by a bare-footed friar, who showed us the famous "St. Michael" of Guido Reni, and then led us down into the burying-ground under the building. Here was a sight to make one shudder. The friar told us that the soil used here had been brought from the Holy Land, and therefore it was considered a great privilege to be buried in it. In order that each of the community shall have the benefit of it, this is the way they manage. When one of the friars dies, the body that has been buried longest is removed, and the new-comer put in its place. As this has been going on for years and years, a marvellous number of bones are accumulated. These have been arranged in the most artistic manner; the walls are lined with skulls, placed tier above tier, the teeth and the holes for the eyes and noses making quite an ornamented surface. These skulls are four or five deep—that is, they stand out about a foot and a half from the walls. Here and there pointed niches are formed by them, in each of which stands an entire skeleton of a friar, even to the fingers, toes, and sometimes beard, dressed in his brown habit, and grinning most horribly. We saw some bony tables, on which were bony candlesticks, containing lighted candles, and at intervals bony lamps were suspended, made carefully and delicately, like rustic work, of the smallest bones. The ceiling was covered with stars, hearts, anchors, and other symbols, made like the lamps, with great skill. In the midst of all these horrors one could not but feel saddened at the sight of two skeletons of little children fastened up near the door. They were princes of the Medici family, who had been dedicated to the priesthood, or, for some reason of the kind, were buried here, and their turn having come to be removed, their bones were placed where we saw them.

Perhaps the good monks make very wholesome meditations in this ghostly retreat; as for myself, the green graves in a cemetery, with the trees, birds, and flowers all around, would be more likely to suggest good thoughts.

XXIII.

A LETTER TO THE CONVENT.

SAINT FRANCIS AND SAINT CLARA IN CONNECTION WITH ASSISI — SHRINES AT ROME — THE CATACOMBS ILLUMINATED — UNDER CHURCHES.

ROME, *Dec.* 7.

DEAR CLARA:—I have been waiting till now for a chance to write to you about some places that I think would interest you. Of course you have heard of Saint Francis of Assisi, but I don't believe you know much about him—I did not until I saw his home, which is at Assisi.

Let me see, I shall have to begin where he began—I mean at the little room in which he was born. It was locked, but our little guide showed us an opening where we might look in. It has been turned into a chapel. In the old cathedral is the very holy-water font at which he was baptized. One day when he was a little boy, he was praying very fervently before a wooden crucifix—a great ugly one, which is still kept in one of the churches—when he heard our Lord speak to him, telling him that the church was falling down, and he must repair it—meaning spiritually; but the little Saint Francis thought the old church must be tumbling to pieces sure enough, so he took some money from his father without saying a word to anybody, and started off for the Church of St. Damian. The sacristan there would not take it, but they showed us the window where Saint Francis threw it in. There, too, is the little corner or niche in the wall where he hid when his angry father came after him to get his money. He must have found him, for there is a funny old fresco on the wall representing the young saint getting a whipping. Wasn't it mean? But then, he did seem to have pretty free-and-easy ideas of taking his father's things, and he was always getting into scrapes. He was sometimes locked up at home because he took all the bread he could lay his hands on to give to the poor, and because he loved to dress in rags and go round begging so the people would laugh at him. Those were days of great luxury, and he wanted to set them an example of poverty.

Then when he gathered around him a few young men as followers, they used to go up to a cave in the mountain just behind Assisi, where they could be alone for their devotions. There they lived until the Bishop let Saint Francis establish the Order of Franciscans, and then they used a little monastery and chapel down on the plain. When our guide took us there to visit it, he showed us where the saint received the Stigmata (but I think he was mistaken, for that happened in the mountains), also the room in which he died. The small church or chapel where he was so often wrapt in prayer and ecstasies, now stands like a little shrine, frescoed by Overbeck, in the centre of the great Portiuncula, a favorite pilgrimage church, seen for miles in every direction. And finally to follow Saint Francis to his tomb, we visited the double church which covers it, and the famous Franciscan Monastery, a magnificent building with tiers of arches, which has long been the glory of Assisi, and is very different from the little cave in the rock where the saint and his first followers were obliged to take refuge.

I suppose you want to know all I can tell you about

Saint Clara, your patron, whose body we saw at Assisi. You must know that I have also had the honor of paying my respects at the tomb of my saint, Helena, the mother of Constantine; and since I have gazed in awe at the colossal statue of her under the dome of St. Peter's, and the reliquary just over her head which contains the wood of the true cross which she discovered; and as I have mounted on my knees the Scala Santa, which, if you do not already know, was brought by her from the house of Pontius Pilate at Jerusalem— our Lord having mounted and descended it during His passion—I feel as if I had done my duty as a namesake of St. Helena. But this is all at Rome, and I was going to tell you about St. Clara at Assisi.

She belonged to a noble family in the neighborhood, and when she heard of Saint Francis, she became very anxious to join him and devote herself to the poor. Under his direction she tried to establish the Order of Poor Claires, as they are now called. Her family made a great fuss about it, and troubled her a good deal, but she finally succeeded. Her only sister, Saint Agnes, wished to join the new Order too, but the family determined to prevent this at any rate. So when they went to the convent and found she would not return with them, they tried to pull her away by force, when, according to the story we heard on the spot, she became miraculously heavy, and they could not move her an inch—so they had to give it up.

We were very much interested in going through the original convent. It was a poor little place, and as we drove up to it, we saw a window in the second story that had been closed. On the boards was a rude painting of Saint Clara holding up the Blessed Sacrament, and all the way down the wall (right on the outside of the house, remember) were painted the startled Saracens tumbling off the ladders with which they had climbed up, and were about to enter the convent. That was the very window where the incident occurred. In the chapel we saw a number of relics, among them the monstrance which she held containing the Holy Eucharist, and also the little bell with which she used to call together the religious (it reminded me of the "novices' bell" at Kenwood). Then we visited the infirmary and the dormitory, with its narrow, bare, brick-floored cells, each door marked on the outside with the name of one of the original band of nuns. We walked down the narrow passage-way until we found "Sister Clara" and "Sister Agnes."

There, too, was the old refectory, with its wooden tables and benches all crumbling away, and the pictures on the wall faded, so it was almost impossible to distinguish them. One of them represented Saint Clara, at a time when they had not food enough for a meal, multiplying one loaf of bread into a sufficient quantity for the whole community. But miracles did not happen every day, and these noble-born maidens suffered all kinds of hunger and cold. When we called at the modern convent in Assisi, the good sisters sent a Brazilian nun to entertain us, supposing, of course, that since we were both *Americans*, the meeting would be a mutual treat. This timid little Poor Claire did not speak English, and it is hardly necessary to say that our nationality, or rather hemispherality, was not sufficiently strong to cause any very great interest on either side. However, we stumbled through a conversation in French, and she showed us the body of Saint Clara, which is enclosed in a crystal case under the church that bears her name.

But when shall I ever be able to tell you about Rome? It is glorious. Not so glorious, however, as to make me want to be left here at the Sacred Heart on the Trinita del Monte to study, while Uncle goes off to the Holy Land and Greece. But perhaps he will take me to a convent in France, probably Tours, which Madam H—— recommends as a pleasant, healthy place. That would be better. But then to be left among foreigners—O, horrors! Besides, there would be some risk, Uncle thinks, in placing me here at Rome, for this Italian government is so uncertain, that the convent might be broken up at any moment. The Jesuits have already been driven from the country. Their headquarters, the Roman College (next door to us here), where have lived such holy and celebrated men as St. Ignatius, St. Aloysius, and Cardinal Bellarmin, has been turned into public offices or soldiers' quarters, and we were not permitted to see their rooms, which have been considered sacred, and visited by pilgrims all these years. But this is not as hard as sending away the nuns from their cloisters to gain a living as they may; those who are sick, and those who have grown old in the religious life, without distinction. The institutions here of different countries for educating priests and missionaries are also being dispersed. They tell us that the Irish College is for sale now—I can not guess what pretext the government will give for taking *their* property—even the American and English Colleges may go next; who knows?

We heard Mass in the Catacombs on Saint Cecilia's Day, when a number of the subterranean passages and chapels were illuminated—the only day in the year. There we knelt on the bare ground close to her tomb, the little excavated chambers being crowded by awed, hushed worshippers, while the priest murmured the prayers in a low voice, and the tapers flickered over the relics of the martyred popes, and down either side of the long galleries lined with bodies. Was not that taking us back to the early Christian days? But no Roman soldiers came stealing down from the daylight above to massacre us, only more bands of pious worshippers to kneel at the virgin-martyr's tomb. Later in the day we went over to the Church of Saint Cecilia in Trastevere, and saw the beautiful statue of her, by Maderno, with averted face, lying dead under the executioner's blow; it is directly under the high altar; we also saw the little bath-room of her house, in which the cruel pagans tried first to suffocate her with vapor. On our way home we stepped into the Church of Saint Agnes, the noble Roman virgin and martyr. Under the church we saw the marble floors and columns of the rooms in which she was exposed and tormented, when, according to the legend, an angel appeared to defend her. Over one of the side altars in the church above is a statue of the saint, by Bernini, I think, which we admired very much. Uncle thought that the artist had succeeded in holding her permanently in one of those fleeting moments of rapt contemplation, or supernatural vision of her heavenly Spouse, which Cardinal Wiseman so beautifully describes in the story of Fabiola.

O, dear! now that I have begun to talk about underground places, I fear I shall never stop—Rome is full of them. The very next day was Saint Clement's Feast, and so all the excavations there were illuminated. It was not very long ago that they discovered under the modern church of that name (modern! did I say? It would be ancient in our country), the old original church, full of bright, clear frescoes. Dr. S—— piloted us among the smoking candles and the eager crowd, explaining them. I remember a very distinct one, representing a priest vested almost exactly as they are at the present day, saying Mass at an altar with candles, altar-boys and all. It was painted in the ninth century, if not much earlier; so you see there is no possibility of any modern improvements! having been made in the church ceremonies for ten hundred years at least. But do not imagine this subterranean church to be at the bottom of the mystery. Further down still they have very recently excavated what the antiquarians have decided to be Saint Clement's house. Think of paying a visit to the residence of the fourth Pope. Not very far from this interesting spot is the Church of San Gregorio, with the porch in front, where he stood and blessed Saint Augustine and his fellow-missionaries when they were about to leave for England. You must tell the Aloysians that I prayed for the society when I knelt at the tomb of Saint Aloysius, in the beautiful Church of Saint Ignatius here at Rome. His shrine is splendid, by the way, all made of lapis-lazuli and silver.

I would like to send you the old Flavian Amphitheatre full of love, but there are so many holes it would all run out.

Your devoted sister,

NELLY.

XXIV.

PAGAN ROME.

A BLIND GUIDE—A MOONLIGHT RIDE THROUGH RUINED ROME—SIGHT-SEERS.

One of the odd characters we met in Rome was an old blind man, who used to make the beds sometimes, and sweep the halls in our hotel. He had been a servant there for thirty years or more, and had become blind by some accident, but he was so attached to the place that they let him stay around and do "odd jobs." One day he asked us if we would like to go up to the observatory of the hotel, and as we were pleased with the idea, he led the way through irregular passages and stairs, of which there were many in the building. It seemed strange to be guided by a blind man. When we reached the top, he showed us the plants he took care of, and picked us each a beautiful flower with as much ease as if he saw it. I think he must have known every one that was in bloom.

The strangest part of this visit was when he pointed out to us each building we mentioned, and described its position among the multitude of housetops stretching around in every direction, just as a man would who had the use of his eyes. We were wondering why we did not see the dome of St. Peter's, when he told us it was hid by the Pantheon, which was much nearer, but that by stepping out on the roof we could see one side of it.

That evening there was a full moon, and the same

party who had been to the observatory decided to take a drive through the city. We took carriages and started for the Coliseum.

No one who has not seen it can imagine how much grander Rome is by moonlight than by daylight. By the former one sees ancient Rome, with all its associations; by the latter modern Rome, with all its dirt and rubbish.

Some one in the carriage is saying:

"What is that lovely little ruin we are passing, with the three columns standing out from the walls, and the richly-carved cornice? See, there is a baker's shop under it."

"That is an old statue of Minerva over the door—it must be her temple, where the noble Roman maidens used to come and spin for the poor, a kind of ancient 'sewing society.'"

Now we are driving through the Forum of Trajan, with its half-excavated ruins. There is a column rising higher than the church towers. It is carved from base to capital with the victories of the Emperor Trajan, and our eyes seek the top, expecting to find a statue of the victor himself; but no! it is St. Peter holding up the keys of Heaven. What a triumph of Christianity over Paganism!

We have caught the first glimpse of the Coliseum through the narrow street, and its arches are rising one above another, until the entire building stands alone. We are in the centre of ancient Rome, surrounded by ruins, and all is quiet. We leave the carriage and enter the great amphitheatre. Armed soldiers are pacing up and down under the arches to protect visitors and pilgrims, for these ruins were once a favorite retreat of robbers.

We walk into the arena and stand for a moment

THE COLISEUM.

Face p. 198.

under the great black cross in the centre, where we can see the moonlight streaming through the cracks and broken windows, over the crumbling seats and lighting up the shrines of the Passion—that indicate another triumph of Christianity. We are thinking of all that has happened here, when one of the party, who has been studying his guide-book, repeats those lines of Byron about the Gladiator, which, I dare say, were very effective the first, and, perhaps, the second and third times they were quoted in this place, but now they bring the red-covered book too vividly to mind.

While we are still in the arena, we see the gleam of a torch through the arches. It disappears, and for a moment there is only the moonlight, then again it flashes out, and this time higher up. At last it appears at the top of the building, and with it a guide and a party of tourists. The same guide, with his piece of burning pitch, scrambles up among the ruins with us. From the top we have a magnificent view, both of the interior of the Coliseum and the ancient part of the city—the Palatine Hill, the Capitol, and all.

We are once more in the carriages, this time driving under the arches of Constantine and Titus, believing ourselves in the train of a triumphal procession. We are passing along the Roman Forum, and now we have reached the Mamertine prison. We have all visited the fearful dungeons before, and now we pass it with a shudder. There is the Tarpeian Rock, and the Capitoline Hill, and beyond are the steps where Rienzi, Last of the Roman Tribunes, was stabbed.

We leave all these and are once more driving through the narrow, lava-paved streets of the city.

We have stopped before the beautiful fountain of Trevi. A commanding statue of Neptune, colossal in size, stands in a shell drawn by sea-horses, and driven by tritons. They are just about to ride over a cataract, and the horses rear back. The water falls into a basin surrounded by rocks, piled up in natural confusion. The silvery stream fairly dances in the moonbeams. According to tradition, whoever drinks of the fountain of Trevi will return to Rome. We lift some of the crystal water in the hollow of our hands and drink, hoping the tradition will prove true—then drive on.

We pass under Hilda's Tower, and see the statue of the Blessed Virgin on the top with the lamp burning before it. It is, properly, the "Tower of the Monkey," and has a legend connected with it, but it has become so identified with Hawthorne's story of the Marble Faun, that among travellers it is called Hilda's Tower.

We are on our way to St. Peter's to see it, too, by moonlight, but we find it is one of the few things in Rome that look best in the daylight.

We then turn towards the hotel once more, pass the Pantheon, and stop in the familiar square with the old elephant and the obelisk.

As Rome is eternal, so it would require an eternal sight-seer to know and tell of everything there.

It is said that those who stay a week in Rome think they know all about it; those who are there three months believe they have seen a great deal of it; but those who spend a year there, find they have only begun.

XXV.

NEAPOLITAN SURROUNDINGS.

OVERLOOKING THE BAY OF NAPLES—STILLNESS OF POMPEII—BEAUTIFUL DWELLINGS AND GRIM INHABITANTS—CAPRI—THE BLUE GROTTO—BAJA—VOLCANIC REGIONS—" ROUND THE WORLD," PERHAPS.

NAPLES, *Dec.* 22.

HERE we are delightfully lodged on the bay of Naples, with the warm sunshine pouring in our windows all day. I can see old Vesuvius puffing away in the gentlest manner possible, with the towns of Portisi, Resina, Torre del Greco, and others, nestled as comfortably at his feet as if such a thing as an eruption had never taken place; while in the distance, at the entrance to the harbor, I can trace the rugged, though graceful outlines of the island of Capri, and all around are numerous curves and high promontories of the coast, making hundreds of little havens and bays within the bay, which give such a charm to this place.

I can hardly realize that it is near the end of December, with weather equal to the brightest days of September. The yellow oranges, now ripening among their dark, rich leaves, are in bright contrast with the withered branches of the other trees. It seems strange to see the beautiful cactuses, that with us are so carefully protected in hot-houses, growing everywhere here like common weeds.

Our first excursion from Naples was to Pompeii, which, I assure you, is well worth a long trip to see.

There you have a real little Roman city, just as it was in ages past, and if the roofs were on the houses, and the furniture and gems of art, that have been carried

RUINS OF POMPEII.

off to museums, were put back in their places, nothing could be more complete. In Rome, of course, you see grander and more imposing ruins in the Coliseum, the Pantheon, and others, but they are mixed in and jumbled together with dilapidated modern houses, dirty streets, wretched, importunate beggars and screeching peddlers. When among the ruins of the Palatine, while your mind is filled with thoughts of the imperial Cæsars in rustling robes and brilliant trains, sweeping through their marble palaces, you stumble, perhaps, across a troop of the most miserable specimens of humanity at the heels of some poor, bewildered tourist with the red book in his hand (all guide-books are red, you must remember), who is trying to study out between the mysterious hints of the guide and the mass of fragments before him which is the Atrium and which the Triclinium, or whether this is supposed to be the temple of Jove, or that other pile of rubbish with its patch of beautiful mosaic. At Pompeii, it is very different; it is almost painfully quiet, except a faint murmur from the distance, where the workmen are continuing the excavations. Such a strange sensation creeps over you on hearing your own footsteps in those deserted streets— you feel that you are in the city of the dead. You do not, as I supposed, go under ground to see it, though the level of the land directly around is, of course, as high as the tops of the houses, being a hill made by the ashes, stones, and lava of the eruption. From the ramparts there is a beautiful view of Vesuvius with the surrounding country, and the sea, which originally came close to the walls of the city.

We entered by the road of the Tombs, lined on both sides with burying-places; we saw the spot where the bodies were burned, and the Columbaria, or places for the funeral urns, with various emblems and inscriptions, among others, the tombs of the gladiators. As we entered the arched gate-way, we passed the sentry-boxes,

BATHS OF POMPEII.

where skeletons of Roman soldiers were found standing at their posts, faithful and stern, amid all the horrors of the destruction of Pompeii. Each thing we saw, or rather the whole together, was so strange and unnatural that it made an impression on my mind never to be forgotten. There were the old Roman paving-stones, with uneven ruts made by chariot-wheels eighteen hundred years ago, with stepping-stones here and there for foot passengers. We visited the most exquisite dwelling-houses, with floors of pictured mosaic, walls most elegantly frescoed, fluted columns, and beautiful fountains of sea-shells and inlaid work in the courts. All is wonderfully fresh and well-preserved. We went into the public baths, the barber's shop, the baker's, and the wine shop, with its dozens of immense vessels, in which three men could easily conceal themselves. I can now understand the story of the "Forty Thieves" who were hidden in oil-jars; if they were as large as these, I think the "Arabian Nights" stories are not so exaggerated as one might suppose.

There was a very beautiful forum, a comic and tragic theatre, and many temples; among the last, a very pretty one of Isis, celebrated for its oracle. They now show you the place where the priest concealed himself under the all-powerful goddess, in order to deliver the wonderful prophecies.

We were introduced to some of the inhabitants of Pompeii themselves, with money-bags tied around a few of them—all in a very hardened condition, and grinning most horribly at all surroundings. There were skeletons of horses, dogs, and chickens, loaves of bread, and vegetables—dried most decidedly.

We went with quite a party, the other day, to visit the island of Capri, in a small excursion steamer. We expected to have a beautiful view, but it was not a pleasant day, and rather rough on the water; we did, however, succeed in visiting the Blue Grotto. We went in very small row-boats, but the entrance is so low that even then we had to lie down in order to get in. It was a wonderful sight; the water inside was of a bright, transparent blue, and the dark, rocky cavern overhead made the effect fairy-like as the boat glided noiselessly around, the oars, when in the water, looking like silver. In one of the dark corners of the Grotto, a man jumped in and swam. It had the strangest effect possible. The only way that I can describe it, is, that he looked like a silver toad squirming around in a beautiful blue glass globe. It is some strange refraction of the light that makes the color, though I do not understand it. We all took dinner at a hotel kept by an Englishman. The table was set out on a terrace overlooking the bay, but it was too cloudy to see Naples. On our way down to the steamer, the whole village turned out to see us off, and try to beg a few baiocchi, or sell sea-shells, or bits of coral. They all looked very ragged and poor, but there were some very pretty little Italian girls among them. Though these people are poverty-stricken and wretched in appearance, they are very good-natured, and amused at almost anything. They all enjoyed it very much when a little dog, belonging to one of the ladies of our party, chased the children over the island and scattered them in every direction.

There is a beautiful drive along the bay toward Baja, a favorite summer resort of the old Roman Emperors and nobles; there are ruins of their villas all the way. It is very interesting as a volcanic country. You see lava everywhere, and numerous extinct craters. We ascended one of them, Mount Solfatara; we walked round the inside of the crater, and the ground or crust is so thin, that when a man threw down a heavy stone, not very large, it sounded hollow, and the earth shook under our feet. It could hardly be called extinct either, for on one side the smoke and sulphur were coming up all the time, and if you put your hand down on the sand, it was very hot. Sulphur, I suppose it was, had made the rock beautiful with brilliant colors, and one of the men got close enough to break a piece off for me. This crater stopped very suddenly not many years ago, and at the same moment another one burst forth very near, and formed the Monta Knova, which we saw too, and which ceased as suddenly as it began. We drove to the lake of Avernus, whose basin is the crater of a still older volcano, which being filled with water, made the beautiful lake before us. Although I have not yet read Virgil (whose tomb, by the way, is near here), I have heard enough about his description of Hell to be interested in the supposed entrance to it. It is a very beautiful place. On the opposite side of the water is an opening to the grotto of the Cumean Sibyl.

There is an old, vaulted temple of Mercury near by, with a strange echo, in which some Italians danced the "Tarantella," a national dance. It is something between a jig and a fancy dance proper; they use the tambourine and castinets; it was a quaint and picturesque scene in the old ruined temple.

We have had views from every side of Naples; they are all very fine. In the museum are many interesting things from Pompeii and Herculaneum, and some beautiful ancient statues, the famous Hercules-Farnese and others.

Uncle went up Mount Vesuvius. He thought it would be too hard climbing for me. He says it was a very easy ride to the foot of the cone. He went with a party of gentlemen, and when they reached the Hermitage, they had a rest and a good, hot bowl of macaroni. The cone is all ashes, and so steep that it takes an hour to go up and about five minutes to come down. Some of the gentlemen tried to go alone, but were dreadfully tired out. Uncle took one man to pull him up with straps, and another to push him, and he was the only member of the party who did not come back exhausted.

I am happy to say that Uncle has given up the thought of leaving me at a convent to study, and says he will take me wherever he may decide to go. He has now taken berths on a steamer to leave Brindisi the twenty-ninth of December for Alexandria. I should not be surprised if we go home by way of the Pacific and California. Uncle thinks the sea voyage will be of service to him. I like the idea of "going round the world," but have little hope of catching letters from home after we leave Italy, which is a drawback to my pleasure.

XXVI.

FROM BRINDISI TO ALEXANDRIA.

BRINDISI; THE HARBOR, THE HOUSE OF VIRGIL, THE APPIAN WAY—THE ADRIATIC; THE "HEEL" OF ITALY, THE OUTLINES OF GREECE—NEW YEAR'S EVE ON THE BLUE MEDITERRANEAN—BAY OF ALEXANDRIA—SCENES FROM AN EGYPTIAN WINDOW.

ALEXANDRIA, *New Year's Day.*

WE arrived here this morning on the steamer Ceylon, from Brindisi. The railroad ride from Naples to that port was dreadfully tedious; we had to rise at five in the morning, and it was half-past ten at night before we reached Brindisi. We found it a most forlorn little place, considering what it must have been in the old Roman times, when it was the principal port for the East. It was there that the armies of the Empire embarked, and there they landed after their conquests, laden with prisoners and spoils. The harbor is very fine, consisting of an inner and outer bay; the first having exactly the shape of a triangle. On Sunday we went to the Cathedral, which, like the rest of the city, is decidedly forlorn. There is a queer, narrow, dirty, crooked, steep—what shall I call it?—it surely does not deserve the name of street; at any rate it took us to the church. On the way we passed all that remains of the ancient Brundisium, a building which is said to be the house of Virgil, now the abode of a washerwoman, and near it two columns, one very high and beautifully carved, the other in ruins. These last mark the terminus of the great "Appian Way," which begins at the triumphal arch of Constantine in Rome, and continues along the coast to Baja, where we saw the old pavingstones when we rode out there from Naples; it then crosses Italy and ends at the two beautiful columns I have mentioned.

The steamer Ceylon arrived on Sunday, and early the next morning we were moving. For a long time we had the flat, uninteresting "heel of the boot" to look at on our right. It protected us from the waves, however, and we were sorry when we got fairly out of the Adriatic, and into the Mediterranean, for it began immediately to be very rough, and the boat rolled most unmercifully. It was worse, I thought, than the Atlantic, and the second afternoon I retired ingloriously from the upper deck to my cabin.

Nearly all day Tuesday we were in sight of Turkey, and then Greece, and great interest was manifested—especially by the gentlemen—in distinguishing the different islands, as they could be traced out against the horizon.

The third day, Wednesday, which was to have been the last, was really charming. Instead of the ugly wind, and gray, dismal, tossing water of yesterday, we had the true blue, blue Mediterranean sparkling in the sunshine, and a soft, warm breeze from the African coast. No land was in sight, but everybody was on deck, playing games or enjoying themselves in a quiet way. Some happy individual was bright enough to suggest that it was New Year's Eve, and, as all were in good spirits (that is, not sea-sick), that we should have an impromptu concert on deck. "No sooner said than done." The captain had the quarter deck enclosed with canvas and draped with flags—British, Italian, Egyptian; the piano was brought up from the saloon, and we had a very interesting evening. There were a great many musicians on board, both ladies and gentlemen, some of them very sweet singers, so the music was remarkably fine, and the rippling of the water along the sides of the vessel made a beautiful accompaniment. There were also readings and recitations, comic and tragic, prose and poetry. I recited Longfellow's "Midnight Mass for the Dying Year." As it was a British ship, the entertainment closed with "God Save the Queen."

It is strange how soon people learn to know each other on board a ship; you are as good friends after a week at sea, as you would be at the end of a year or more on land. After the three or four days the Ceylon passengers spent together on the Mediterranean, they were sorry to part at Alexandria—some to go up the Nile, some to Australia, and others to India or Palestine.

The scene in the harbor here at Alexandria is something I shall never forget. How some boys I know who love ship-building would have enjoyed it! There were vessels of every description—for pleasure and business, passengers and freight—schooners, yachts, sailing vessels of every kind; among them the graceful, sweeping lateen masts and sails, steamboats of all shapes and sizes, men-of-war—indeed, it would take a more experienced sailor than I am to name them all. Then the flags of many countries floating at the sterns and mastheads made it very gay and lively; most frequent and most beautiful was the crescent and star of the Arab countries.

Our vessel had scarcely anchored, when there swarmed around from every direction the row-boats that take passengers ashore. From this moment we felt that we were in an altogether different and strange world. I could no more describe the various costumes of these boatmen, than I could help laughing at them. Some wore the regular turbans and baggy knee-breeches; others wore dark-red caps with black tassels, and still more baggy-looking gowns, fastened at the knee, or flying loose; then there were those who wore the most baggy garments of all, with peaked hoods or cowls, like Capuchin friars. Some of their remarkable disguises looked like night-gowns sewed up at the bottom, with two holes left open to put their feet through. As for dirt—that is not the name for it; but, fortunately, these fellows are so black anyway, that one does not notice it anywhere but on their clothes, which are mostly light-colored or white, or at least intended to be so. These are the poor people. The higher classes wear very beautiful dark colors, and their costume is rich and graceful, such as one sees in pictures, pointed shoes and all. Some of them, with their long, white beards, swarthy faces and venerable appearance, take one back in imagination to the days of wonderful Egyptian priests, magicians dealing in the black art, fearful genii, and all sorts of mysterious people.

As I look down from my window into the narrow street below, I can see all these costumes, and many more. I see large men riding on tiny donkeys, and their feet reaching almost to the ground, while the sleek, mouse-colored animals, much more intelligent than the European donkeys, pace along with wonderful rapidity. I see, now and then, a camel come walloping along, with his awkward, sea-sickening walk, and some odd character perched upon the summit of his hump in the midst of numerous bundles and bags. Then there are women hurrying along with their veils wrapped closely around them and reaching to the ground; they also wear another small black veil that covers the lower part of the face, generally attached to the larger one by a gold or brass ornament resembling a spool, right over the nose; thus their eyes are the only features that can be seen.

It is difficult to give my impressions of this strange people. Our dragoman, who has guided us to all parts of the city—Pompey's Pillar, Cleopatra's Needle, the Catacombs, the Khedive's Palace, the Bazaars—showed us a queer set of beads, a kind of rosary called a comboloio, which the Mussulmans use. Friday is their sacred day, and he has just come back from the mosque, and is now waiting to take my trunk to the cars. We shall be in Cairo to-night.

XXVII.

EGYPT.

A WORLD OF WONDERS — PALM-TREES — SPRING IN THE VALLEY OF THE NILE — ORANGES EVERYWHERE — ARABS AT WORK — THEIR HOUSES — DONKEY-BOYS, COSTUMES, SAIS — A GREAT MOSQUE — CAIRO IN GENERAL — THE PYRAMIDS AND SPHINX AT GHIZEH — TOMBS OF THE CALIPHS.

CAIRO, *Jan.* 10.

I THINK that Egypt is the strangest and most interesting place that can be imagined; it is as different from Europe, or any country that I have seen, as if I had made a journey to the moon. On our way here from Alexandria, by rail, we passed the delta of the Nile. The land was, of course, fertile and flat, and for the first time we saw palm-trees growing in any number. By the way, I did not know, until the other day, that dates grew upon palm-trees (green, wasn't I?), still I wondered that people took so much care to cultivate them and cultivate so many, if it was only for ornament, for they are so tall and slender that they do not give much shade. I have a much better opinion of the palms now that I know they yield the delicious fresh dates, which are as plentiful here as the burrs are at "Pine Grove." We could not have chosen a better season for visiting Egypt; everything is beautiful. The early spring crops are just springing up, spreading a green carpet along the valley of the Nile; the sugar-cane is now ripe, and the cotton waiting to be picked, while the trees are weighed down with oranges.

They are everywhere—on the table at each meal, at every street-corner are piles of them, and along the road-side one sees donkeys and camels in long lines laden with them, bringing them to town. No matter where we are, indoors or out, on foot, in a carriage, or

EGYPTIAN WOMAN.

on a donkey, taking a short ride in the desert or crossing the river in a ferry-boat, there are always plenty of Arabs, men, women, and children, who are ready to give us a whole lap full of sweet, juicy mandarin oranges for a ha'penny or piastre, as they call it.

Although this country is so rich and verdant, the people who cultivate it are very poor, as we can see by their wretched appearance and the miserable little mud villages we pass, scattered here and there over the ground.

We went into one of the huts the other day to see the Arabs making the little clay water-jugs that are so generally used here. We had to bend very low to enter the door-way, and even when inside, the gentlemen could not stand up straight. The workers put a lump of wet clay on a wheel which they turned round and round with one foot, shaping the jug with their fingers in a very expert way. By this simple process they made more than half-a-dozen of these neat, well-shaped bottles (even ornamented on the outside) during the two or three minutes we were watching them. All around the villages there were piles of them drying in the sun. Some of the huts are covered with straw or old matting, while others are moulded up in the form of haystacks. They are so low that as you pass rapidly by in the cars, you would take them for mere heaps of rubbish among the green fields, were it not for the sleepy-looking inhabitants squatting Turkish fashion under the trees, lazily smoking their pipes; and now and then a woman coming from the well with her dark veil falling gracefully over her shoulders, balancing a large jug on her head.

The country women do not cover their faces, and are generally barefooted and bare armed, wearing anklets, bracelets, and necklaces of colored glass or gilt beads. When they raise their dark blue dresses, you can see their loose trousers, of red or yellow, gathered round their ankles. Some of these women are beautiful, and many a lovely picture could be made of them, with their jugs, or baskets of oranges on their heads, or what would be more characteristic, with a baby astride their left shoulder, while the little thing lays its head

SHEPHERD'S HOTEL—CAIRO.

on its mother's, and sleeps as comfortably as if it were rocked in a cradle.

I have not yet told of anything that I have seen in Cairo, for all of these things are to be found in the country. As for curious trees, plants, and birds, I shall not remember half of them. There is a large banyan-tree in front of my window, with the lower branches growing downward.

Jan. 11.—I never tire of sitting out on the piazza in front of the hotel, and watching what passes in the street. On the opposite side there are always about a dozen boys with donkeys waiting to be hired. There are white, gray, black, and mouse-colored ones, neatly shaved and taken care of like horses, with bright saddles of red leather. The donkey-boys, of every shade and cast of complexion and features, from the almost white skin of the Turks and Circassians, to the coal-black Nubians, are all dressed in loose blue or white tunics, each wearing a red cap or fez with a tassel, and carrying a long reed with which to strike the donkey. The moment you make your appearance they all rush toward you and begin talking in broken English. The donkeys go alternately by the names of "Yankee Doodle," "Prince of Wales," "Flying Dutchman," or "Macaroni," according to the country from which the boys imagine you come. They are generally very quick, too, about guessing, though the other day one of them came up to me with a very comical-looking animal, such as one sees in pictures. He began, "See, Yankee Doodle donkey, gude donkey," then as I did not take him, he decided that he had made a mistake, that I was not an American, so he went on, " Dis Prince o' Wales' donkey; he name it Yankee Doodle; Prince o' Wales ride on dis donkey."

It is astonishing to see what large men and great burdens these little creatures can carry. We frequently see the native ladies on the donkeys, and always astride, though with very short stirrups. This, however, does not look at all out of the way, with their style of dress.

At first, these people seem to have no regular fashion, but all dress to suit themselves; but one soon finds that there is great regularity about their costume. Among the women it is principally by the material that one knows their rank. The dress of the higher class seems to be always of silk; one never sees alpaca, merinoes, or any woolen goods, I suppose it is partly because the climate is so hot. This dress is of a single color, either green, red, yellow, blue, purple, or brown. This is entirely covered with a black silk veil, and it is only when the wind blows it open that one sees the robe at all. The poor women use cotton or calico, the outer dress and veil being always dark blue, the trousers alone are bright. The six hundred wives of the Viceroy, and the ladies of the harems of the Pashas rarely go out in the street, and when they do, it is in close carriages. The couriers or sais who run in front of the carriages of rich people, have, I think, the most beautiful costume of all. They wear black or red velvet vests richly embroidered with gold thread, white trousers reaching only to the knee, and very long, flowing sleeves that resemble wings as they bound swiftly ahead, scarcely seeming to touch the earth. These runners are generally rather dark, beautifully formed, and graceful in their movements. They must be trained from childhood, for they seem never tired, never out of breath. While running, they hold themselves perfectly erect, and carry a light rod in the right hand, calling out to the people as they pass, something that means "clear the road," and it is wonderful how the Arabs, camels, and donkeys scatter right and left to make way for the carriages. If it is the Khedive's son who drives out, there are frequently four sais with spears in front, and several horsemen behind.

Among the Mohammedans, the descendants of the prophet are distinguished by their green turbans and

MOSQUE—EGYPT.

gowns. The Copts, who are all Christians, wear black turbans.

Sometimes one meets with startling combinations of the European and the Eastern dress, such, for instance, as pointed slippers, tight pantaloons, a colored jacket, and a formidable turban; or what is more frequent, Turkish trousers and a black cloth coat on the same individual.

After seeing, in some of the cities of Italy, a small column of Egyptian alabaster pointed out as a great treasure in some church, it seemed strange to visit an immense mosque, that of Mohamet Ali, with a large dome and dizzy minarets made entirely of this beautiful material. The architecture was grand and imposing; the interior was carpeted with rich rugs, and five hundred lamps were suspended from the dome and ceiling by heavy chains, although the vastness of the building made them look like threads.

Whole volumes could be written about what one sees in and around this one city of Cairo; the curious little streets or lanes; the houses projecting farther out at each story until the sky is almost hidden, latticed windows and balconies, beautiful oriental doors; bazaars where each shop is but the size of a child's playhouse, and all the people are trading in the streets, as it would be impossible for more than one man to stand inside the shop. When no customers are around, the shopmen are smoking their pipes or drinking little cups of Arabian coffee, and always seated cross-legged on the counter. Then there are the old mosques, with miraculous pillars sent through the air, and footprints of the prophet on stones; primitive Coptic rites and shrines of saints where devils are cast out; Mohammedan dervishes spinning round like tops to honor the Great Allah; funeral processions struggling through the donkey carts and traders; curious burying places in the desert with the heads of the tombs toward Mecca.

Everything is a dizzy whirl of wonder and excitement; being dragged up the steep steps of the Pyramids by wild-looking Bedouins of the desert; resting on the top hot and panting; eagles soaring right above our heads, and desert, desert, desert far away to the westward; the green valley of the Nile and desert,

A Street in Cairo.

desert, desert beyond to the eastward; tombs half buried in the sand at our feet, and the sphynx, stern, sublime, and broken-nosed. Then scrambling down over the crumbling stones, crawling into the interior of the pyramid, down a slippery inclined plane, and

up another inclined plane; pushed, pulled, and carried
through narrow passages and low holes, nearly suffo-

DAHABEIH. NILE.

cated for want of air and by smoking lights. Coming
at last to a large chamber made of immense blocks of

granite, and containing an empty sarcophagus, the Arab guides yelling, squabbling, aud interpreting, tell us this is the tomb of King Cheops. A magnesium wire lights up the vast room and shows the Bedouins running here and there with the frightened and bewildered party, dusty, tired, and nearly choked, but glad to recognize each other by the bright gleam of light. If I forget everything else that I have seen on my journey, I shall always remember that wild scene in the centre of the great pyramid.

Another day took us once more to the desert, but this time on the opposite side of Cairo. I can now see the fairy-like cupolas and oriental honeycomb-work of the tombs of the caliphs, the same color as the sand, and seeming like a beautiful fossilized growth of the desert. Everything is in keeping — long strings of camels plodding through the sand, looking twice as picturesque on their rightful ground, and strange birds flying overhead. The old monarchs did, indeed, choose a wild and solemn place to build their wonderful tombs.

To-morrow, again, we shall make a distant excursion to the site of Memphis. The donkey ride will be long and tiring, and it is already after nightfall, so I must leave Cairo as it is, with this jumbled-up description; for we leave for Suez on Wednesday, to embark for Ceylon and Hong Kong.

•

XXVIII.

UNCLE'S CHAPTER.

HIS ACCOUNT OF THE COPTIC CATHOLICS AS WE SAW THEM IN CAIRO —AN ANCIENT RITE—CATHEDRAL OF THE SCHISMATIC COPTS—THEIR QUEER CUSTOMS—TRADITIONS OF THE HOLY FAMILY IN EGYPT—THE HOUSE THEY OCCUPIED—THE SYCAMORE TREE.

CAIRO, *Jan.* 11.

DEAR FATHER H——: Since leaving the United States I have seldom touched pen to paper. Some things, however, which I have witnessed in Cairo have brought you so forcibly to mind that I can not resist the impulse to write, and tell you of what I have seen while the memory is yet fresh. I have often heard you speak with great interest of the Coptic Catholics and their rites. Well, I have assisted at several Low Masses in Coptic, also at two solemn, or at least sung, Masses in the same language. The church of the Catholic Copts is a very pretty building, recently erected by the care of the Franciscan missionaries, who share in its use with their Coptic brethren, and are subject like them to the Coptic bishop. [There is another community of Franciscans here who devote themselves to the European residents of the city of various nations.] This church is surmounted and lighted by a dome, and in general form is not unlike the Pantheon at Rome, except that it has no portico and that the facade is in the ancient Egyptian style, so cleverly imitated that at first sight I believed myself to be entering some ancient temple which had been adapted to Christian worship. It has two altars in addition to the high altar. I noticed nothing peculiar about the construction or furniture of these. There is no communion rail. A small square cloth is handed to the communicants by one of the boys.

The vestments of the officiating priest are, so far as I could observe, the same as our own, except that instead of a chasuble they wear the pluviale, which is without a cape, and a far more flexible and graceful vestment than ours, and reaches to the feet. They do not appear to keep any distinctions of color; for, although within the octave of Epiphany (Christmas with them), violet, red, yellow, and green were all used. The pattern of the pluviale is rich and variegated. It has a cross in the centre of the back—but small—and by no means showy like the huge cross-bars of the French chasuble.

The head of the celebrant is bare, but the rest of the clergy and all the congregation keep their heads covered throughout the Mass. Turbans, fezzes, and caps of various kinds are as much in order here for men as are the hats of women in American churches. There are benches in this church, but some of the people prefer to sit on the floor cross-legged whenever they can find a carpet or clean place.

The missal is placed at the left hand of the celebrant, as with us during the canon, and is never changed. The text is in Coptic, the rubrics in Arabic; the text reading from left to right as in English, the Arabic characters from right to left. The offertory is at the beginning of Mass, before either epistle or gospel—before even the lavabo. The celebrant turns and shows to the people the bread which is to be consecrated, and walks to the end of the altar and back, holding it in his hand. At High Mass he makes an entire circuit about the altar, the altar boys accompanying him in procession. At some of the incensings likewise he goes around the altar. After the epistle has been chanted, it is repeated also in Arabic for the benefit of the people who do not understand the Coptic. One little boy who did this was only six years old at most, and another day I saw a little fellow of four years old perform the same duty. He was dressed in a flowing cassock or gown of blue and gold, with a cross upon the back. He put me in mind of little Samuel in the temple. The gospel also, after being sung in Coptic, is interpreted in Arabic to the people, and at High Mass a homily from one of the Fathers is also read to explain its meaning. The priests who assist at High Mass, whatever office they may perform, wear no other vestments than their ordinary every-day habit, a loose black gown with flowing sleeves, and black turban. The altar boys wear gowns of similar form, but of various colors.

The celebrant often gives his benediction to the people, turning first to the left and then to the right, but only turning partially around to either side. From the consecration until after communion, each hand was covered by a pall, which he still retained when giving the benedictions. There was no elevation of the host at the time of consecrating, the priest kneeling once only at each consecration. But just before communing he turned around with the host in his hand, elevating and showing it to the people, who adore it with an outburst of enthusiasm which, to a stranger, is perfectly startling. The censer among the Copts is like our own, and handled very much in the same way, but so far as I saw, by the officiating priest only.

When High Mass is finished, that is, immediately after communion, the celebrant comes forward toward the congregation, when all—clergy, assistant, and people—gather around him, and bend their heads to receive his blessing, which he gives by laying his hand upon the forehead of each. There was a beauty and solemnity about this final act which I found very impressive.

I speak, you understand, of the Catholic Copts, who recognize the authority of the Holy Father, and are therefore in communion with us. I said my own Mass in the same church, but, of course, according to the Roman rite. It was a great joy for me to stand at the altar surrounded by these descendants of the ancient Egyptians, and see them worshipping with me on the same ground where Joseph and Moses once trod, and where Pharaoh hardened his heart against God, and almost under the shadow of the same pyramids where their fathers drove the enslaved Israelites to their task. Now these remnants of that ancient race are numbered with the people of God, united with the Vicar of Christ, and mingle their tears and prayers with his against the European Pharaohs and Egyptians of our day.

What delights me most in these Coptic services is the chanting. At first it was difficult to distinguish between the *missa cantata* and *missa privata*, for even the Low Mass is recited in a chanting tone, and with cadences as sweet and musical as anything I have ever heard in the plain chant; and the altar boy responds in the same manner. These responses are so frequent, and chime in so readily, that it seems more like a running accompaniment than a way of responding, and I liked it better than the chanting of the choir of priests and deacons at the High Mass. At one point of the latter, however, I was completely enchanted. It was just before the communion, when the celebrant turned toward the people and showed them the sacred host, singing all the while. All—priests and people—joined their voices to his in a sort of low, murmuring chant, and when the still louder, clearer, and higher voices of the boys rose in the air above the rest, the effect was simply transporting. At the communion also a hymn is sung—sometimes by the clergy, sometimes by a small choir of boys, and sometimes by alternate voices of both—and this last combination especially is very beautiful and effective.

Communion was given to the women through a latticed window at one side of the altar, not always by the celebrant, but also by another priest, both before and during Mass. The women are separated from the men, places being assigned to them in latticed galleries, so that in church they are not only closely veiled, but cloistered. I saw a devout and venerable old man communicating. He took off the large shawl with which he had been covered, came forward and kneeled on the altar-step. After communion he returned to his place and, covering again his head and entire body in the ample folds of his shawl, he remained so for a long while, like a bundle of clothing, motionless and apparently inanimate. I know nothing of the interior dispositions of these people, but their appearance in church is certainly very edifying. A little boy of three or four years ran forward and kneeled by the old man's side, and bent his head beneath the Sacrament. He seemed to consider it as a means of receiving a special benediction. Neither the priest nor the others present seemed to notice this as anything unusual. To me there was something very beautiful and touching in the incident. I assisted also at a Low Mass celebrated by the Coptic bishop. There was nothing about it different from what I have already described, except that he was attended by two deacons in dalmatics. These dalmatics reached to the floor, and had long, loose sleeves.

They were of light blue color with dark stripes. A *priedieu* was placed before the altar where the bishop made his preparation and thanksgiving as our bishops do. He had no mitre, but a black cap precisely like the ecclesiastical cap of the other priests, except that it had attached to it a black veil which fell back over his shoulders. This cap, or biretta, he wore at the altar, except at the gospel and the more solemn parts of the Mass, when it was removed by the deacon. The cap is shaped very much like an old-fashioned bell-crowned hat, but without the brim, and more expanded at the top. His crozier was in the form of an actual cross, the extremities of the two arms being bent upwards. This he only used when walking to the altar before Mass, and retiring to his throne at the end. He vested at the altar and unvested at the throne. Whenever he gave benediction to the people, it was with a small silver cross, which was kept beside him at the altar. On entering the church, besides the cap, he wore a purple gown, covered by a short black cassock, over which he wore his pectoral cross. At the altar he put on an alb, a stole, and then the pluviale. I saw no maniple nor any other vestment. After Mass he stationed himself in front of the high altar, where every one came forward and received his benediction, kissing first the little silver cross and then his ring. So far as regards the communion of the laity under both kinds, and the giving communion to infant children, the Catholic Copts have conformed to the usages of our Church. They preserve, however, their own ancient rite, and almost all the religious usages which they observed before their reunion.

The schismatic Copts have also a cathedral here, and another church at Old Cairo. Since the death of their late patriarch, the government has not allowed them to elect a new one, from a superstitious idea (so it is said) of the Viceroy, that when a new patriarch is chosen, he himself must die. These ceremonies are, with very little apparent difference, the same as already described. The cathedral has a close rood-screen, and there is a similar screen also to the small chapel adjoining it, where it is customary to say Mass except when a Sunday or some high festival occurs. On the morning of January 9, I visited this church at the time of the services, and had a good seat brought in for me, just in front of the screen door, where I could see the celebrant and the altar. I was allowed, also, to look through a small square window or opening in the screen, where, by standing up, I had a complete view of everything which took place in the sanctuary. The altar was simply an oblong table, and covered by a rich dark green cloth, reaching to the floor on all sides. Upon it stood a beautiful carved tabernacle, a small square box to contain the Blessed Sacrament. This was also so low as to be within easy reach of the celebrant. On the top of this stood the chalice throughout the Mass; while the paten (a large vessel about the size of a tea-plate, and shaped like a shallow pan) was placed on the table of the altar, as with us. The congregation all sat cross-legged upon the floor, on carpets and mats. All took off their slippers on entering the church, but kept their heads covered. The celebrant himself sat down in the same fashion outside of the screen door, while the epistle was read, and the homily after the gospel. He interrupted the reader, from time to time, correcting him, as I supposed, or sometimes, perhaps, making a brief explanation. Other priests present did the same.

The celebrant partook of the sacred element at three distinct times for each species. The two altar boys who communicated did the same, each boy walking entirely around the altar and returning to receive again. The priest received the precious blood by means of a spoon, and communicated to the boys in the same way. Finally he consumed what remained by drinking from the chalice.

All this seemed to me very strange, but I had an excellent post for observation, and could not be mistaken.

A still more remarkable thing was the giving communion to a little infant about a year old. A young man brought the child in his arms to the door of the sanctuary, and the celebrant, after emptying the chalice at his own communion, put in his finger, pressing it carefully around the inside of the cup, and then touched it to the child's tongue. One of the altar boys then gave the child a drink of water from a small jug. Both of these usages, namely, the triune-communion, if I may so call it, and the communicating to infants, were confirmed by the testimony of the superior of the Franciscan missionaries, who told me that such is the custom among the schismatic Copts. When a layman wishes to communicate, he brings his own altar bread with him for that purpose, which is thereupon put on the altar and consecrated with the rest. One of the breads was shown to me at the convent of the Christian Brothers. It was of the size of an ordinary tea-biscuit, but much thinner, and sacred words, in Coptic characters, were stamped upon the top. At the end of the Mass, which followed close upon the communion, the celebrant took a small tumbler in his hand, holding his thumbs and forefingers over the top, as we do over the chalice, while a boy poured in water. Then, with a quick motion and surprising dexterity, he threw the contents of the glass into the air in such a way that it fell like a spray over all that stood near him. All, by this time, had gathered about the door of the sanctuary, and he gave them his blessing in the manner already described.

The church of the schismatic Copts at Old Cairo is a very ancient one. It is built over the house in which, the tradition says, the Blessed Virgin and St. Joseph lived with our Saviour during their abode in Egypt. The pillars and walls of the little house remain still. They showed us the place where the Divine Infant lay —a sort of deep recess or niche in the wall. On the other side of the city, to the northward, not far from the great obelisk which is the sole mark of the site of the ancient city of Heliopolis, is shown also the sycamore-tree under which the Holy Family reposed on their way hither. We plucked some leaves from it, and also a ripe orange from a tree near by. It is a fertile spot. We saw the cotton growing there, and the sugar-cane nearly ripe, while a well of sweet water, a few steps from the tree, refreshed our thirsty lips. The line of the desert is also very near. This must have been a welcome resting-place to these blessed pilgrims, and was, I suppose, the first fertile spot they found after their weary flight across the sands. Cairo possesses, also, other churches in union with the Holy See, which have their own peculiar rites, namely, Armenian, Greek, Syrian, and Maronite. The head of the last is a mitred abbot. The others are governed each by a bishop or vicar-apostolic of its own, and so is the Coptic. All these are independent of each other, making a strange confusion here of jurisdiction as well as of rite.

I have not seen Father H—— since last October, when I met him at Geneva. I find, however, his name registered here in the sacristy of the Franciscans. He was here in the beginning of December, and is now far away up the Nile. I shall return home, please God, by way of the Red Sea, India, China, Japan, and San Francisco. Adieu, and kind remembrance to the whole circle of dear friends around you.

Your affectionate friend and brother in Christ,

C. A. WALWORTH.

XXIX.

THE DESERT AND THE RED SEA.

A BASHFUL YOUNG MAN — MOUNTING A CAMEL — LAND OF THE CHILDREN OF ISRAEL—DESERT SCENERY—SUEZ CANAL—THE STEAMER —MOSES' WELL AND MOUNT SINAI—DOWN THE RED SEA—ENTERING THE TROPICS—STRANGE LIGHTS.

STEAMER "AUSTRALIA," RED SEA, *January*.

THE last day we spent at Cairo we visited the tombs of the Caliphs a second time. A young Holland gentleman, Uncle, and I rode thither on donkeys. While we were in the streets of the city we could not go very fast, because they were so narrow and crowded with people; but the moment we were outside the gates, in the desert, we went at a full gallop. The idea of riding at that rate on a donkey seemed so funny that we were laughing all the time. The stirrups on the gentlemen's saddles were arranged in such a way that they slipped from one side to the other, and the riders had to balance themselves carefully to keep on. The young Hollander was of rather a timid disposition, and his face would get red, and he looked anything but comfortable, when one leg slipped up and the other down, alternately.

While we were at the tombs we had a camel ride. When you are placed on a camel's back and he begins to rise, you have the strangest sensations imaginable. All of a sudden one crank in the hind legs will unbend, and bunk! you will go nearly over the creature's head;

then up go the fore legs with the same sudden motion; and this time you find yourself in the neighborhood of the animal's tail; one more bounce from this hind quarter, as he gets fairly on his feet, sets you once more on the middle of the hump, where you first seated yourself.

You are very high up by this time, and, as the camel starts off with long strides, your body bowing backwards and forwards furiously, while you hold on with both hands to—you don't know exactly what—you begin to wonder which is farthest away, the desert below, or the heavens above. After riding a short distance, you are very glad to go through the difficult operation of being lowered. This is something like mounting, except that the movements are still more surprising and unexpected. There is an astonishing number of joints in a camel's legs, and he seems to fall from one crook to another until he has those long limbs of his folded under him, and you are near enough to the ground to be lifted off. They have a most distressing cry when they think they are to be loaded. The only way I can describe it is by suggesting something like a mingling of the noises made by a horse, a cow, a cat, and a baby, if you can possibly imagine such a sound.

It takes a whole day to go by rail from Cairo to Suez, but we were so much interested in the country we passed through that it was not at all tedious. About one-third of the way we followed the fertile valley of the Nile, through the very country that is supposed to be that part of Egypt which was occupied by the children of Israel. It is the richest soil in the country, often producing six crops in the year; every field has tiny canals traversing it in all directions, so that whenever the ground needs watering, these are filled from

A Caravan.

the small branches of the Nile that stray off from the two main streams of the delta.

The railroad followed one of these branches as far as the station of Zagazig, and on the way we frequently saw the inhabitants watering the fields. There were generally two boys standing in the stream swinging a tight, basket-looking bucket into the water, then emptying it into one end of a little canal. They did it very rapidly, and without moving from their places; the water ran from one canal or channel into another, until the whole field was moistened.

Soon after leaving Zagazig we were surrounded on all sides by the desert, and then really appreciated its vastness and grandeur. The sloping sand-hills, in every direction, as far as the eye could reach, reminded one of the waves of the ocean, but were doubly imposing from their very stillness. In some places the sand was beautiful, where the wind had made ripples along the banks, and it had hardened in that way.

We had not gone far when we saw a very large caravan slowly winding along from the direction of the Holy Land. There were between forty and fifty camels, very heavily laden, and evidently proceeding to Cairo. They looked natural and graceful, for they were walking on their own proper ground; their great, baglike feet that seemed so gawky on hard ground, now sank into the sand easily and were as readily lifted up again, while horses and donkeys would stumble along most awkwardly.

We reached the Suez Canal at Ismailia. This is a town right in the desert, without a green thing in sight. The houses, the streets, and even the inhabitants, looked sandy, the last both in complexion and clothes. Sand-colored cane fences surrounded the place to prevent the sand from covering up the town, and, still stranger, there was a lake in the sand. Very pretty it is, too. On one shore is the Egyptian desert, and on the other the Arabian; it divides the two countries and forms part of the Suez Canal.

Further on are the Bitter Lakes, which are much larger, but like this one, without the least vegetation.

Several times during the day we passed small oases,

SUEZ CANAL, AT ISMAILIA.

and saw different kinds of birds, among them the ibis and the eagle. We reached Suez in the evening. The next morning as we were walking on the roof of the hotel (quite a favorite promenade in this country), and looking every now and then toward the great canal to see if the "Australia," our vessel, was in sight, we noticed on a neighboring roof two or three Franciscan Fathers walking up and down, saying their rosaries. It was a pleasant surprise. We soon found the Convent, had a delightful visit, and later in the day one of the Fathers took us through the Egyptian part of the place.

The harbor of Suez, where the large vessels anchor, is some distance below the town; so on Friday, January 16, we left the hotel early in the morning in a small sail-boat to go down to the ship. This boat was no larger than an ordinary row-boat. We progressed very well for some time with the sail, and as the water was very shallow, the men pushed us along occasionally with poles. Before we had gone far, however, it began to rain, and to increase our troubles the wind ceased. There we had to sit in the wet, while the boatmen went through the slow process of towing us along. The two men took turns running on the breakwater and pulling the boat with a rope. It seemed as if they must hurt their bare feet on the rough stones, but they did not appear to mind it at all.

We have secured cabins on the steamer in the best possible position; it is not crowded, and we have each a whole room to ourselves. I believe the ship is one-sixteenth of a mile long—how many feet that is, I have not tried to calculate; at any rate, it is very roomy, and as comfortable as can be.

We left Suez Friday morning, and have had delightful weather ever since.

The place was pointed out to us at which the Israelites are supposed to have crossed the Red Sea. There is a narrow strip of land between the mountains and the sea, where an army might easily have been hemmed in. Just opposite, on the Arabian side, is a small oasis, consisting of a few trees and a spring. They call it Moses' Well.

All the way down the Gulf of Suez the shores are

very interesting. To be sure there are nothing but mountains and desert, but the sun makes such a variety of light and shade that we never weary of looking at the coast. In the afternoon we watched very carefully for Mount Sinai, but we were not quite certain which of the high peaks we saw was the right one.

The crew of the ship is composed of Indians and Chinese. The Hindoos look quite picturesque, with their red turbans and sashes, working about the vessel; some of them wear rings on their big toes. The Chinamen wear queer, broad-brimmed hats.

Jan. 17.—We have left the Gulf of Suez and are fairly out in the Red Sea. The lines of the shore are no longer visible. During the morning we passed two little coral islands, called "The Brothers;" there was nothing peculiar about them except that they were very narrow, long, flat, and regular—two small slices of land out there all by themselves. They were covered with grass, or something green, but no trees or shrubs grew on them.

This evening we passed a lighthouse, the only one in the Red Sea, although there are a great many shoals and ugly places which keep the captain well occupied.

Jan. 18.—We are now in the tropics, and it is constantly getting hotter. Everybody is beginning to appear in summer clothing, and we spend the evenings on deck without any wrappings. The heavens are very brilliant; the stars seem so near. The phosphorescent lights in the water—the glow-worms of the sea, one might call them—become more beautiful every evening; they brighten up the water around the vessel as far as the foam, caused by the motion, reaches on all sides. The zodiacal light is seen in the sky every night long after sunset, when the stars are all shining; it is a strange, white light that reaches from the western horizon almost to the zenith. The cause of it is, I believe, unknown, although they tell me it is thought to be some refraction of the atmosphere of the sun.

Jan. 19.—St. John's Island is the only land we have seen to-day.

We are entering the region of the flying-fish, though as yet we have only seen some very small ones around the steamer.

They have an invention on this ship for fanning the passengers when they are at dinner. There are long poles suspended horizontally from the ceiling by heavy cords; a piece of white linen, made double to catch the air, about a foot and a half wide, is attached to the poles; the whole contrivance is moved by means of cords and pulleys, and there are little Hindoo boys who swing them back and forth, making a refreshing breeze the whole length of the saloon; they are called punkahs.

It is pleasant to think that we are on our way home, although just now every day takes us further from it. It requires no small amount of patience to write at sea; a gentle breeze every now and then making my paper dance around the saloon.

XXX.

INDIAN OCEAN.

TROPICAL DREAMINESS — SHAM DANGERS — A DINNER THAT WON A FORTRESS — MERMEN AND THEIR CHANT — THE HEAT — PECULIARITIES OF ADEN — INCIDENTS OF OCEAN LIFE — THE "SOUTHERN CROSS" — A DITTY.

     STEAMER "AUSTRALIA," INDIAN
      OCEAN, *January.*

WE are gliding on and on in a dreamy way. There is a wonderful fascination in doing nothing, when you once get accustomed to it. Indeed, the climate of the tropics takes all the energy out of one, so that it is impossible to do anything but dream. It requires an effort to make up one's mind even to write a letter

We lounge on deck all day and far into the night, only coming down to our meals and to bed. There we sit, eager to catch every breath of air made by the motion of the ship—the monotony broken once in a while by a sudden exclamation and a rush to the side of the ship in order to see some new wonder of the deep, or some strange effect in the sky. Everybody is supposed to have something to keep them busy—a book, or a piece of work, or a game of some kind; but if you glance around the deck, you will find they have little interest in their occupation, but spend most of the time gazing listlessly at the water and the clouds, or in following the sailors with their eyes, as they climb among the rigging of the ship, ever busy at something—loosening or fastening, tying or untying—for if there is no work for them the captain makes some, no matter what, so it keeps them from becoming lazy and good-for-nothing. For instance, they pretend that the vessel is on fire, sound the alarm, and rush around, arranging the machines and working the hose, just as if it was really so; a band of sailors are sent to man the boats, the numerous fastenings are undone with wonderful rapidity; the oars are placed, and all made ready to be lowered at an instant's notice. By this time the hose has done its imaginary work, the fire is extinguished, and they all go about arranging things in their accustomed order. These sham dangers are very lively and amusing.

The last day or two we were on the Red Sea, we signaled passing vessels with colored lights. In the evening it looked very pretty to see the blue or red glimmer appearing way out in the darkness. There have been several wrecks on this treacherous sea within a short time. One we passed near Suez, and another much farther south; the last one was still lying against the rock where it struck.

Just at the mouth of the Red Sea are twelve islands in a cluster, called the Twelve Apostles. Judas, a barren little one, is some distance from the rest. There is another interesting island right in the middle of the straits of Babel-Mandeb, so that all ships have to pass it either on one side or the other to leave or enter the Red Sea. The English have a fort and garrison stationed on it, for it is the key, one might say, to all their colonies in India and the islands of the Indian Ocean, since the Suez Canal has been opened. A few years ago it was uninhabited, and no one claimed it. While the canal was being talked about, the French Government sent out a vessel to take possession of the island in the name of France. When they reached Aden, the officers of the French ship were invited to dine with the British Governor of that place. Under the influence of the good dinner and the wine, one of the Frenchmen chanced to let slip their intention. Then the Governor very quietly took a card and wrote out orders to send a British man-of-war immediately and take possession of the island of Perim, as it is called; he then took care to entertain his guests un-

NIGHT AT SEA.

til a very late hour. You can easily imagine the dismay of the French captain on arriving there the next morning, to find the flag of Great Britain waving triumphantly over the island. There it has remained ever since.

While we were at Aden, all the ships from different countries that were in the harbor fired off salutes to the English, in honor of the Duke of Edinburgh's wedding. It sounded like a bombardment, and we were right in the midst of it.

January 22, early in the morning, we found ourselves lying in the harbor of Aden. I hurried on deck as quickly as possible. There were about a dozen little Somali boys, with log canoes, diving and swimming about the vessel like fishes. They came from the African coast just opposite Aden. They wore scarcely any clothing, and their skin was a pleasing bronze color, not coal black like the Nubians, nor yet yellow like the Arabs. Their limbs were slender and graceful, and their faces very bright and intelligent. We have no idea of real Africans in America; we do not see fair specimens. This race have their own chiefs or sheiks, being much like our Indians, and they are quite free and independent, though I believe they are nominally subject to the Sultan of Turkey.

How we enjoyed watching these little monkeys in the water. They swam around us all day; in fact, they are as much at home in the water as on land. They would go through all sorts of antics, pretending to fight with their fists and feet, shoving each other under the water and popping up again, rolling over like porpoises, and sliding in and out of the canoes like eels. Sometimes the gentlemen on board our ship would throw over, one at a time, silver sixpences or rupees; as quick as a flash five or six of them would dive after it, no matter where they happened to be, in the canoe, on the steamer, or in the water, they seemed to go down all in the same spot without interfering with each other in the least. When the money went in, we heard half a dozen splashes or so—saw several pairs of feet kicking just under the surface; then all was silent for a moment or more, after which the heads would begin to pop up, one after another, each boy taking a long breath and dashing the water from his eyes. The one who got the silver would stick it in his mouth and be ready for the next opportunity; if it came immediately, down they all went again without stopping an instant. They had picked up a few words of English. I think I shall always remember their song as they floated around, with only their heads in sight, asking if any one wanted to see them dive for a sixpence. It was more like a rude chant than a song, reminding me, not of mermaids, but of mermen. One would begin,

"Hab a dibe? Ho! ha!"

Then they would all join in,

"Ho! ha! Ho! ha! Hab a dibe? Ho! ha!
Ho! ha! Hab a dibe?"

The tune is ringing in my ears yet. Hearing them speak their native language, it seems made up of r's, they roll and prolong them so; it is musical though, especially when spoken by the boys.

We went ashore for awhile during our stay in the harbor. Aden is dreadfully barren and sandy, and oh! such a scorching sun; I think if I had remained half an hour longer I should have had a sunstroke; as it was, my head seemed on fire all day, and it made me feel faint and sick even after we were on board and under the awning. The sun beat right through my hat, and the sand was so hot that I could feel it burn through my shoes. I don't wonder that the inhabitants live half of the time in the water and wear scarcely any clothes; but their skulls seem to be so baked they don't mind the sun any more. They have a queer fashion of twisting up their hair so it looks like short ropes hanging around their heads. They are very fond of dyeing it red and yellow, which they do with some kind of clay which they put on their heads. We saw one fellow with his head all plastered over, and we thought at first it was to protect it from the sun, but we learned that he was going through the operation of dyeing it.

The town of Aden, together with the British cantonment, are situated in the crater of an extinct volcano. There are some very ancient tanks near by that supply them with water. I believe they are quite curious, and so old that nobody knows when or by whom they were built, so (as is generally the case with such things) they are called Moses' Tanks. The sun was too hot for me, however, so I did not attempt to visit them.

If we were on land now instead of the water, I think the heat would kill us outright. As it is, we are not any too cool, I assure you, and we shall be continually approaching the equator until we reach Singapore.

Jan. 23.—We weighed anchor. "A life on the ocean wave"—nothing very eventful—no land.

Jan. 24.—Still in the Gulf of Aden, but we have had the African shore to the south of us; and passed a queer-shaped promontory, called Elephant Hill, from its resemblance to that animal. By looking through the captain's spy-glass we have been able to see some small Somali villages, and also two or three very antique-looking boats that trade along the coast of Africa. The captain tells us they are made just as they were hundreds of years ago, and are about the only vessels that can land along this coast in many places; they are used altogether by the natives.

At sunset we saw the Cape of Guardafui; early tomorrow morning we shall pass south of the island of Socotra and take a direct course to Point de Galle, Ceylon.

Jan. 25.—This morning we saw a hundred or more fishes jumping in and out of the water, one after another in a long line; the drill they seemed to be in was wonderful. I am told they hunt their prey in this way; they are something like porpoises and are called Bonitas.

There are so many crosses among the stars here that there has been some dispute as to the true one; but last night, or rather this morning about four o'clock, I saw the genuine Southern Cross for the first time. The captain showed it to us; it is really very beautiful. I have never until to-day seen a rainbow on the ocean; it made a perfect arc, rising out of the water in one place, and falling into it in another.

Jan. 26.—More flying-fish, and very pretty jelly-fish around the vessel.

Jan. 28.—We shall probably reach Ceylon on the first of February. In the meantime, the days come and go unconsciously to us—we can scarce tell one from another. I have just been singing—all by myself—to the music of the ripples against the ship's-side, this little

SEA-SONG.

Dreamily, dreamily, glide we along—
The waves never ceasing their murmuring song.

Lazily, lazily, flit the days by,
As we gaze on the varying ocean and sky.

Gently, so gently, we're rocked on the wave
That I can play jackstraws and Uncle can shave!

XXXI.

A CINGALESE HEROINE.

ODD SIGHTS AND SCENES—MAHOMETAN SAILORS—CHRISTINA THE CINGALESE GIRL, AND LITTLE EVY — SAVED FROM DEATH — BROKEN ENGLISH—A PASSING CLOUD.

How like a beautiful romance seem those days and weeks we spent in sailing down, down the Red Sea and through the Indian Ocean! How unlike anything I have ever seen were the sky, the sunsets, the strange fish floating past us in the water, and the very sailors themselves—grim, solemn-looking Hindoos—who moved around the vessel as noiselessly as ghosts (only not as white by any means), following the voice of the boatswain as he gave his orders in their own language; now all pulling together at the ropes, then creeping, singly, among the rigging, always busy and always quiet. How different from our own "jolly tars," who are continually singing and calling out to one another!

What a laugh we had one day to see these funereal-looking men jumping around and running up the ropes like so many monkeys, to get out of the way of a pig. They were all Mahometans, and this poor animal had just escaped from the butcher, who was about to kill it for dinner. It was a strange scene—the little pig rushing over the deck and squealing, with the butcher, and a few Chinese sailors, "pig-tails" flying, trying to catch him, and the Mahometans in great distress, lest they should be touched by so unclean an animal, scrambling down the hatchways and up the rigging. All the passengers were in a roar of laughter.

The vessel, called the "Australia," which bore us from Egypt to Ceylon, was one of the largest belonging to the P. and O. Company, which carries the mails between England and the East Indies. It had come all the way from Southampton, passing through the Bay of Biscay, the Straits of Gibraltar, the Mediterranean, and the Suez Canal before we boarded it. Most of the passengers were English people.

The first person who attracted my attention, when I began to look around at my fellow-travellers, was a beautiful Cingalese girl, who stood on the deck with a European child of about two years old in her arms. They made a more beautiful picture than any I had seen in all the Italian art galleries.

The Cingalese inhabit the southern part of the Island of Ceylon. This girl was sixteen or seventeen, though small for her age; her complexion was of a soft, decidedly brown tinge, and she had such beautiful dark eyes, and so sweet and intelligent a face that one could not help being drawn towards her. Her silky, jet-black hair was twisted in a coil and fastened with a small tortoise-shell comb. She had the prettiest little dimpled hands, and bare, brown feet that just showed under her red petticoat—a garment that readily dispensed with what are to us indispensable bothers—dressmaker, pattern, needle, thread, and thimble—being simply a straight piece of cloth wrapped around the waist and lapping over. A little, loose white jacket barely reaching to the waist, and cut half low in the neck, completes the Cingalese costume which she wore. In addition to this I noticed on her neck a coral necklace with a handsome gold locket attached.

The child she carried was no less attractive than the

nurse. She seemed to be a delicate little creature, white as a lily, with those deep, violet eyes that seem as if you could look far down into them, and with that spiritual expression you sometimes find in a delicate child. Her little white arms were clasped tightly around the nurse's neck, and when I went up and spoke to her, she tucked down her fair curly head; but we soon made friends.

The mother of the child, Mrs. M——, and her little son, who was seven years old, with the nurse and baby, were returning from England, where they had gone to escape the hot months in India. She was now bound for Point de Galle, Ceylon, where her husband resided with her other children whom she had left there.

It was Mrs. M—— who told us this story of the Cingalese girl. The baby, whom they called Evy, was born in Ceylon, and like most European children raised in these hot climates, was delicate, besides which, an accident happened to her when she was very young. The woman who had always been her nurse, a native of the island, went out one day for a walk with the baby in her arms.

All the roads around Point de Galle wind here and there among the cocoa-nut groves, the luxuriant foliage drooping over them in such a way that one may be in a very secluded and wild place, though within a few minutes' walk of the settlement. It was in some such spot that the nurse met her father, who was, by the way, a hanger-on of the foreigners, and professed to be a Christian, though he was, in reality, a disgrace to the name. Being either intoxicated, or in a frenzy of passion, he attacked the woman with a club and murdered her. While he was beating her, she, in the pain and agony of death, was squeezing little Evy tighter and tighter, and would have killed her in this way—even if the child had been so fortunate as to escape the blows, any one of which would put an end to her frail little life—had not the Cingalese girl I have described, then nearly fifteen, who happened to be passing at the time, rushed bravely forward, and, at the risk of her own life, wrenched apart by main force the arms of the now dying woman, and escaped unhurt with the child. In a short time she appeared before Mr. M——'s house, panting with excitement and the run through the burning heat, and put little Evy in her mother's arms.

The girl could not speak a word of English at that time, but her looks and the blood-stains on her dress told enough. The story was soon spread; but imagine the gratitude of the parents to this little heroine! They took her into their house, that she might still take care of the child she had saved, and had her baptized a Christian. Mrs. M—— gave her the name of Christina in honor of this event, and that is what we called her on the ship. I wish I could remember her pretty Indian name; she told me what it was, but I have forgotten it. The locket she wore contained on one side a picture of little Evy, and on the other these words: "To Christina, from Mr. and Mrs. M——, in grateful remembrance of her heroic conduct in saving the life of their child." Then followed the day of the month and the year in which it happened.

I used to like to hear her talk in broken English. Sometimes she would sing Mother Goose's melodies to the baby with a real quaint, pretty accent. She had a sweet voice, and once in a while I could hear her singing softly in some language I did not understand, what I supposed were some of her rude, native songs.

I asked her how she liked England. She said, "It

very nice, zey very kind to me, but ough! it zo dreadful cold—I most freeze zare."

"Why!" said I, "I live in a country that's colder than England."

"Oh!" she said, opening her large eyes and looking as if she hardly believed me, "colder zan England, how can live zare?"

We had just begun to get acquainted so that she would talk to me, when the little baby was taken sick, and for several days we thought it would die. The bright little creature had enlivened the whole voyage, and a gloom fell over all the passengers during those few days. Christina stayed with it all the time, and I saw very little more of her until a day or two before we reached Point de Galle, when the child was well enough to be brought up on deck.

When we bade them "Good-bye" there were hopes of Evy's recovery, and Christina was in great glee at the idea of being once more on her own beautiful island.

XXXII.

SCENES IN THE TROPICS.

A SUNSET ON THE ARABIAN SEA—POINT DE GALLE—AN OLD SPANISH PRIEST—A BUDDHIST TEMPLE—A COUNTRY RIDE IN CEYLON—THE "AUSTRALIA" AND THE "DELHI"—BAY OF BENGAL—PENANG LAWYERS —HOT, HOTTER, HOTTEST!

STEAMER "DELHI," *Feb.* 9.

WE are now in the Straits of Malacca, steaming on toward the China Sea.

In the Arabian Sea, the evening before we reached Galle, I saw a real tropical sunset, and a rare one too; all the colors of the rainbow, and many strange combinations besides, that I have never before seen, nor expect to see again. The principal color in the western sky was a lurid, burning red, while from the exact spot where the sun touched the horizon, rays of bright, delicately-shaded green shot off and upward in every direction, growing wider and wider until they mingled with the innumerable tints that extended around. We all stood gazing over the stern at the fiery reflection on the ocean and the glowing sky, when I turned, thinking to follow the colors until they faded gradually toward the west; but instead of this, the whole heavens were aglow with a warm, soft tinge of pink, and directly in the east appeared the full moon, as bright and glorious as in the middle of the night—its beauty rather enhanced by its ruddy setting. And now we could not complain of the monotony of the ocean, for if we turned toward the west it seemed bathed in fire, and toward the east danced the cool, silvery reflection of the moon, reaching to the very sides of the vessel. The effect was magical; even the tall masts and spars of the ship, marked against such a sky, seemed weird and unearthly. Any one looking at the passengers then would have thought some mischievous water-witch had been at work, for we all stood as if spellbound, scarcely daring to breathe freely until the last tinge had vanished, and the moon and stars had the sky all to themselves.

I really begin to feel tired of seeing so many wonderful things. It seems as if I were galloping through some wild dream; there is almost too much for one poor little head like mine to manage.

On the first of February we were at anchor in the harbor of Point de Galle. It seemed a beautiful spot after the long stretch of sand and sea we had been passing through. We had hardly seen a green twig since we left the banks of the Nile. Here the cocoa-nut palm grew down to the very edges of the bay, which makes a complete circle, with the exception of the narrow passage by which we entered.

Galle, on the Island of Ceylon, is built on a small peninsula, surrounded by fortifications. We walked to the hotel, where we found a cool veranda to rest upon, for one can not move about five minutes in this climate without being exhausted, at least it is so with foreigners. We were there in the cool part of the year, with the thermometer nearly a hundred in the shade; imagine what it was in the sun! We got a banana-leaf (which, by the way, is three or four feet long), and tore it up in pieces large enough to cover the tops of our heads. It is very thick and smooth, and turned out to be a splendid thing to keep the sun from baking our skulls. Hats and parasols are not of much use by themselves here.

The native waiters at the hotel wore English sidewhiskers and had their long back-hair tucked up and fastened with a tortoise-shell comb.

As it was Sunday morning, the passengers, as soon as they had landed and begun to look around them, started off for the different churches. We drove up to the Catholic chapel, which is situated on a hill outside the fortifications, hoping to hear Mass. We had not been in a church since we left Suez, and would not have another chance for at least a month, perhaps never! (That last misgiving was occasioned by the broken masts and spars which we could see sticking out of the water at the entrance of the harbor, where small boats were going and coming, while men were diving for crew and cargo). When we reached the summit of the hill, we found that the last Mass was over, so all that we could do was to make a visit to the Blessed Sacrament. A little native Catholic boy, with a single short white garment wrapped around his waist —none of the Cingalese children we saw wore *more* than this—and a large rosary hanging around his neck and dangling against his dark skin, led us to a mere shed made of rough boards. This was the chapel! The little Christian who guided us, having obtained the key, unlocked the padlock which secured the door, and opening it for us to enter, kneeled reverently, pointed to the rude lamp burning before the small wooden altar, and left us. In an instant, by some strange freak of association, I thought of the gorgeous interior of St. Peter's, which we had so lately seen. What a contrast! There, we could imagine the glory of Mount Tabor; here, the stable of Bethlehem.

The same Cingalese boy who had opened the chapel door for us, took us to see the priest, who lived close at hand. He led us to a little bungalow, consisting apparently of two rooms. The one in which he left us while he ran around behind the house to announce our arrival, contained benches and a centre-table. That was all. The walls were only built up about five feet from the ground, the roof being supported several feet above them on square pillars, thus leaving the upper part of the room open for the air to circulate through. The walls of the back room—which was, I suppose, the sleeping apartment—were built up to the roof all around. While we were noticing these tropical arrangements, one of the quaintest, the most picturesque figures I have ever seen, entered from that back room, in the person of our host, an old Spanish priest. He was a man of large frame, with a fine head, a whole-souled, genial smile, and a long gray beard that rested on his flowing white cassock. He addressed us first in Spanish, which we did not understand, and then in French. In that language the conversation was continued, a little uneasily at first, for none of us felt at home in it; but the next moment when he learned that we were Catholics, and that Uncle was a priest, his delight knew no bounds. He became very animated, his eyes lighted up, and he began to talk very fast, telling us ever so many interesting things about the country and the missions, and gesticulating vehemently where his French failed him. He would also interrupt himself every now and then in the midst of a strange account of some young Cingalese saint he had visited shortly before, to say, "O, if you could only speak Spanish!" or, "Can you understand my French? It is so bad." Perhaps it was because he noticed how eagerly I listened and how I strained my attention to catch the meaning of his excited words. Surely this old missionary's heart was in his work. He had spent years in the interior of the country, laboring among the natives, and he spoke enthusiastically of the converts to Christianity.

"They are so fervent, so brave, so anxious to be taught," he said.

Now in his old age he had been stationed here at the foreign settlement, and after his ardent apostolate, he seemed to be grieved beyond measure at the negligence and dishonesty of the European Catholics, who were mostly in the employ of the British Government, and held positions which they had gained more or less at the expense of their religion. It was hard to preach Christianity to pagans who were constantly cheated and imposed upon by Christians. However, in spite of every discouragement, he was building a pretty stone church on this same hill, and he showed us his school-house where the Cingalese children were taught. We saw quite a number of them running around with little skirts and beads, like our first acquaintance. Before we left, the old Spanish priest offered us some wine from his own country, which he considered very choice, and only brought out on special occasions. He also showed us his little garden or terrace on a crest of the hill overlooking a dense grove of cocoanut palms.

We next saw a Buddhist temple, which looked like a toy-shop, or a museum of curiosities; there was everything you can imagine, or rather you can not imagine in the way of charms, offerings, and idols, elephants' tusks, tigers' claws, beads, pictures, snake-skins, every kind of monstrosity carved in wood and stone, and painted with glaring colors.

There being an English settlement so near, they had even got European knick-knacks, among others some French dolls, and quite a large picture of a Prussian soldier in full uniform, colored in glowing style, something like the circus bills one sees stuck upon fences. These last seemed to be highly prized, and were put in a conspicuous place to be worshipped with the rest. There happened to be a great festival going on that day; the place was full of people, and two priests were reading Sanscrit from leaves, instead of books, in a monotonous, whining chant. In another apartment we saw Buddha in every size and shape, made of bronze, marble, or ivory, all of beautiful workmanship, but anything but beautiful in form. It was difficult to distinguish the sex of the idols, and the men were very indignant when we asked if one of these seated deities was a woman. The women are all slaves here, more or less. We did not venture to ask many questions after that. In front of the statues were offerings of flowers and eatables. In another place we saw them arranging the image of the sacred elephant, with silver chains and bright clothes, to be carried in a procession, which took place at night, but unfortunately we could not wait on shore to see it.

We had a long ride in the afternoon through the Wakwalla valley, and a fine view at the end of it. How can I tell about a drive in the tropics? I might talk for a week without telling all I saw, that I had never seen before, or the many things that I had not even heard of. It was so strange to see all those tropical fruits growing; there were cocoanuts, pineapples, breadfruit, coffee-trees, cinnamon-trees, nutmegs, jack-fruit.

We saw a stick which, when whittled, smelled at one end of camphor, at the other of cinnamon, and in the middle of cloves. These different kinds of wood had been grafted on the same tree. Then there was the traveller's tree, which looks like an immense palm-leaf fan, and contains water that is drinkable, which you obtain by cutting into a certain part of the leaf. I think it is well named. I could imagine some poor traveller getting lost in one of those tangled jungles and coming across such a tree—what a God-send it would be!

At intervals along the road we saw the pretty little bungalows, with their open verandas, nestled among the foliage; and the native huts of bamboo and palm-leaves, with the naked little black children running around and looking like monkeys, or at least just as wild. Among them we saw a boy who had the leprosy so severely, that his skin had turned as white as an Englishman's. There is another dreadful disease we saw a great deal of here—it is elephantiasis. The foot and ankle swell until they are the size and shape of an elephant's.

We took the "Delhi" at Galle; it is a small ship, with a cargo of opium, but there are only about eight passengers for China, and we have had a very pleasant time playing croquet and whist, with the usual amusement on board ship of indulging in perfect laziness.

The "Australia," in which we came from Suez, is a faster ship than the "Delhi," especially when she had discharged a quantity of her cargo at Galle. We saw her leave the harbor of that town about half an hour after us, but before we were fairly clear of the coast she overtook us. Instead of lessening her speed a little and passing behind us (as her course was north to Calcutta and ours east), she deliberately swept ahead of us and crossed our bows only a few yards in front—which we considered a very cool and uncivil proceeding indeed. It seemed to afford our old fellow-passengers great amusement, and they cheered tremendously, while we of the "Delhi" good-naturedly answered them by making as much noise as our small number would permit.

The only event I remember that relieved the monotony of the voyage through the Bay of Bengal, was one day when a flying-fish flew in at one of the port-holes, which gave us an opportunity of examining it very closely. Uncle kept one of the wings as a curiosity. Afterwards the first mate found a little fish not more than an inch long, with tiny wings, that had been washed on board by the waves. He gave it to me, and the doctor put it up in a vial of spirits of wine, so that I might carry it home.

We have had Bombay pomeloes for dinner several times on board. It is a fruit I never heard of before, though in some of these eastern countries they believe it to have been the "forbidden fruit" of the Garden of Eden. It is a species of orange, only much larger; one would be equal to a dozen ordinary oranges. They have a slightly bitter taste, but are very cool and refreshing, and we found them a great luxury in the hot weather.

Penang is a beautiful little island in the Straits of Malacca, and here we had a second drive through the tropics as interesting as the first. The country was like a continuous park or grove, the roads winding off in every direction. The settlement is called Georgetown, and besides the Europeans and Malays, there are quite a number of Chinese inhabitants. A characteristic of the place are the "Penang Lawyers." They are very strong canes, with great rough, heavy heads, made of a wood peculiar to the island. I dare say they are well named, for when a mighty Briton gets into a quarrel with a native, it is with some such instrument as this that he administers the law.

On February 9th, as I said at the commencement of this letter, we were passing through the Straits of Malacca. If it was hot at Aden and hotter at Galle, it was certainly hottest here, where we were not two degrees from the equator. (When we were so near, it seemed too bad that we could not cross it). Do not imagine I have been writing all this in that latitude; no, indeed, I gave it up in despair before I had written two pages. It made me dizzy to try to think. I did not touch my pen again until we had turned our backs on the equator.

XXXIII.

CHINESE TOWNS AND THE MONSOON.

SINGAPORE — THE MERMEN AGAIN — CHINESE PAGODA — ALMOST AN ACCIDENT—THE CHINA SEA—HONG KONG—CHINESE NEW YEAR— SAMPANS—A FEW PEOPLE—BETWEEN CHINA AND JAPAN.

MONDAY morning, Feb. 10, we found ourselves winding in and out among the hundreds of lovely little islands surrounding Singapore. There had just been one of those short, heavy rains that are, I believe, common to the tropics; it had both cooled the air and made the foliage fresh and green. Near the landing is the "Spirit's Island," which the natives believe to be inhabited by "His Satanic Majesty," so they are very careful not to trespass on his domain.

We saw a ship lying at anchor which has particular charge of the telegraphic cable between Galle and Hong Kong. It was a curiously-shaped affair, with great wheels at each end for drawing up the cable, and all appliances for repairing it, should a break occur. It seems strange to think that telegraph wires run around the world from San Francisco to Japan, and only need to cross the Pacific in order to complete the circle.

When we were moored, what was our surprise to hear the old tune from black heads floating round the vessel, "Hab a dibe, Master—trow sixpence in wat'r—a' right." These Malay boys turned out to be more expert than the Somalis, diving under one side of the vessel and coming out on the other, and being possessed of various marine accomplishments; but I did not think they were as handsome as the little divers at Aden.

The wharf was about two miles from Singapore, and all along the coast were fishing villages. These were nearly all on swampy ground, and some were built out

SINGAPORE.

into the water, on high poles. I do not know what the idea was, for there seemed to be plenty of dry land about.

Singapore is a real Chinese town. We went through streets and streets of their stores, with red and yellow signboards and immense paper lanterns hanging out.

We saw them working at every kind of trade—and the water-carriers, with a bucket hanging at each end of a pole, which they carry across one shoulder. In fact, everything is carried in this way — sometimes with baskets instead of buckets—even animals, as pigs or chickens. The costume of the Chinese coolies, or day-laborers, is very simple. Imagine a garment about the length of the skirt of a Highlander, with a straw hat as large as a parasol, coming up to a peak in the centre, and you have the whole rig. The babies are dressed up in scraps of different-colored cloth, so that they constantly reminded me of the blinking monkeys who go around with organ-grinders.

After great difficulty in making ourselves understood, we succeeded in seeing a Chinese Pagoda. The building looked just like the queer pictures of such things I had seen, with curved roofs and rich, twisted carvings.

When we went in, the devout heathen were lighting fire-crackers, burning paper with Chinese characters on it, and making a great noise and smoke. The building was quite large, having several courts, one inside of another. There were big gods and little ones, devils red, black, and blue. Tables were set before them with offerings of meat, vegetables, fruit, and candy. The evil spirits have the best of everything, for they need to be propitiated and kept in good humor, otherwise they get mischievous, while the other gods are too good to harm any one.

On the opposite side of the road from the temple, as if they too were to honor the gods, theatrical performances were going on under a pretty pavilion. The dresses of the performers were very rich and fantastic. One man evidently represented a clown, and we saw the people laughing at his jokes. The men always sang in a false voice, very high and squeaky. Of course we could not understand what was said, but it was very amusing to watch the acting.

The vessel had received her coal, and we were all ready to leave port at four o'clock in the afternoon, that we might get clear of the islands before dark. How it happened nobody knows, but certain it is that the "Delhi" came within an inch of sending a Chinese junk, or fishing vessel, to the bottom of the sea. Either the fishermen had neglected to hoist their lights, or their nets prevented them from steering. At any rate they were under our bows before the steamer could be turned, and just grazed along the whole length of the vessel, as near as was possible without being knocked to pieces.

The poor fellows were dreadfully frightened, and set up a howl that rang in my ears for days; we were all glad to hear the quarter-master call out from the stern, "All's clear, capt'n!"

My remembrances of the China Sea are very stormy. The second day we were out, the north-east monsoon or trade wind caught us, and we had to struggle against it the whole way up to Hong Kong. The forecastle was raised above the main deck, and most of the time we had a perfect Niagara pouring over there and rolling the length of the vessel.

On the 17th we saw a vessel coming toward us, with her sails all set, and with great speed. It was so provoking to think that the very wind that was taking her along so fast, was keeping us back to the pace of an old lame horse. The wind quieted down, however, as we got under protection of the land, and about eight o'clock that evening we were lying outside the harbor of Hong Kong for the night.

The Chinese New Year's festivities were going on about this time, February 18, and as we appeared before the town, we heard noises very much resembling those of the Fourth of July. The shops were closed,

CHINESE TOWERS.

and everybody out enjoying themselves. The people ride in sedan chairs, carried by two coolies—so did we.

Englishmen and Chinese talk to each other by means of " Pigeon English " (Pigeon means business). To go up-stairs or up a hill is " go up top-side." Bring my hat is " go catchee my piecee hat." If you wish to convey the idea that a man died and went to heaven, you must express yourself thus : " He make sky-pigeon go up top-side."

As we were not well versed in Pigeon English, we had considerable difficulty, and were glad to be back on the vessel, where we could watch the little boats of the natives. They are called sampans, and have two eyes painted — one on each side of the bow; for the Chinese say, " If boat no have eye how can see ? " I am afraid the eyes are not of much use, for when we tried to go ashore in one, it seemed to be knocking and banging into everything. They have bamboo masts, and sails which they manage with great dexterity. These fishermen families seem to be born sailors ; they cook, sleep, and live entirely in the sampans. The women and children manage them perfectly. You see a woman (dressed like the men) with loose pants, and a gown that comes almost to the knee — with a baby tied on her back, sound asleep, with its head bobbing about, while she pulls away at the oars, or attends to the sail; and perhaps half a dozen youngsters are rolling about, making you think every moment they will fall into the water. These little boats are larger than row-boats, with a cover like that of a cradle over one end of them.

Feb. 19.—Left Hong Kong at eight o'clock this morning in the steamer " Behar," commanded by Captain A——. We have a New Zealand quarter-master and Malay crew — fine-looking sailors. The servants are all Chinamen. There is not even a stewardess on board. I am the only human being of the feminine gender on this ship. At each port since we left Egypt, we have dropped some of our old passengers, so that as we continue sailing on around the world, we are

CHINESE VISITING.

thrown more and more on our own resources for amusement and occupation.

At Ceylon we parted with the greater number of our fellow-travellers, among them the interesting Cingalese girl, and the lively English clergyman who wrote poetry about watering-place belles and railroad conductors. At Singapore, if I am not mistaken, we left the enthusiastic little Puseyite who was going to convert the Farther Indians, and who believed in everything Catholic except the Pope. He had his calendar of saints, kept all the fast days, shocked the solid Episcopalians with his very high-church notions, felt hurt when I, as a matter of course, spoke of Catholics when I. meant Roman Catholics, and finally, that he might not become inert and unfit for his calling during the hot and lazy voyage through the Indian Ocean, he chased a cat up and down the deck every evening until he was completely exhausted and in a profuse perspiration. Then at Hong Kong we said farewell to the pleasant young Englishman and his charming bride (my only lady companion for weeks) who had come all the way from Southampton by water, who had both been sea-sick the greater part of the time, and who, in spite of these trying circumstances, had remained just as devoted and as attentive to each other as true lovers could be. Japan was to have been their final destination, but the China Sea had tossed them so unmercifully that they had to land at Hong Kong to recruit their strength before attempting to cross the Eastern Sea. So now our companions have dwindled down to two or three oddities, among them a young English sportsman on his way back to Japan after a trip to his native land. According to the story of the purser on the "Australia," he once shot two cormorants and presented them to a lady in Yokohama, having been persuaded by a friend that they were wild ducks. Discovering his blunder, he sent his office-boy to buy some ducks in the town, and hasten to change them for the cormorants which he knew to be still lying on the lady's back piazza. The stupid boy bought live ducks. The next time that the gallant young hunter dined with his lady friend, she called him to account for the remarkable fact that his game had resurrected shortly after being presented to her. This is only one of the stories we heard at the expense of our sportsman.

Our particular friends on the ship, however, are two other young men. One of them is very business-like; he has been sent out by one of the great English foundries to establish branch houses in the colonies, and he talks learnedly about guns, locks, and all kinds of iron things. He is accompanied by his brother-in-law, a very sentimental young man, with a trunk full of the works of the poets. He repeats poetry of all kinds by the hour on star-light nights, but he is principally devoted to the effusions of Eliza Cook, a volume of whose works is ever in his hand. Uncle and I have been trying to teach these two to play whist with us. The iron genius has learned to play quite a good game, but the Eliza Cookist, who is generally my partner, when any question of "thirteener" or "returning the lead" comes up, looks piteously across the table, rolls his eyes, and begins to spirt poetry. If predictions come true, we shall have too much tossing between China and Japan to play many more games of whist. At present we are sheltered by the Chinese coast, and the scenery is very interesting. We have once more crossed the boundary line of the North Temperate Zone, and it is getting very cold.

Feb. 20.—Still following the coast to keep out of the monsoon as long as possible. We are passing islands,

islands, islands, all mountainous—this is broken China sure enough. The captain is splendid. He mimics Chinese songs to perfection, and sometimes he sings with the sailors as they haul the ropes.

Feb. 21.—We have now cleared the island of Formosa and are out in the Eastern Sea. It is rough.

Feb. 22.—Rougher—bumps, bruises, and broken dishes. It was fearful to watch the sailors trying to furl one of the large sails during the gale, by clinging to the masts and rigging with their legs or with one hand, while they unfastened it with the other—suspended, as they were, high in the air and directly over the water. Some of the pulleys got out of place and the ropes tangled, while the great, loosened sail was flapping back and forth in a wild fury. It added to the clamor of the wind and the waves. The captain had to fairly roar out his orders from the poop-deck, and I thought every moment that some of the men would be knocked off into the sea.

Feb. 25.—The last three days have been very much alike. The monsoon beats against us. The vessel leans more than ever. The swinging lamps in the saloon make an angle with the posts of about forty-five degrees; the floor is a steep hill. Uncle and I sit on the high side of the table, and our soup, tea, and oranges go over into the laps of the iron genius and the Eliza Cookist. Occasionally the ship makes a jerk the other way, then we are at the bottom of the hill. To-day my trunk was dashed against the door of my state-room, so I could not get in until the steward came to my assistance. The other evening I neglected to put my shoes, comb, and brush in the little brackets made to hold them, so they were banging about the cabin all night at the risk of my eyes and nose.

Feb. 26.—Off the coast of Japan; beautiful scenery:

Fusiyama in the distance, snow-peaked; it is the sacred mountain. Anchored near Yokohama at night.

ANCHORED NEAR YOKOHAMA AT NIGHT.

XXXIV.

UNCLE'S OTHER CHAPTER.

THE MARTYR-FIELD OF JAPAN—THE MODERN MISSIONARIES AND THEIR WORK—RESULTS OF ST. FRANCIS XAVIER'S LABORS—TWELVE THOUSAND NATIVE CHRISTIANS DISCOVER THEMSELVES TO THE BISHOP—OTHERS INACESSIBLE—JAPANESE SIGHTS—VESTIGES OF A JESUIT MARTYR AT YEDO.

YOKOHAMA, *March* 7.

DEAR REVEREND FATHER:—I trust long before this you have received my letter written at Cairo, in which I endeavored to give you, in some sort, a graphic representation of the Coptic rites as they appear to the eyes of an uninitiated observer. This present letter finds me on another ground of equal interest to Catholic Christians, namely, the martyr-field of Japan. I send you a few items of intelligence, hastily enough picked up and jumbled together, which may, nevertheless, have something of the attraction of novelty. To me, at least, there is a holy charm in the thought that I am in Japan; and as I say my early morning Masses in the little Catholic Chapel of Yokohama, beneath the statue of St. Francis Xavier, I can easily fancy myself surrounded by invisible eyes that watch over this sacred soil with intense interest as the scene of their missionary labors, and I feel that the breath of martyrs is in the air. I do not mean to say that any early Catholic history is connected with the precise spot where I now write. I am not aware that the early missionaries penetrated to this side of the island of Nippon, nor do I know the contrary; but this I know—that I am in Japan, and that the names of neighboring towns and islands which I hear pronounced in every day's discourse, are familiar names in the history of St. Francis Xavier, and of the early missionaries and martyrs of Japan. I will tell you personally all I know of the remains of this earlier Christianity. First, however, a few words in regard to what the Catholic Church is doing here in our day.

The missions in Japan were re-opened in 1858 by the French missionaries of the Congregation called Les Missions Etrangères, an Order distinguished in the annals of the propagation of the faith, and which, to the best of my knowledge and belief, has given more martyrs to the Church in our day than any other society. These fathers at first commenced their labors on one of the small islands south of Nagasaki, called Loo Choo. In 1870, when by treaties with different nations, Japan was opened to some extent to foreign occupation and commerce, the fathers came to Yokohama, then called Kanagawa. They now number thirty missionaries, and have seven stations; namely, at Nagasaki, Kobi, Osaka, Yokohama, Yedo or Tokio, Hakodate, and Niigata. They are presided over by Monsignor Petitjean, from Autun, in France, both as Superior of the Order and as bishop. The church and mission at Yokohama, where the bishop resides, is committed to the more immediate charge of the Rev. Père Pettier, who has learned to speak and preach in English, and devotes his personal attention to the foreign population.

Every one of the towns above named (Yedo excepted) has about twenty miles square assigned to them by treaty as limits within which foreigners are allowed to reside, and beyond which they must not venture without an epecial permission and passport of the government. This, of course, constitutes also the boundary to which the labors of the missionary are restricted. The government is especially jealous of all Christianity, and stands ready to check any appearance of successful propagation of it, although to a certain extent it is tolerated. Christian schools are not allowed by law. The Catholic seminary at Yedo exists only by toleration, and the first students were taken into the house in the nominal capacity of servants.

I said a little while ago that I did not know of Christianity having spread in earlier days to this part of the island. From the Rev. Père Pettier, who has just left my room, I now know that it did extend to Yedo, which is only twenty miles to the northward on the same coast and in the same bay. Only a few days ago one of the fathers of the Yedo seminary discovered in that city a small bridge, called by the people, the Christian Bridge; and near by it a declivity or side hill which goes by the name of Christian's Hill, which contains the grave of a Christian martyr. The pagan population have not only preserved this tradition, and these relics, but (what is far more remarkable) they consider the spot to be sacred. They come there to pray, and, if their statements may be trusted, these prayers are sometimes answered by the healing of their diseases, and in particular by the restoring of sight to the blind. There is, moreover, in the same city a street which has always borne the name of Christian street.

It is well known to the Catholic missionaries that Catholics are still to be found in the northern part of this island. Not long since, an attempt was made to establish a communication with them and furnish them with a priest. A catechist went up there and commenced a school. He then petitioned the government for permission to bring one of the fathers of the Missions Etrangères to his school as professor, which was at first granted. This was not favorable to the views of certain officials of the Russian Empire, which loves Japan as bears love honey. They represented that the object of the petition was not to promote education, but to teach religion, and the Japanese authorities were induced to retract their permission.

It was, however, in the southern parts of Japan that St. Francis Xavier and the missionaries who followed his footsteps had succeeded best in the establishment of the Catholic faith, and there it is one would most naturally look for any remaining evidences of their work. During a visit of Mgr. Petitjean to Nagasaki in 1864, he saw one day in the mission church an old Japanese woman, who was praying beneath a statue of the Blessed Virgin. Something peculiar in her manner attracted his attention, and, on inquiring, he discovered that she did not belong to Nagasaki, and was not known to any of the missionaries.

She seemed to be afraid to be spoken to, and answered questions with great reluctance. On being pressed, she acknowledged that she had a religion which was not like the religion of the country. Holy men had taught it in the land, she said, long, long ago, but these were all dead and gone, and there were no teachers of her religion left. Being confident that she was a Catholic, and one that derived her faith from the old plantation, the bishop endeavored to assure her. He told her that he knew all about these early teachers, that he himself was a priest of the same religion, and that he and others like him had come to preach that religion once more, and establish the old worship again amongst them. It was not until she had catechized him very closely that she gave him full confidence, and became satisfied that she was in a true Catholic church, and in presence of a real priest. She then acknowledged openly that she was a Christian, and said that the neighboring islands were full of others like herself who held to that faith, though secretly and in constant fear of persecution. She had heard of the arrival of strange missionaries at Nagasaki, and had come there, though with great fear and caution, to see if perhaps they were not like those who had brought the faith to Japan three hundred years before. Joyfully now she returned home to announce the glad tidings to the rest. The missionaries soon found themselves surrounded by a multitude of native Christians, very ignorant indeed of many things belonging to their religion, but nevertheless clinging to it most firmly and affectionately. About twelve thousand of these have thus far reported themselves in the small islands near Nagasaki. But unhappily the enthusiasm with which they crowded to welcome the fathers aroused the attention of the Japanese government, and gave rise to a new persecution. Great numbers of the native Christians were arrested and imprisoned. They could no longer come to Nagasaki without punishment, nor were the fathers allowed to visit them at their houses. It is supposed that at least sixty thousand more Catholics are in Japan who are afraid to make themselves known. Without priests, without any authorized or qualified teachers—without any means of offering the Christian sacrifice, or maintaining any public worship, without the succor and consolation of the sacraments, and all the while in constant dread and fear of persecution, is it not wonderful that this poor hunted and isolated band of believers should have maintained the Catholic faith for so many generations? Only one sacrament was left to them—the sacrament of baptism—and this has been perpetuated amongst them by a class of men whom they call baptizers, who know what is requisite to valid baptism, and transmit the knowledge to others.

It is to be hoped that ere long these Japanese Christians will be able to communicate freely with the missionaries who are so near them. At present those who come over to Nagasaki to visit the church, to hear Mass and receive the sacraments, dare only come by

TEMPLE, WITH TOMBS OF THE MIKADOS, AT KAMAKURA.

night, and are instructed to come in bands of not more than twenty at one time. When the fathers go to the islands to visit the sick, it is by night also, and dressed in the native costume; any open attempt to propagate the faith, or even to communicate with the native Catholics outside of the treaty limits, would arouse the jealousy of the government, and draw down its anger upon their heads.

I shall not attempt to give you any description of Japan or the Japanese. In a stay of twelve days in a strange country, one does not become very learned, although he sees a great deal that is novel and interesting. We have been to Yedo and to Kamakura; the latter is said to have been once the capital until it was destroyed by an earthquake.

We have seen the great sphinx-like bronze idol of Daibootz, who holds his head some seventy feet high (so I am told, but I could not measure it). He has the same brooding, introverted look which characterizes the sphinx. We went inside of him, but did not find much there worth contemplating. Exteriorly regarded, however, he is a grand thing to see, and really a wonderful piece of art. It is a far more colossal figure than the great statue of Bavaria at Munich, for that is standing, while Daibootz is represented in a sitting posture. We saw from the eastward, as we entered the gulf of Yedo, the sacred mountain Fusiyama, 14,000 feet high, with its foot in the sea, and its head hooded with snow—a perfect cone of grandeur and beauty, and superior to anything of the kind I have ever seen or ever conceived. We have wandered about among the native booths both in Yedo and Yokohama, and seen much that is strange, curious, and beautiful. But it would take too much both of space and time to tell of these things as they should be told, and I therefore leave it all until some day when, God willing, we two may have the privilege to sit together once more, and talk the time away at leisure. For the present, farewell, and may God have us both in His holy keeping until we meet again.

Ever faithfully, your friend and brother,
C. A. WALWORTH.

In connection with Uncle's allusion to the spot known as the Christian's Hill at Yedo, and the miracles said to be performed there, I have taken the liberty of adding another account of the same place, written by a Protestant missionary. It was clipped from the *New York Evangelist*, and is, I think, quite *apropos:*

"It seems that over two hundred years ago, a Jesuit missionary, an Italian, by the name of Jean Baptiste, attempted to enter Japan in disguise (after the Christian religion had been rooted out at Nagasaki and elsewhere), and being discovered, he was brought to Yedo, and confined a prisoner on this 'slope.' He had come to Japan in a Portuguese vessel, and was smuggled ashore at night; but after this nothing was heard of him, although there have been several mentions of his mysterious disappearance in some Italian books on the subject of Jesuitical missions. However, while engaged in translating some years ago, Dr. Brown came across an old Japanese volume marked, 'Whoever reads this, please don't tell,' (!) and in it he found a complete and minute record of all that ever happened to this Jesuit 'Jean,' and the entire account of his mode of capture and long confinement on this very 'slope' where we were then talking. It told of the methods used also by the Japanese to gain information from him concerning foreign countries, and of the strict manner in which he was guarded, lest he should induce others to embrace his Christian heresy; even as it was, I believe he was instrumental in converting two or three persons about the prison! Dr. Brown sent an account of this man, and a partial translation of this curious book, to an Asiatic society in China some years ago. But I do not know if any information on the subject has ever been published."

XXXV.

THE JAPANESE.

QUEER !—FUSIYAMA—JAPANESE ART — CURIOSITY — JAPANESE HOUSES AND CUSTOMS—GIN-RIK-SHARS—DAIBOOTZ.

PACIFIC OCEAN, STEAMSHIP "ALASKA."

JAPAN is a funny place, though there are a few very beautiful things; Fusiyama, the Temples of Shiba at Yedo, and the great idol of Daibootz, are grand, but everything else we saw was funny, even we ourselves were funny, at least to the Japanese. If we showed ourselves in public, we caused as much amusement as a Kentucky giant or a baby elephant.

The first sight of Fusiyama (burning mountain) was glorious, as we neared it from the sea. Imagine, if you can, a volcanic mountain fourteen thousand feet high, standing entirely alone, sloping down to the water's edge, with its summit covered with snow, and directly behind it the setting sun. Can you wonder the Japanese call it "Sacred Mountain," and worship it? I am sure I would too, if I had nothing better to adore than their old, sleepy-looking gods and dancing demons. It is very seldom you see a Japanese picture or work of art without Fusiyama in the background.

Yokohama is a queer mixture in the way of nationalities. From the window of my room, which overlooked a part of the foreign settlement, I could see the British, French, and United States garrisons, distinguished by the flags and the uniforms of the sentinels. They are all situated on a steep hill or cliff, washed on two sides by the bay, and separated by a creek from the town.

One could not help thinking that, with this well-chosen little corner, and the half dozen men-of-war lying in the harbor, the "foreign barbarians" might protect themselves against the "Mighty Empire of the

FUSIYAMA.

Rising Sun," should the latter feel inclined to resent their presence.

I had not a very grand idea of Japanese art, judging from the specimens I had seen in America on paper fans. Now I can fully appreciate their genius and correctness of drawing from nature—those fans give you a better idea of the natives of Japan than the most learned description possibly could. The dress, the attitudes, the expressions are perfect. I can not say as much for their landscapes, though Uncle admires them very much.

I really believe the Japanese are the most direct descendants of Eve, and each one has inherited twice her share of curiosity. We amused ourselves often, just counting how many top-knots would pop in at the door of our room during the course of an hour, to see what we were about. Fortunately, they expect other people to be curious too, and are rather pleased than otherwise, to show you everything they have. We walked out several times into the country around Yokohama, among the rice fields. They would let us go into their houses and look at whatever we wanted to see, and they, in turn, looked at us; we examined their costume and they ours; we amused ourselves laughing at what was comical about them, as they did with us. It was a mutual entertainment. Their houses are all low, rarely more than one story, and built of very light wood, on account of the frequent shocks of earthquakes. We only entered the dwellings of the common people, of course; those of the nobility and princes are on a much grander scale, though, I believe, the general plan is the same. The houses we saw were mostly made very neatly of clay or earth of some kind, plastered into a light bamboo framework, and sometimes over this a kind of rough matting. The roofs are thatched with rice-straw, made into a pretty ornament at the top, and the entire front of the house consists of paper screens, that slide backwards and forwards, serving for both doors and windows. These same contrivances form the divisions of the different rooms, so that they all can be slid aside, making the house into a single apartment. If the cottage is large, a hall, or rather pathway, runs through it from front to back, which has no other floor than the bare ground. The rooms on each side are raised about

A Garden.

a foot and a half above this, and are covered with a very pretty white matting, that is always most scrupulously clean, serving for both chairs and table. It is considered a great want of politeness to enter a person's house without first leaving your sandals at the door. The people all wear a sock or shoe (of dark blue cloth generally), which fits the foot just as a mitten does the hand, leaving the big toe separated from the rest. A strap passes between the toes in a way that will hold on the sandals, which are made either of wood or of thick braided straw. The little children observe this rule as strictly as the grown people, and as you pass by you see the different-sized sandals of all the family standing at the doors. The houses are nearly always thrown open, so you can watch the people sitting on their mats and working away at their various trades, or if it happens to be chowchow time, the chop-sticks are flying. The only fires they have are made of charcoal, in little, highly-polished boxes about a foot square. They are sometimes very finely carved, and, among the wealthy, cast in bronze.

We would sometimes sit down in a tea-house to rest and watch the Japanese as they came in, take their small cup of clear, strong tea (without milk or sugar), while warming their fingers over a little charcoal-box. Then they would begin to smoke. The bowl of their pipe holds about half as much as a thimble, and after every puff, they knock out the tobacco and put in fresh. As they have to light them so often, they could not manage very well without the charcoals.

I am sure our American friends would laugh if they could see Uncle or me riding in a gin-rik-shar. It is just like a baby-carriage, with two wheels, except, instead of a handle in front, there are shafts, and a man runs between them to pull you along. The gin-rik-shar holds one man, but it is "*the* thing" in Japan—everybody uses it, natives and foreigners. I laughed as much the first time I tried one as I did when going through Belfast in a jaunting-car. The men who draw them are wonderfully strong. (They are small, too ; it is so with all the Japanese ; none of them seem to be much larger than I am.)

One day Uncle and I rode forty miles—out to Daibootz and back—in gin-rik-shars, with two men to each. We started at eight o'clock in the morning, were on a good trot all day over mountains as well as meadows, and when we reached Yokohama in the evening, the men ran through the streets as fast as if they had been perfectly fresh. It was wonderful. We only stopped twice on the way—once at a tea-house, where they took their chowchow of rice and tea, and a short smoke ; then started off for Kamakura, winding among the rice-fields for miles and miles on narrow paths, where it would be impossible for a horse to go. As we got farther into the country, we became more and more objects of curiosity, many of the people probably never having seen a European lady before, though, of course, there are often gentlemen travelling within the " treaty limits." The peasants would run to the doors as we passed by, and once we found ourselves right in the midst of a crowd of children just out of school. Oh ! what a shout they raised. You see, boys are the same all over the world.

At Kamakura, which was the old capital of Japan before Yedo, our gin-rik-shar boys (all Japanese and Chinamen are " boys " or " Johns " in Pigeon English) took their second rest, while we went to visit the temples. Besides a meteoric stone, which they worship, and a vast number of hideous idols, we saw the triumphal sedan-chairs in which the daimios or princes of Japan are carried in grand processions. They were very rich with gilt and lacquer, that peculiar

Japanese varnish that makes wood look like colored ivory.

About noon we reached Daibootz, the great object of our excursion. It is an immense bronze statue, at least seventy feet high, as it sits cross-legged on a low pedestal. It is in the centre of a sacred grove, quiet

DAIBOOTZ—THE GREAT STATUE OF BUDDHA, JAPAN.

and beautiful as can be. As you approach it through an avenue of spreading trees, the branches drooping gracefully around the figure, as it sits with its hands lying together in its lap, and the eyes cast down, with a meditative expression on the features, the whole effect is solemn and enchanting.

After seeing so many ugly monsters, not only in the

temples, but in every private house, all of which have little shrines, it was an agreeable surprise to find such a work of art as Daibootz, the Jupiter of the Japanese gods.

At the end of the long avenue was a curiously-shaped gate, peculiar to the country, guarded on either side by a fiery-red devil or evil spirit. We sat down under one of these and ate our lunch, under his special superintendence, I dare say. On our way home I learned another new thing—the Japanese use that soft paper of theirs for pocket-handkerchiefs. Good idea, saves washing.

XXXVI.

YEDO.

MUD—TEMPLES OF SHIBA—HAIR TOP-NOTS—ATOGAYAMA—THE "BURNT DISTRICT"—A CHOWCHOW HOUSE—A JAPANESE THEATRE—A DAY GAINED.

UNFORTUNATELY we chose a rainy day for visiting Yedo. The streets are not paved and they have no sidewalks, so we were covered with mud, and missed one or two sights. We would have stayed over night, but there are no good European hotels in the city, and we did not like the idea of "putting up" at a Japanese house for fear of being embarrassed with chopsticks and such things.

However, we saw much more than we expected, and had a merry day of it. The only railroad in Japan runs between Yokohama and Yedo, so that part of the trip was easily accomplished. We had a paper given to us before we started, with the names of what we wanted to see, written in English and Japanese, so we could show it to the driver and point to the latter. First of all, we went to the temples of Shiba, which are, really, the principal things to be seen in the great city. They are a number of temples built over the burial-places of the Tycoons or Emperors of Japan. Like all of their sacred buildings, they are in a grove, and in examining them one can not help admiring their good taste; inside and out, everything is in such perfect harmony. Though they are very richly ornamented and colored, they do not look gaudy. When we were going to enter the largest temple the little shaven-headed Bonze (priest) who showed us around, informed us that we must take

A Chinese Street Scene.

off our shoes—rather an unwelcome request on such a cold, damp day. At the appearance of a boo (about twenty-five cents) his conscientious scruples vanished, and we were allowed to enter at a side door, boots and all. The American Minister at Yokohama told us he had not thought of the boo expedient, and so rather than take off his boots went away without seeing the inside of the temples at all.

We saw more shows and temples, pagodas, and pleasure grounds during the day than I can remember. Among other things at Asakusa, was an old wooden idol, with the features all worn off so that his head looked like a round ball. While I was looking at it a woman with a child came up and began rubbing his face and hands in an affectionate way. I afterwards heard that he was one of their gods of health, and they believed some virtue from the part of the idol they rubbed would be imparted to the sick man and cure him. Another curious custom is this: when a man is very sick and expects to die, he will cut off the little top-knot the Japanese always wear, and send it to the temple of the god of health as an offering. This is the greatest sacrifice he could make. Not very far from Yedo there is an old temple where there are thousands of these hair top-knots hanging around the walls.

After we had seen Shiba we ascended the hundred steps of Atogayama to an elevation from which we could have had a fine view of the city on a clear day. As it was, we saw the low houses stretching off in the distance, far as the eye could reach, with here and there a pagoda towering up. I have a better idea of the size of the place from the hours we spent in riding through it. I thought we should never reach the castle, which was at the other end of the city from Shiba. It is here that the present Mikado resides. I think it is surrounded by six distinct walls and moats. We went inside of three, which is as far as strangers can go without a permit.

The next thing on our programme was to find something to eat. We looked over our "interpretation paper" and found the words "chowchow house," "foreign food." The driver understood what we wanted and started off. We drove for at least three-quarters of a mile through the "burnt district," where a great conflagration had taken place, not a year ago, and now there was not a vacant space to be seen—every house was built up. The spot was only distinguishable by the clean, new wood-work. Great fires are as common in the cities of Japan as earthquakes; I am told they have from three to five a month.

We found the chowchow house to be very nice, and though nobody spoke English, they had a table set in European style, with knives, forks, and spoons. All the family came to have a peep at us, and though we could not speak a word which they could understand, they took it for granted that they knew what we wanted, and before long the courses began to come one after another. I thought they would never stop; at last we had to call out enough. Not only call out, but gesticulate in the most decided manner, before they ceased bringing up something more. There was only one dish we had any misgivings about—it certainly savored of kitten! Perhaps they thought they were giving us a great treat. When we were ready to leave, the man brought us a bill written out in Japanese, which Uncle keeps as a curiosity. As this gave him no clue to the price, he began pulling out the rios and the boos until the man appeared satisfied. The house had two stories and we were up-stairs, the first floor being the Japanese tea-house. With so much paper and light work it seemed more like a doll house than a real dwelling, and one could not help wondering how they keep the children from knocking them to pieces, and kicking holes in the screens.

We had been to see everything that was marked on our paper, but we still had several hours before us, so we decided to find out a theatre. Somebody had told us it was very amusing. After wasting a good deal of time we succeeded in reaching the theatre. From the front it looked like all the other houses, but we went up a flight of stairs and found ourselves in the gallery, looking down on the audience and the stage. We were seated on mats in little places about three feet square, separated from each other by divisions about a foot high. The pit was crowded with people, sitting cross-legged on the floor, which was partitioned off the same way in little squares holding four persons each. We noticed them passing around Japanese sweetmeats and tea during the performance. The people seemed very much interested; at one time they would be in tears, then again they would cry out indignantly, as the piece changed from pathetic to cruel. To us, however, it was all comical, and, being in a conspicuous place, in constant dread of offending the sensitive Japs, we suffered the most excruciating pangs of suppressed laughter. The acting seemed to be most extravagant, with a great deal of raving and flourishing of swords, and the piece ended by somebody's head being cut off and rolling on the stage. Between each scene a band of musicians made very squeaky, noisy music on strange instruments.

The scenery was very rudely represented, and there were men in black masks who crept around to arrange it. For instance, there was a blind man in the play who was wandering around and came to a river, or rather the river came to him. It was represented by a long piece of cloth painted with wavy blue lines, which was jerked slowly up by a string from the far end of the room opposite the stage. This wonderful stream flowed right along through the audience on the passage-way or aisle, which was raised about a foot from the floor, and was on a level with the stage. It was ridiculous to see this thing coming up to the place where the crazy actor was groping his way. As soon as the would-be river came near enough, he rushed madly towards it, put his foot in the blue waves, and then shrank back affrighted. At another time in his wanderings the old man was to fall off a precipice. This was represented by a green box perpendicular on one side and sloping on the other with a tree stuck in the top, which the supposed-to-be-invisible men in masks pushed into the middle of the stage. The old man climbed up the sloping side and fell off the other, when the hill once more disappeared in a supernatural manner. They had also a remarkable way of pushing stools under the actors when they wanted to sit down, giving a most comical effect. I enjoyed that theatre more than anything I had seen for a long time. We laughed over it for a week or more.

On the 10th of March we left Yokohama in the Pacific mail steamer "Alaska," which is paddling instead of screwing us across the great ocean while I write. Just as we were leaving Japan we met and exchanged news with the "Colorado" from San Francisco, and since that we have had the whole ocean to ourselves until to-day, March 30, when a vessel was seen on the horizon. Perhaps you will wonder what we have been doing with ourselves all those twenty-one days. That is answered in a few words—trying to make the time pass. There are about six hundred and thirty Chinese coolies in the steerage. These, with a cargo of Japan tea and eight first-class passengers, have been our fellow-travellers, together with the birds, a species of albatross, that have followed us all the way. The day we crossed the 180th meridian of longitude, was Sunday, and as that is the place where the extra day is tacked on, which one makes in going around the world, we had two Sundays in succession, both being the 22d of March. Had we kept on with the usual way of counting we should have been a day wrong at San Francisco.

There are two Japanese young men on board who are going to America to study engraving. They do look too ridiculous in European clothes! One of them made an India-ink sketch on Japanese paper of our little boy passenger. It is a very good likeness, with one exception; he made the little fellow's eyes slant like a Jap's—just imagine!

During the voyage a Chinaman died, and his body is being taken with us to be sent back to China by the next steamer. It is so with every Chinaman that dies abroad, for they believe they can not go to heaven unless buried in China.

XXXVII.

TWENTY-FIVE DAYS ON THE PACIFIC.

THE WAVES RISE AND THE RAIN FALLS — HOW WE PASSED THE TIME — "YOU SAVEZ" — SEA-BIRDS AND THEIR FLIGHT — APRIL FOOL'S DAY.

TWENTY-FIVE days at sea—a long time without seeing a foot of dry land, and not even a vessel to keep us company on the waste of waters. Yet such was our voyage from Japan to San Francisco—a part of our journey we had long looked forward to with a vague dread, and when the time came, it was with some misgivings that we bade adieu to Yokohama and its inhabitants—for even if they were heathens they were human beings and better company than the fishes—and consigned ourselves to the tender mercies of the winds and waves of the mightiest of oceans—the broad Pacific.

But we were homeward bound—a thought that did much to keep up our spirits during those first stormy days, while the great steamer puffed its way slowly through the tossing water and the dreary rain, for it was the equinoctial season, and nothing can be more forlorn than drizzling, rainy weather at sea. Everything was so fearfully damp, the waves slushing against the sides of the vessel, the rain dripping, dropping everywhere, running in little streams over the deck, trickling from the masts and shrouds, hissing against the steampipes, and soaking into the clothes of the sailors, who looked like drowned rats hurrying around; while every thing one touched on the vessel seemed damp and sticky; and the few passengers huddled together near the steam-heaters, until really one began to think we would all be absorbed or sink away into rain-drops or mist like Undine and her mysterious old uncle.

Many times a day our thoughts, too eager to keep pace with the plodding motion of the steamer, would span an airy bridge across the hundreds of leagues that separated us from the coast of America, across which we could travel backwards and forwards at will and refresh ourselves with imaginary glimpses of what was going on in our "ain countree."

We did many things to hurry up old Time, who seemed to have lost his flying propensities, some of which would make one smile.

I remember one day when Uncle and I, in a desperate effort at amusing ourselves, resorted to "tit-tat-toe" on an old slate that happened to be near, and spent several hours at this novel and interesting game.

At another time, the table-cloth in the saloon being checked in red and white squares, we played checkers on it by portioning off a certain part of it for the board, and using silver dollars for the white men and large copper pennies for the black ones. Any one not understanding the idea might have supposed we were gambling in some outlandish fashion, "a la Japanese," for instance.

The carpenter of the ship, finding us so destitute of games, kindly volunteered to make us a backgammon-board and checkers, which, though rude, were quite a success, especially as he had only his heavy carpenter tools to work with. The board consisted of a square piece of wood, planed on one side, on which the points were painted in red and black, with a long strip of paint down the centre dividing the two parts of the board, which did not fold over. The checkers were little round blocks of wood, and for dice-boxes we used Japanese boxes of bamboo. As the eight cabin passengers — all gentlemen except myself and one lady who had a little boy — became better acquainted, we played whist, bezique, and backgammon as regularly every day as the sun rose and set. I doubt if any of them have as great a relish for those games since then.

I varied these occupations by building block houses for the little boy and telling him stories until my ingenuity was almost exhausted. He was a bright little fellow, who had been born in China and had always been under the care of a Chinese nurse, so he spoke "Pigeon English" with as much or even more fluency than his mother-tongue, and always began or ended his sentences with "you savez," a combination of English and French, which is sprinkled most plentifully through every conversation in "Pigeon English," that remarkable mixture of languages. "You savez" is the key to everything; it is the first thing an Englishman learns on going to China, and indeed new-comers are apt to think that if they open a phrase with these words, and say all the rest in good English, that no Chinaman can fail to understand them.

One day our little friend went to the stewardess to get something to eat, and said :

"Stewardess, mamma say give me bread and butter," then a happy thought having struck him, he added, looking up at her with "a smile that was childlike and bland," "butter on two sides, topside and bottomside, you savez?"

"No," said the stewardess, "I don't savez."

An invariable source of interest on board were the birds, a species of albatross, that followed the vessel from coast to coast, during the whole twenty-five days, now gathering around in great numbers, then scattering off and lagging behind, sometimes disappearing entirely except one or two, then flocking in again from every direction. They would fly for hours and hours without resting, until one would think that they must drop from sheer exhaustion; but they only lighted on the water when something was thrown overboard to them, or to devour some unwary fish that came too near the surface. They would then settle on the waves and fold down their great wings, which were about four feet from tip to tip, so that they looked something like ducks. In resuming their flight they would run along on the water for some distance with outstretched feet and wings and start from the top of a wave.

What renders the flight of these birds so majestic and impressive is that they sail along quietly and noiselessly without flapping their wings, except when they raise or lower themselves or turn off in a different direction; they seem to tack with the wind like a sailing vessel, taking a zigzag course when it is not fair. We noticed that when there was no breeze at all they flapped their wings much more frequently. Some of the passengers tried to catch them by fastening pieces of meat to the end of a long cord and letting it dangle behind the vessel. The idea was that the bird would swallow the meat and they could then draw it in by the cord. A cruel, mean way, it seemed, to take such splendid creatures. They were not, however, successful. The motion of the steamer was too rapid to allow the birds time to swallow the bait. Several times they caught it in their hooked beaks, but it was jerked out before they could be taken.

We had a great deal of fun among the passengers on April Fool's day. In the morning we had cotton fish-balls for breakfast. This put us on our guard at dinner, but everything went on as usual until it came to the dessert. A very tempting frosted cake was placed before the captain and he began to cut it. He tried and tried with several different knives, but all to no purpose. He made no impression on the cake, and thought it must be very stale. Finally he succeeded in knocking off a piece of the icing and the knife struck something with a ringing sound. The captain now turned the cake upside down, showing an empty tin-pan, which disclosure was received with a roar of laughter.

The baker made very nice white cream candy, which had been frequently on the table. Noticing its resemblance to chalk, I suggested to the captain a day or two before that it would be a splendid chance for an April Fool. So when I saw the dish of candy on the table I followed it, as it was being handed around, with great interest. One or two of the passengers tasted it, discovered the joke, but very prudently kept it to themselves. A young Englishman just opposite me, however, took the largest piece on the dish and put it all in his mouth. He instantly snatched it out again, showing his tongue and the inside of his mouth perfectly white. Those who knew the joke now fairly shouted, calling the attention of every one else to the fearful faces he was making over the dose he had taken. In the midst of our merriment the vessel suddenly stopped, and the faces all changed from laughter to a look of seriousness and alarm. Ignorant of the cause, it was with a strange thrill that we found ourselves arrested in mid-ocean, a deadly stillness succeeding to the rumbling of the machinery. It was, however, only a slight breakage in the engine and we were soon moving again, though less rapidly than before.

XXXVIII.

CHINESE EMIGRANTS.

THE "ALASKA" AND HER CAPTAIN — THE CHINESE KITCHEN, CABINS, AND OPIUM-SMOKING-ROOM — JOYFUL MESSENGERS — THE GOLDEN GATE — COUNTING THE CHINAMEN — ASHORE AT LAST.

The steamer "Alaska," which stopped so suddenly with us in the midst of the Pacific, and which has since been driven ashore on the coast of China, though we have not been able to learn any of the particulars, was a magnificent vessel of unusual size. But it was not a very good ocean steamer either for speed or safety, having paddle-wheels instead of a screw. It had six distinct decks—even a house six stories high is a rare thing; imagine then such an one, lengthened and moulded into the form of a ship, what a monster it would be floating on the water. The "Alaska" was fitted out with all the magnificence of a Hudson river steamer.

The captain was proportioned in size to his vessel; he had a gigantic stature and great strength, a very commanding appearance, and was an experienced seaman—in fact, had run away from home when a boy to become a sailor, and had fought his way up through every kind of hardship. He seemed just the man to take the charge and responsibility, and a heavy one it was, of that great vessel with its rich cargo and its hundreds of human lives. Counting Chinamen, crew, and all, there must have been very nearly a thousand souls on board.

To see that everything was right and in order, the captain made a complete tour of the steamer every evening at eight o'clock, when every man was obliged to be at his post, and each department ready for inspection. One evening the captain took us with him on this visit, and it was very interesting.

We went through the bakery, the pantry, and the kitchen, where the cooks and waiters were on hand, with every drawer open for inspection, and all the dishes and cooking utensils shining on the shelves, the perfection of neatness and order. We then visited the butcher's quarters, where we heard the various noises of a farm-yard; there were cows, chickens, sheep, and pigs, whose late companions, killed and quartered, were suspended from the ceiling near by. In another place we saw a small dining-room, with a table all set for those officers who were on watch during the night, and took their meals at different times; we also got a peep down the hatchway into the forecastle, where the sailors sleep, but it was not very inviting and the captain did not ask us to visit it. We went in to see the Chinese kitchen and eating-room, and read the bill of fare for the next day, which the captain always looked over. It seemed to be all rice, with variations. The Chinamen had tickets for their food, one of which they gave in at each meal, and they eat there standing.

We used to sometimes watch them at a distance as they came, one after another, like a flock of sheep, to get their bowl of rice.

In the course of our trip around the vessel, which took us at least an hour, we saw their small cabins, containing six berths each, and also their opium-smoking-room. Although it was not much larger than a piano-box, it was packed just as full as it could be with Chinamen, drowsy and stupid with opium, the smoke of which filled the room. They prefer being shut up in a close place like this, for they get the benefit of each other's opium. The six hundred Chinese emigrants who crowded out to see the passengers the captain was taking round, were very dirty, ragged, and disagreeable-looking specimens; but far different did they appear when we reached San Francisco.

It was a glorious day. The sun glittered on the waves and on the sails of vessels, the first we had seen for weeks. Our great, dark, noiseless sea-birds, companions of our voyage, had gradually disappeared, like our doubts and fears, which had risen with the angry waves, but vanished as we neared land; and we were surrounded by countless numbers of snow-white sea-gulls, with pink bills and claws, rending the air with their flapping wings and calling backwards and forwards to one another with their one odd note. They seemed like joyful messengers who had come out to welcome us and accompany us to land. Other land-birds soon began to skim over the water, great sea-lions stuck out their heads around the vessel, and strange to say, I saw for the first time three or four whales spouting their spray into the air. I had been wishing to see some ever since I left the harbor of New York, but it was not until the last day of our ocean travel that I saw them.

While we were watching all these things the Golden Gate opened before us; the tall black cross in the cemetery on "Lone Mountain" stood out against the sky; we saluted the flag of the white light-house on the cliffs, just over the raging surf; our arrival was telegraphed from there into the city; a pilot came to guide us in, and we were soon anchored in San Francisco Bay, waiting for the health officer to come on board.

GOLDEN GATE—CALIFORNIA.

When he arrived we all went "forward" to see the Chinamen counted, which was done to be sure that no more than eight hundred, the lawful number, were on board, and that they were all in good health. A sailor stood at one side of the narrow hatchway, and at the other one of the mates, who counted out in a loud voice, as the Chinamen came pouring up the steep ladder: "One, two, three, four, five, six, seven, eight, nine, ten—tally! one, two, three," etc.; and each time he said "tally" the doctor made a mark in his book. Thus they were counted by tens, up to the number of six hundred and thirty. They were all dressed for the occasion of landing, in fresh green, yellow, red, and brown clothes, their pigtails newly braided, and their faces, which had been besmeared with dirt during the voyage, were shining yellower and more heathenish than ever. They had not the slightest idea what was being done to them, and it was comical to watch their expressions as they were pushed and pulled up.

The sailor and the officer who counted were not very gentle in handling them. When they came up too slowly they were caught hold of by the arms, clothes, or pigtails, whichever came first, and were carried into daylight with such impetus that they landed on the deck in a heap, and scrambled up the best way they could, some with a broad grin, seeming to consider it a good joke, while others took it more seriously.

Some of them seemed to think their rice-tickets were wanted, and most of them came out with them in their hands. While looking around for some one to give them to, they were hoisted in the above manner, and their tickets scattered to the winds. As they stood crowding around, some of the sailors drove them down to the other end of the deck with ropes, with as little ceremony as if they were a herd of cattle.

After a very annoying examination by the custom house officers, we were soon riding through the streets of San Francisco, and took rooms at the Lick House where we slept soundly, though still dreaming of being "rocked in the cradle of the deep."

XXXIX.

FROM SAN FRANCISCO TO SARATOGA.

THE GOLDEN CITY—A KIND OLD DUTCHMAN—THE SEA-LIONS—ACROSS THE COUNTRY—SIERRA NEVADAS — SALT LAKE CITY—PRAIRIES — HOME!

No sooner were we registered at the hotel than old friends seemed to turn up in every direction.

It was such a treat to see familiar faces after being among strangers for nearly a year. Senator C—— and his wife were particularly kind. They took us a drive through the park and to most of the sights in the city, and Mrs. C—— went shopping with me. It had been many months since we left the civilized part of the world, and as most of our travelling had been on shipboard, which every one who ever tried it must know is very destructive to clothing, our purposely small stock had become rather dilapidated.

During our stay in San Francisco, we visited the old Mission church established among the Indians by Spanish priests, and made an expedition to the "seal rocks" near the Cliff House. We started in the street cars, intending to take the omnibus at Lone Mountain, but we were too late for it. An old German landholder, who lived somewhere out near the Cliffs, was in the street cars, and on learning we had been to Germany, he became very much interested, talking about his "*Vaterland*," and when we reached the end of the railway, finding no conveyance, we were about to return, but he protested—"No, no, you must see the sea-lions, it would never do to go away without," and declared that if nothing else could be found, we should go in his own buggy, and he would wait till we came back.

MISSION CHURCH—SAN FRANCISCO.

Leaving us with a country shop-keeper, a friend of his, who invited us into his private parlor, and entertained us with an account of his six months' trip across the country before the great Union Pacific Railroad was thought of, our new friend, after some time, returned with a horse and buggy he had hunted up for us, and which we hired for the ride.

After a hearty good-bye, our good-natured German drove off in his direction and we in ours, probably never to meet again, but leaving in our minds a pleasant remembrance of the genial kindness we met with in this part of the country.

When we reached the coast we looked far out to sea at the sails on the horizon, thinking that a short time

MISSION CHURCH RESTORED—SAN FRANCISCO.

before our position was just the reverse; we had been out there ourselves, looking eagerly in toward the place where we now stood. Beneath the cliffs were rocks worn into queer shapes, and even pierced through in great holes by the waves, over which countless numbers of seals or sea-lions were scrambling, the din of their hoarse bellow almost drowning the roaring of the waves. While we were there watching them, a heavy fog enveloped us, hiding the water, the sails, the sunshine, and the sea-lions; and wrapping ourselves up, we drove rapidly back to the city through the dense dampness.

After making all kinds of inquiries and plans for going to the Yosemite Valley and the Big Trees, we finally decided to give up the project.

It was too early to go then, and as we were impatient to get home, we did not wish to wait for several weeks. A party that started while we were at San Francisco found the roads snowed up, and were obliged to return.

The trip from San Francisco to New York is so familiar that I will only give a few extracts from my diary, written with a pencil as we jolted along in the cars.

April 11.—Left San Francisco this morning at seven o'clock. Very much interested in the California scenery.

Quantities of mustard plant growing along the road. Watching the forms and peculiar tints in the clouds; made Uncle admit that some of our American skies are as beautiful as those of Italy—a question we had often disputed. Have a little table in our section so we can play cards. Crossing the Sierra Nevada Mountains. Passing through the snow-sheds and tunnels. In the dark of the evening we pass the Hydraulic Mines— miners at work by torchlight.

12th.—We are going through Nevada. Mostly barren plains; cattle in great numbers grazing on the green and prickly sage and the stubble. Palisades.

13th.—Stopped at Ogden. Took the train for Salt Lake City. Visited the Tabernacle, shaped like the back of a monstrous turtle. Great interest is manifested in the beautiful new house which Brigham Young is building for Amelia, the latest favorite.

Salt Lake City is not as pleasant a place as we had

heard it was; with the exception of the Tabernacle, it looks to us like any other raw, Western town. As for harems, they may be, to a certain extent, picturesque and romantic in the rich, hazy light of an oriental city; but they are certainly disagreeable and repulsive here, in the practical, matter-of-fact, broad daylight of a New World settlement. These were our impressions of Mormondom.

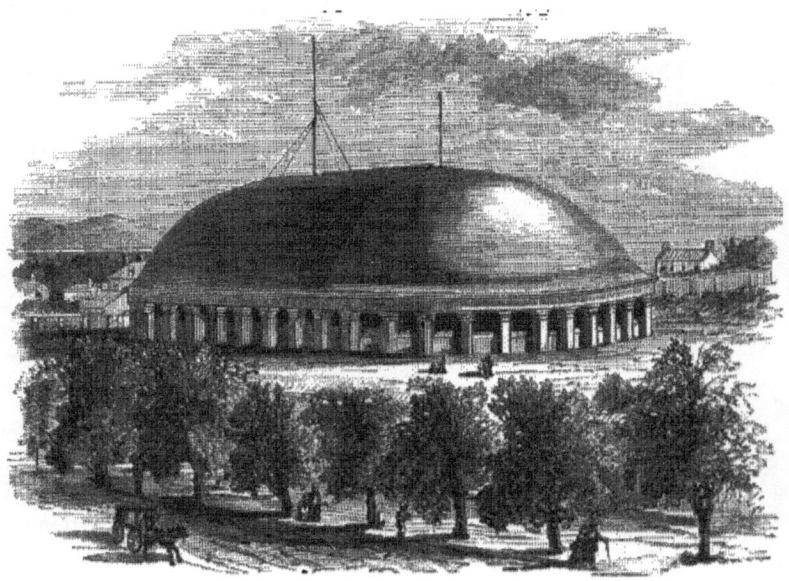

THE MORMON TABERNACLE.

Returned to Ogden to spend the night. Such a relief to have a night's rest off the cars.

14th.—Travelling again. Snow storm; the first we have seen since we left home.

Warsatch Mountains; beautiful wild scenery. We leave them behind and the ride becomes barren and uninteresting.

Beginning the ascent of the Rocky Mountains.

15th.—Passed the summit of the Rocky Mountains—strange to say, we saw no mountains, only a rolling country, the ascent had been so gradual.

NIAGARA FALLS.

16th.—Prairie, prairie, prairie—all day.. At Chicago we stopped for a few hours and drove through the new part of the city—whole streets of magnificent buildings, fresh from the workman's hands—little thinking that in a few months they would be again razed to the ground by the fiery scourge of that city. We hurried down to the train and were once more travelling. At Detroit I awoke with a start from a sound sleep, for after six nights we were used to the sleeping-cars. Bewildered and uncertain where I was,

RAPIDS OF NIAGARA.

I felt sure that the shock I had felt was caused either by a steamboat explosion or a railway collision. But it was only the train rolling onto the ferry-boat with a fearful thump! The stormiest day on the ocean had not given me such a fright.

At Niagara we walked across the bridge while the train puffed slowly over, but Uncle and I had both seen the falls before, so we continued our journey.

We did not stop again until we reached our final

destination, and were ready to settle down once more to quiet life. Thus June, 1874, finds us where June, 1873, left us — Uncle absorbed in the duties of his parish, I intent on my studies, and more strongly convinced than ever of these three things: that the world is round, that the finest country in the world is the United States, and that the brightest spot in the United States is Home!

WALWORTH HOMESTEAD, SARATOGA SPRINGS.

For p. 316.

www.ingramcontent.com/pod-product-compliance
Lightning Source LLC
Chambersburg PA
CBHW021338300426
44114CB00012B/990